Frigga Haug and Others

Female Sexualization

A Collective Work of Memory

Translated from the German by
Erica Carter (Material Word)

VERSO
The Imprint of New Left Books

**British Library
Cataloguing in Publication Data**

Haug, Frigga
  Female sexualization: a collective work
  of memory. — (Questions for feminism)
  1. Women — Social conditions
  I. Title   II. Sexualisierung, *English*
  III. Series
  305.4'2   HQ1154

  ISBN 0-86091-162-4
  ISBN 0-86091-875-0 Pbk

First published as *Sexualisierung: Frauenformen 2*
© Argument Verlag 1983

This English translation first published 1987
© Verso 1987
Reprinted 1992

Verso
6 Meard Street London W1

Typeset in Times by
PRG Graphics
Redhill, Surrey

Printed in Great Britain by Dotesios Ltd
Trowbridge, Wiltshire

Contents

List of authors

Sünne Andresen is a student of sociology doing research into the relationship between the working-class movement and the women's movement. She is also a member of the Hamburg Socialist Women's Association (Sozialistischer Frauenbund, hereafter SFB).

Anke Bünz-Elfferding works as a music teacher and is doing research into feminine aesthetics and cultural theory; she is a member of the West Berlin SFB.

Frigga Haug lectures at the Hamburg *Hochschule für Wirtschaft und Politik*; she is currently researching into automation, as well as the women's movement and women's socialization. She is a member of the SFB.

Kornelia Hauser is studying sociology, and doing research into women, ideology and the State; she is a member of the Hamburg SFB.

Ursel Lang works as a psychologist in a home for adolescents; she is doing research into the family and ideology, and is a member of the West Berlin SFB.

Marion Laudan is a student in adult education.

Magret Lüdemann is a student of sociology; she works in the *Argument* women's studies project, and is a member of the Hamburg SFB.

Ute Meir works as a psychiatrist.

Barbara Nemitz is a doctor working on and doing research into automation and its effects on health; she is a member of the West Berlin SFB.

Erika Niehoff is studying sociology; her research is on the working-class movement and the family, and she is a member of the Hamburg SFB.

Renate Prinz works as a teacher of maths and sport; she is doing research into the family and ideology and is a member of the West Berlin SFB.

Nora Räthzel works in a project with unemployed foreign workers in Hamburg; she is doing research on automation and writing a doctoral thesis on women in male occupations.

Martina Scheu is studying philosophy and psychology.

Christine Thomas is studying sociology, and has done research on forms of cultural resistance amongst girls. She is a member of the West Berlin SFB.

Translator's Preface: **Erica Carter**

Preface to the English edition: **Nora Räthzel**

Memory-Work: **Frigga Haug**
Introduction to the Projects: **Frigga Haug, Kornelia Hauser, Erika Niehoff, Nora Räthzel**
Hair Project: **Ursel Lang**
Body Project: **Frigga Haug, Christine Thomas**
Slavegirl Project: **Sünne Andresen, Frigga Haug, Kornelia Hauser, Erika Niehoff**
Legs Project: **Barbara Nemitz, Renate Prinz**
Notes on Women's Gymnastics: **Renate Prinz**
Sexuality and Power: **Kornelia Hauser**
Church and Sexuality: **Frigga Haug, Kornelia Hauser**
Women and Bodies: **Nora Räthzel**

Marxism and Sexuality: **Frigga Haug, Kornelia Hauser, Nora Räthzel**.

Translation: **Erica Carter**, with special thanks also to **Chris Turner**.

The translators would also like to thank **Ann Pawling, Sue Kent** and **Claire Laudet** for their timely assistance with typing.

Translator's Foreword

Any reader who has spent time living in a foreign country, perhaps speaking a foreign language from one end of the day to another, will be familiar with the sense of incompleteness that later accompanies day-to-day life 'back home'. Photographs never quite capture the smells, sounds, tastes or sensations of a foreign city; the piercing intimacy of transatlantic friendships dulls over distance and time. Above all, there is the difference of language. Clusters of memory may be trapped in a foreign language (in my case, German) that remains for the most part incomprehensible at home.

More seriously, (in Great Britain in particular, less obviously in the intellectual life of North America) there is no framework of cultural knowledge within which narratives of 'foreign' experiences might become meaningful. In the Anglo-Saxon world, 'Germany' is popularly construed as a rag-bag of Nazi stereotypes (the two German phrases most firmly embedded in the British schoolboy vernacular are '*Achtung!*' and – sadly – '*Heil Hitler*'), alongside a few antiseptic images of post-war West German efficiency (the German Democratic Republic having meanwhile melted in our mental geography into the amorphous mass we term the 'Communist world').

On the Left and within feminism, there have been attempts to counter this kind of insularity; to realize the internationalist project of socialism and feminism, by opening up to cultural and intellectual influences from the non-English speaking world. Here too, however, importation has been selective. What passes for 'French feminism', for example, tends to be limited to a handful of writers (most often Kristeva, Irigaray and Cixous) whose work has been used to resolve very specific problems – problems of language and textuality in particular – within the theoretical practice of academic feminism. This is not to say that these writers have no more general usefulness for feminism; only that their prominence has tended to obscure the diversity of other feminisms in the French-speaking world.

Closer to home, selectivity has thankfully become more diffi-cult to practise. Black women amongst others are demanding now of white feminists that they (we) adjust their political and theoretical agendas, not simply in order to accommodate 'race' as a single issue, but to recognize the necessary plurality of positions occupied by women of differing ethnic origins and languages, different religions, different generations of cultural experience.

Clearly, writings emerging from white European feminism cannot be equated with works by women who write often from outside, and certainly against Eurocentric traditions. What Western feminism's gradual acknowledgement of difference – not only racial difference, but class and generational, national, regional, hetero- and homosexual – has however created is a more fertile context for the reception of works of both European and non-European, 'black' and 'white' origin. It is now possible to look to non-Anglophone writing, not for the affirmation of our own entrenched positions, but for a disruption and critical questioning of our assumptions about feminism's political – or indeed linguistic – potentiality.

The Discourse of *Frauenformen** in Translation.

Here, translation becomes a formidable responsibility. In the first instance, since so little work from West German feminism has appeared in translation,[1] there is a danger that each new book will be read as representative of the whole. More seriously, the translator finds herself called upon to select pivotal cate-gories, to rehabilitate, redefine or if necessary invent terms which – if the book is successful – may pass into more widespread usage within and beyond feminism. In the case of *Frauenformen 2*, the task of sculpting an English version has often proved

---

* Roughly translatable as 'women's forms' (Ed.)

difficult. Not only is this a text whose focus is frequently on language itself (particularly in the final three theoretical sections of the third chapter); it shifts also in tone and register, moving rapidly between narrative and theoretical reflection. The book records a collective's attempts to analyse women's socialization by writing stories out of their own personal memories: stories within which socialization comes to appear as a process of sexualization of the female body. In the first chapter on what is called 'memory-work' *(Erinnerungsarbeit)*, the reader is introduced to the method of collective work undertaken by the group. Described as a method for the unravelling of gender socialization, this involves choosing a theme connected with the body – legs, hair, stomach, height – and calling on members of the group to write down their memories of past events that focus on this physical area.

In the second chapter, we pursue the process whereby the stories are circulated amongst the group, discussed, reassessed and rewritten. The group searches for absences in the text, for its internal contradictions, for clichéd formulations covering knots of emotion or painful detail. Rewritten in the light of collective critique, the final version becomes a finely textured account of the process of production of the sexualized female body. And finally, the third chapter examines the theoretical implications of a study in which women's 'sexuality' has been revealed as constructed within practices apparently quite separate from 'the sexual': walking across a hotel foyer, having a haircut, crossing legs demurely under the table. The problem of sexuality is 'displaced' here from the sexual act itself onto the practices of everyday life whereby girls learn to become women. More particularly, those practices are seen to centre on the female body, which appears in *Frauenformen* as the axis around which sexuality is organized in childhood. Ultimately, then, the political project of the book becomes what one member of the collective terms 'moving the body into the world': extricating the female body from its constricted framework of sexual meanings, and relocating it within more fully 'socialized' areas of concern.

What then does the notion of a 'socialized' body mean for feminism in practice? In the first instance, it entails a rejection of naturalistic and ahistorical conceptions in which the body appears as the guardian of femininity's ultimate truths. The practice of a politics of the body often takes the form of struggles (fruitless, since their goal is an impossible one) for a return to the 'natural' body from which patriarchal civilization is deemed to have isolated us as women. A friend in West Germany told me recently of a conference she was organizing on 'women and work'; while on the one hand, she had difficulty finding contributors proficient in, say, economics, or trained in technical skills, she had on the other to fend off advances from umpteen self-taught masseuses, women's self-awareness groups and natural childbirth circles. Fair enough, in a sense; 'body-work', as the *Frauenformen* collective point out, is also *social* labour. Yet the seminars on offer were no different from those proposed by the same groups for different conferences in previous years.

It seems, then, that a preoccupation with the cultivation of the body does indeed limit drastically feminism's horizons. In opposition to this trend, the authors of *Frauenformen* propose, not only to 'denaturalize' the body, by rewriting the narratives through which their bodies have historically become what they are; more, they use the analysis of those narratives to reconstruct a theoretical discourse and a methodology within which 'body politics' can appear as a thoroughly *social* preoccupation. I believe this constitutes the most innovative aspect of the book. No other feminist work has examined in such detail the means by which memory may be mobilized collectively to chart the progress of women through discourse, via their subjective experience of the body. The only related studies that spring to mind are Rosalind Coward's *Female Desire: Women's Sexuality,* and Susan Brownmiller's *Femininity,*[2] both of which contain sections on the female body and its sexualization. Neither however attempts a systematic reading of memory (their use of memory is more impressionistic), nor do they submit their individual recollections to collective reading or critique.

Memory-Work: a Theoretical Framing.

Since 'memory-work' is explicitly presented as a bridge to span the gap between 'theory' and 'experience', the collective's work will clearly be assessed in relation to theories currently dominant on the Left and within feminism conceived to explain the process whereby women, as subjects within culture, are 'made'. However, the theoretical terrain onto which the book will enter is currently occupied by discussions of the disappearance of *any* subject whose history (individual and/or collective) might be mobilized as a force for political action. These discussions centre increasingly on the core term 'postmodernism', which is held to define the field on which all cultural interventions must now make their way. In the broadest of terms, 'postmodern culture' is seen to be characterized by a superabundance of mass-produced cultural artifacts which, though their origins are dissimultaneous, are endlessly reproduced in relations of simultaneity. The dominance of 'the postmodern' is said to have particularly grave consequences for political movements such as socialism and feminism, which have traditionally worked with notions of a linear historical development towards liberation. In our contemporary culture, by contrast, 'history' – or its image – has been made instantly retrievable: so fashion revitalizes the cravat for men, and calls the style 'New Edwardian': pop music producers re-release old songs as film themes from the latest box-office record-breaker.

Within the framework of a cultural logic that anaesthetizes history, reducing it to a synchronic assemblage of aesthetic objects, there seems little room for socialist and feminist projects for collective emancipation. For feminists, developing a perspective on 'postmodernity' is difficult. On the one hand, the postmodern irreverence for history does disrupt many of the conventions we have traditionally considered oppressive. Thus when the bustle, once a symbol of bourgeois women's prim immobility, recently returned to the fashion spreads of *Vogue*, it made its appearance only as a playful allusion to gender conventions long since disavowed. On the other hand, the same disdain for any history beyond the image has profoundly disorganized feminist culture, indeed radical culture in general. A politics played out amongst media images holds only little of the promise of sociality or cheerful affection for which socialists and feminists have traditionally striven. And, as the authors of *Frauenformen* suggest, liberation cannot consist in the propagation of solitude.

Clearly, then, sites do have to be identified and practices elaborated for a critical cultural production that both engages contemporary images of femininity, and re-places them in contexts over which we have control. How then does *Frauenformen 2* contribute to what the authors call this project for liberation? In the book, a vision is presented of the political possibilities of assembling, from the autobiographical texts to which memory gives access, a coherent representation of each female body – which is offered then in the final chapter as a springboard for social action. On the basis not only of their new theoretical knowledge of themselves, but of the new narratives now spun around the body, women, it is suggested, may take control of their bodies and their sexuality. In rewriting stories of the body, and subjecting them to critical analysis, the authors attempt to construct a new discursive framework, a *usable* theoretical language for their readers and themselves. Theory, they insist, enters into and meshes with everyday narrative, defining the context within which our 'selves' – physical and psychological – become meaningful. What the book offers, then, is amongst other things a set of terms designed not only to further our theoretical understanding, but to enrich our physical existence as women.

Theoretical Encounters: West Germany and Great Britain.

The work of the collective starts, interestingly, from a theoretical position first marked out in Britain in the mid-1970s; the authors cite British work on youth cultures as a crucial influence on their research. Broadly, their interest focuses – as did this early work on youth culture – on the practical engagement of social subjects with the 'structures' into which they are born: an engagement viewed as a practice whereby social subjects secure their own eventual subordination. (Angela McRobbie speaks in an early article of girls as being 'saved by and locked within' a culture of femininity which they themselves help to reproduce.)[3]

British youth culture analyses emerged at a time when Marxist and feminist academic theory in Britain was strongly influenced by Althusserian structuralism. Althusser's work on ideology in particular seemed to explain the lack of a popular revolutionary consciousness that so vexed the New Left. His harnessing of psychoanalysis for a theory of 'ideology' offered new ways of conceptualizing the process by which individuals came to desire their own subordination – or at least it seemed to.

The problem with the structuralist paradigm was that the 'structure', particularly in many derivative accounts, came to figure as an ideal construct within which cultural positions were always already given; 'class', 'gender', 'race' and 'generation' were often presented as immutable categories of social analysis. Thus 'subordinate' cultural practice, even in its apparently oppositional manifestations, was seen ultimately only as reproductive, not however as productive of new configurations of social relations.

By the end of the 1970s, challenges were being posed to this model. Within academic feminism, they had arisen in part out of a sympathetic reading of French theories of language and its part in the production of subjectivities (later grouped under the catch-all title of 'discourse theory'). The most unsettling contention of 'discourse theory' from a feminist point of view was that the categories hitherto deployed by cultural analysts as 'givens' – class, gender, race, generation and so on – were constantly being produced anew within different and competing discourses, and that they were therefore more fluid and shifting than had previously been assumed. To return to Angela McRobbie's formulation quoted above: what was implied by this emphasis on the production of social categories on multiple sites, within multiple discourses, was that there was no such thing as a fixed 'femininity' which women could either be 'saved by' or 'locked within': 'youth', the 'working class', 'femininity' and 'masculinity' were seen now as produced historically in far more complex constellations.

The crucial point about these theoretical realignments within academic feminism was that femininity was no longer seen necessarily as a position of subordination. 'Women' may in fact be produced in a variety of contexts as the *agents* of historical processes, the holders of power. Power may be accorded to women for example by virtue of their class position – think of the rise of the 'ruthless' female manager; or, more ambiguously, women may derive power from the very practices of femininity that feminism has always abhorred – their use of fashion, their manipulation of the codes of romance and sexuality. More problematically, it is becoming clear that feminist discourse *itself* may have served in the past to obscure, or indeed to consolidate the relations of power within which feminists (largely middle-class, largely white) have been able to operate. Afro-Caribbean and Asian women in Britain have, for example, forced the issue of race to the top of the feminist agenda (this, I think, is the most striking point of difference between contemporary feminisms in Britain and West Germany). As a result, white feminists have begun to re-evaluate earlier political positions in which women were located always as the victims of a totalizing patriarchal oppression.

It is on this issue that the work of the *Frauenformen* collective meshes once again with Anglo-Saxon concerns. While they would not agree that the power accruing to women is either extensive or indeed desirable in its present forms, the authors do argue against a definition of femininity as exclusively passive. They are led to this position in part through the work of Michel

Foucault, of which there is an extended and very lucid discussion in the opening section to Chapter 3. More centrally, however, the question of how to conceptualize the contradictions of women's subjectivity has been approached by the collective from the dual perspective of a theory of ideology (elaborated within the *Argument* circle by the *Projekt Ideologie-Theorie*), and of what is known in West Germany as 'critical psychology' – an attempt by Marxist psychologists, most notably Ute Holzkamp-Osterkamp and Klaus Osterkamp, to produce a theory of subjectivity framed in scientific Marxist terms.

Choosing terminology to fit a theoretical framework largely unknown in the English-speaking world has been particularly tricky. In theoretical terms, it is assumed by the authors that the social relations into which individuals are born are always pre-patterned in given ways; they are not the result of individual choice or self-determination. The term they use for this state of affairs is *'Fremdbestimmung'* – literally, 'alien determination', or 'determination by others'. I have chosen instead, in consultation with the authors, to use the term 'heteronomy', meaning 'subjection to external laws'. 'Heteronomy' describes, not a set of actions (as does 'determination by others'), but a state of social relations that marks out structural barriers to women's strivings for autonomy and liberation. Using the notion of heteronomy also allows the translation to reproduce a similar bipolar terminology to that of the original German, in which *'Fremdbestimmung'* is frequently counterposed to *'Selbstbestimmung'* – 'determination by the self', or autonomy.

A second theoretical assumption underpinning the original is that social subjects are never 'passive', but instead constantly engaged in practice. 'Individuals,' it is stated at one point, 'are always active.' Since there are however structural limits on what critical psychology terms their 'capacity for action' (*'Handlungsfähigkeit'*), social subjects by and large look for ways of living within their limitations, and thus of escaping the dangers of deviance or breakdown. Neither critical psychology nor what is known in the *'Argument'* context as 'ideology theory' offer ways however of defining 'how social relations are concretely lived by individuals, and in particular by us as women'. Searching then for new metaphors in which this process can be encapsulated, the authors turn eventually to the image of the Arabian Nights slavegirl. She is by no means passive – on the contrary, she develops all manner of competences to seduce her master – yet the limits on her capacity for action are absolute. *'Sklavinnen-*

verhalten' ('slavegirl conduct') has thus been translated in the following as 'slavegirlishness', since this seemed to me to suggest the degree of conscious coquetry involved in women's exclusive focus on their own sexual attractiveness, and its constricting nature.

I hope that these two terms that seemed to me most 'strange' in English will, framed by the text as a whole, lose their incongruity. For the rest, the terms used are, I hope, self-explanatory. It remains only to invite the reader to put them to use as instruments of knowledge and – hopefully – pleasure. I would like also to thank the authors for their patient explication of the text: Michèle Barrett, Ann Rosalind Jones and Anne Phillips for their support as editors: and Chris Turner of 'Material Word' for collaboration on research and translation.

Erica Carter

Preface to English edition

It may perhaps be most interesting for a British readership if we begin with an account of who we are, what our theoretical and political background is, and how we came to write this book. A number of us have been active in the Women's Liberation Movement for many years, some only since becoming involved in the writing of this book. Frigga has the longest history of engagement; during the time of the student movement in the late 1960s she was among the founders of the Socialist Women's Association *(Sozialistischer Frauenbund)*, one of the few women's organizations formed in opposition to the male-dominated movement of 1968 that attempted at the same time to hold on to a socialist vision. Frigga also worked with and later became co-editor of the journal *Das Argument*. The other women in the group came to *Das Argument* over a period of several years, either through the Socialist Women's Association or through courses on Marx's *Capital* at the Free University in West Berlin.

Das Argument is the oldest journal of Marxist theory in the Federal Republic. It was launched in the anti-nuclear movement of 1959, and enjoyed a temporary heyday during the student movement. The impetus for a return to Marx initially derived from the circle around *Das Argument*. In 1970, the first *Capital* course was offered at the Free University by W.F. Haug, editor of *Das Argument*. In its prime, the seminar was attended by 600 students; today, the participants number around 200.

In the course of the 1970s, left politics in the Federal Republic fragmented, and the left divided amongst communist groupings,

21

left-wing social democrats, non-aligned socialists, left splinter groups and of course women's organizations. A number of new socialist or feminist social-scientific and political journals were launched. *Das Argument* expanded to encompass a small publishing house, in which we published both individual books and series, each under the auspices of different project groups within *Das Argument*. Areas of research within the projects included automation and qualification, discussions of international socialism, ideology theory and of course women's studies. *Das Argument* is neither affiliated to, nor supported by, any one political party. This represents a disadvantage from the point of view of material security, but an advantage for the development of theory. Within our present political culture, alliance with a political party would mean subordinating the development of theory to a single line.

It was not until 1982 that women working with the journal were able to bring together the two sides of their lives: our commitment to the women's movement, and work within *Das Argument*. Following the publication of the first volume of *Frauenformen* (Women's Forms), it seemed necessary to many of us to establish a framework within which women's issues could be debated continuously. We were already working within *Das Argument*, and so already had a readership – female and male – in this context. What was also clear, on the other hand, was that only 10 percent of the journal's contributors were women, and that even in the *Argument* context, the issue of women had been only tangentially – albeit relatively regularly – addressed since 1962, in part in the context of the journal's debates on sexuality and domination (to which we refer later in this volume). Once the dimensions of the problem had become clear, our efforts to establish an autonomous women's editorial board within *Das Argument* were given new impetus. Although men on the editorial board had always recognized the seriousness and weight of the woman question, most of them were unconvinced of the necessity for an autonomous editorial group. One argument they put forward was that this would mean recognizing the necessity for all social groups, unions or young people for example, to have similar autonomy in editorial policy. Admittedly, the same men had already reached the theoretical conclusion that women could not be considered one social group amongst many, but that the 'woman question' was one that touched all classes. Now however, they were being asked to relinquish a part of their control over the journal. Our aims were to take autonomous control of the content of two of the six issues produced annually; to take charge of one topic area in the review section of every issue; to publish conference reports, and to place at least one feminist piece in all the issues not specifically concerned with questions relating to women. Each of these aims, with the exception of the last, has since been realized – and will continue to be pursued in future.

For us, the autonomous women's editorial group represents an opportunity to work at the reconstruction of all disciplines from the standpoint of women. Our reference-point here has been and remains Marxism; our stated aim is to inscribe feminism into the Marxist framework. In time-honoured female tradition, then, we have set ourselves a dual task: that of reconstructing scientific work along feminist lines, and that of remodelling Marxism to open up a place within it for issues concerning women.

In the initial stages, the women's editorial group set up separate projects in which women could work specifically in their own area of expertise. Thus the editorial group consisted at first of delegates from ten different projects, working on themes as diverse as women in trades unions, health, language and literary studies, the women's movement and the working-class movement, the family, culture, sexuality and domination, women's studies, economy and therapy. Since then it has emerged that an orientation to traditional disciplines obstructs rather than facilitates analysis of the issues raised. The most successful projects were those that had drawn from the start on different disciplines for the analysis of problems. At the same time, it also became clear that we had planned to do too much. Research, writing, defending our arguments at conferences, then also planning and editing issues of the journal: for the many women who had simultaneously to pursue a 'normal' job of work, or their studies, this was simply too much. The editorial meetings became unproductive; numbers of women had to sit through them plagued by a guilty conscience over their incapacity to take on particular responsibilities, or to fulfil those they had assumed. In addition, the large number of editorial members (30 in all) meant that no individual women felt individually responsible for the tasks in hand.

As a result, we reduced the editorial board to twelve women, all of whom had expressed, not only enthusiasm, but also a desire to make time for editorial work. We were also forced to set our sights a little lower and accept that women could not be required to take on such a broad range of responsibilities. The editorial group is thus now made up of individuals who all – and we insist on this – have some anchorage in the women's movement. Many of them belong to the Socialist Women's Association which, based now in a number of different towns across the Federal Republic, offers a context in which women can learn for themselves to make active interventions into the contemporary political situation.

Our original hope was that all members of the group should learn everything. The differences in our backgrounds, our needs and lived practices, made it impossible to develop the kinds of egalitarian relationships capable of supporting such a project. Nonetheless, we have attempted to work collectively, in other words to unite the process of teaching and learning within each individual woman. In this volume we have attempted to dismantle the kind of division of labour found in Volume One of *Frauenformen*,* in which stories were written and rewritten by one set of individuals, for which others then elaborated a theoretical framework, more or less on their own. In what follows, by contrast, each individual has been allocated work both *on* and *with* the experiences related. The method has been a productive one, in that it has allowed each of us both to work on one special area, while at the same time participating in discussions of the more general issues raised.

Our first attempts at developing a method for memory-work are outlined in the first volume of *Frauenformen*. Here, women write stories based on their own lives, stories of events in which they have learned to behave in 'feminine' ways. The whole project arose out of our fundamental unease with all the theories of socialization previously developed within psychology and sociology. On the one hand, girls are said to be accounted for by these theories – and yet they barely make an appearance. On the other hand, if and when girls do appear – as they have done in various socialization theories under the influence of the women's movement – they surface only as objects of various different agencies (the family, the school and so on), which are seen to act upon them and force them into a particular range of roles. The question of how individuals make certain modes of behaviour their own, how they learn to develop one particular set of needs as opposed to certain others, is never addressed. In no existing work did we find any indication of the existential afflictions and obstacles facing girls in their attempts to become 'grown-up' women. (Our critique has since been radicalized further; we now see that such analyses are full of absences on the concrete experiences of young boys.)

In this first volume, we researched a number of different forms of feminine socialization: love, happiness, marriage, the desire for children. In the process, we learned to understand women as active agents who are not simply stamped with the imprint of their given social relations, but who acquiesce in them and unconsciously participate in their formation. The first volume also had a politicizing effect on women who attended the public readings we gave; the excitement they expressed stemmed from a new perception of themselves, not as fully-formed beings moulded in the first three years of their lives, but as beings who desire and have a capacity to become something they are not as yet. The book generated a new mood of dissension; in many of the readings we gave, there were heated discussions over possible ways of making the transition from the attitude of victim to that of active agent, or over the precise ways in which the relationship between what we call heteronomy and autonomy can be understood, and above all changed.

What was missing from our first book was an analysis of sexuality as a form of socialization. It was out of our recognition of this absence that plans for the second volume emerged. (Our transition from discussions of sexuality as the 'theme' of the book, to investigations into the sexualization of the body, is documented in the preface to the German edition, and in the opening section of the second chapter below.)

What effects, then, did this second volume have? How was it received by women? Given the paucity of theoretical discussions within socialist feminism in the Federal Republic, debates around the book could not take place in an academic group concerned with questions of method, or of our understanding of sexuality. Feminists who do theoretical work are not only generally uninterested in writing from a socialist perspective; they also rarely engage in any significant way with socialist positions. Our work has usually reached women who are attempting to advance the discussion of women's issues within the Communist or Socialist parties of the Federal Republic. Another audience has been found among women students attempting to make links between their formal studies and women's issues: amongst a generation, then, no longer so directly affected by old arguments between dogmatic Marxist women and dogmatic feminists, and which no longer closes its ears at the merest mention of socialism. We have been invited to innumerable readings by bookshops, universities and political organizations. In all the discussions, without exception, our experience has been that our topic has struck a chord. Hardly any of the women we have spoken to have felt that their external appearance, their relationship to their bodies and physical 'deficiencies' has had anything less than a formative influence on their relationship to the 'external' world. We have been showered with a whole barrage of examples to support the arguments of the book, some more devastating than any we had encountered in our work on our own lives for this volume. The question of how to develop perspectives for the future has also been raised with increasing urgency, precisely because women have been able to identify with the issues outlined in the following pages. Should women for example suppress any kind of pleasure in their bodies, simply because it is in that pleasure that we subordinate ourselves to socially prescribed forms of femininity? For us – entangled as we are in the nets we describe and analyse – it is clearly no simple matter to produce recipes for a new way of living. But we can at least point to a number of things which to an extent changed the way we worked on this volume. In the first instance, we developed a consciousness of the extent to which our attitudes to the world are at least partially moulded by our relation to our bodies. Until this point, it would never have occurred to us to claim that even explicitly political forms of behaviour, or rather their lack of productivity, might have been generated through our relationship to our bodies.[1] We came to see other aspects of the world too through different eyes; never before had it been so clear to us how impossible it is for a woman to eat without this being accompanied by some kind of implicit comment on her figure – usually formulated by herself, or perhaps by a male or female companion. We certainly have no intention of falling euphorically into the deceptive trap of assuming that any problem that has been made conscious can be solved immediately. On the other hand, if we do not assume that there is a degree of truth in this, then no change at all will be possible.

What we ourselves have gained in writing this book is a degree of self-confidence, an increased ability to deal more matter-of-factly with our bodily 'defects'. In addition, we have gained a new goal for ourselves: to capture for ourselves new bodily pleasures (and other pleasures too) by making our way in a world to which we gain access by routes other than those that lead across our bodies. It is not until women have learned to grasp life and its opportunities with greater passion that they will learn to trust in their capabilities to live life fully – and only then will external physical appearance take on new meaning.[2]

We have also often been asked whether we are not leaving an important dimension out of account by viewing exclusively as a problem the centering of women around their bodies. Is it not clear, we have been asked, for example, that women also gain in power by making use of their 'charms', either in work or in relationships to others? It seems to have been difficult to transmit the fact that our theory is founded on precisely this insight.[3] It is precisely because we gain in competence through our bodily practices that we cling to them as we do. The drawback, however, is that in exercising this power, we simultaneously confine ourselves to one part of a wider world and one particular relationship to it. Even if we ignore the loss of living-time we suffer in learning to exercise this kind of power; even if we leave out of account the inexorable curtailment of that power with the onset of old age; even then, the pleasure we take in this kind of power still seems to us to drag us ever deeper into quicksand, digging us in further with every move we make. The marshland corpses we become may be attractive and well-preserved; but they are the bodies of women who, in the course of their lives, have influenced nothing save for the handful of men in their immediate surroundings.

In the context of our group, new research has been conducted since the publication of this volume on the significance of the female body in the process of socialization. In 1984, new work by Frigga Haug established a framework within which it was possible to articulate the relation between class and war in terms of women's orientation to their bodies, and of the notions of morality to which that orientation gives rise. In taking on responsibility for their bodies, women relinquish responsibility for the reproduction of society as a whole. In our third volume of *Frauenformen*, we have then attempted to trace the ways in which a centering on the body occurs in the process of identity formation. Here we have tried to unravel the process whereby women's notion of doing things 'for themselves' comes to signify, or to contain within itself a notion of acting 'for others'. Our conclusion has been that women feel responsibility neither for themselves nor for society, but exclusively for other individuals (husband and children). Bourgeois society has created a state in which each individual is required to take care of herself or himself; there is no longer any guild or estate that takes on this responsibility. For women, this has led to a division of labour that focuses their attention immediately on their bodies, while perceiving all social processes in ever more abstract and mediated ways. By these means, it seems to us, the structural exclusion of women from the social processes of decision-making, as well as their acquiescence in that exclusion, are secured.

The electronic and technical revolution has ushered in a paradigmatic change in the social sciences and in philosophy. As Donna Haraway has suggested, 'traditional, white, western male philosophers are beginning all of a sudden to identify with the animalistic body, perceiving their human identity threatened by the decision-making processes of the computer'.[4] Under the influence of universally disruptive developments in the forces of production, the mode of domination articulated to the division of labour finds itself in a process of constant (and, currently, chaotic) reconstruction. Whereas previously it was the 'mind' that was to gain mastery both over the body and over nature, it is now the body that is to be saved from the ravages of the scientific and technical revolution. For us as socialist feminists, there is great potential in this development. The fact that the dualisms of body and mind, together with the division of labour between head and hand, have themselves been laid open to debate, can clearly be traced to their incapacity to explain the world as it is today. For us, this represents an opportunity to produce articulations of the relations between human beings and the world that overcome the present relations of class, race and sexual domination. In seeking out these new relationships, the female body, with its ideologically constructed and yet also practical proximity to nature, will be one means of intervention among many.

Introduction

Encirclement – Noise – Silence

The same painful mixture of repugnance and attraction remains. Since we as a group of women began working on the subject of sexuality, we have been confronted almost weekly with some new book or other: advice-givers for the advice-seekers. It becomes intolerable, all these admonitory gestures, enjoining a 'sexual liberation' that amounts to little more than a programme of physical jerks. Is it our bourgeois morality that surfaces here? Or perhaps our longing to rid ourselves of the guilt that self-gratification produces, coupled with a restlessness, a secret thrill – will the written text tell us something we have never yet known or experienced? And so we continue to rummage amongst a pile of books marked ultimately by perpetual repetition. Boredom, tinged with embarrassment. Again the old morality within us, in spite of everything?

And now here we are proposing to throw another book onto the mounting pile, as if it weren't large enough already, as if it didn't already obscure our view of so many different questions. Yet this too is not an adequate objection. We will not fall back on the alternative of treating questions such as wage differentials as more important than sexual matters. We refuse the kind of ordering and hierarchization of problems that assumes without further investigation that there are certain difficulties whose pain we must necessarily suffer; that we must conform to a hierarchy of 'correct' causes of suffering. Our discussions have shown sexuality to be a crucial area of unhappiness (and of silence) for us as women, an area in which our speechlessness prevents us asking questions. Even if we felt that thinking about sexuality and happiness took up too large a space in our lives we would still have to clarify the process whereby it assumes such proportions, and to attempt to find solutions.

It is important for women to abandon their attitude of pensionable dependants: not so much to declare an interest in sexual gratification whatever the cost, but instead to attempt to forge new links between social competence and happiness, love and sexuality. In an attempt to avoid reviving old notions of morality in the process of our examination we decided to subject all these books on sexual liberation, as well as feminist hopes for a 'natural female sexuality', to critical scrutiny.

In the course of our investigations, our sense of boredom with tediously repetitive arguments was linked, not only to a heightened awareness of ourselves, but also to a fear of having actually to live the demands we make of ourselves. We require of ourselves that we experiment continually with a body we treat as something external. Who are we then, we whose shame is dispelled the moment someone tells us it is unnecessary? What indeed does necessity mean to us? If for example we remove our clothing, it is possible to see how much too fat or too thin we are; to see our breasts as sagging, overly large or diminutively small, our legs as short, fat and hairy with varicose veins, our hips as too wide, our waistline almost invisible – and so on. Discussions along these lines in the course of our work immediately triggered memories of the advice with which they were associated: 'show off your best side', 'hold your breath for firmer posture', 'pull back your arms, it looks better that way . . .'. We concluded that our relationship to our bodies is the product of a careful self-ordering into a feminine position inimical to our happiness as women. We set out, then, to focus on ourselves in an attempt to investigate the historical process of our constitution as women. We were concerned not only with the question of how we have become women in the social sense,[1] but also with the way in which the female body is *made* as a socio-biological unity. Our aim was to identify the ways we live ourselves in bodily terms, the ways we live in our bodies, and in so doing to define and determine our relation to other human beings and to the world.

We decided therefore to write what we called 'stories' of the body. What came immediately to mind were the laborious attempts of our educators to drill us not only in washing, teeth-cleaning, hygiene, but also in posture, the proper position of the arms and legs, the proper position of the mouth ('don't just sit there with your mouth open . . . !'). And so our field of research – originally devoted to discussions of sexuality – expanded to encompass the body in its entirety, its ordering into the social, and the role played by upbringing and education. It was at this point that we began to suspect that the books on sexuality we had looked at, in restricting themselves to the 'erogenous zones' and sexual organs, had necessarily mistaken their object.

On our Method of Working

The process of our work was a collective one – a fact that allowed us to turn our knowledge of numerous different fields (we worked as sociologists, psychologists, teachers, musicologists and natural and medical scientists) to fruitful use. What this meant concretely was that all the women involved made some sort of intervention into, or participated in writing, all the texts we produced; it allowed us also to bring together a vast range of ideas in our discussions. We were able too to use our association with projects around *Das Argument* to give our group work a common theoretical foundation – in Marxism, critical psychology, theories of culture and ideology. Our work on these theoretical systems involved us at the same time in reconstructing their foundations: our attempts to confront them with the issue of the specificity of gender inevitably changed them.

Our reading of Foucault was important for us, insofar as it allowed us to rethink our conception of sexuality. To make the book correspond to the actual process of research, we originally reproduced our debate with Foucault in the very first chapter. Our women typesetters recommended, however, that we draw a distinction between the actual research process and the process of its representation – and that we begin with a less difficult text. The book now begins with a chapter on memory-work, which outlines the method of investigating sexual socialization used in the projects discussed in subsequent sections.

We were unable in these projects to achieve all we had originally planned. They lack more detailed historical research, and studies of the construction of femininity in art and other related areas. Much that we have touched on in passing remains to be investigated further. Where perhaps solutions might have been expected, there is only questioning, tentative advances, experimentation. In our view this is not entirely a deficit, but also an invitation to ourselves and our readers to think and work further in this area. Much will have been gained if this book is read, not as a completed product sufficient unto itself, but as a preliminary outline worth taking further: if the gaps in our research are read as a challenge, both to us and you as readers to work together in future.

CHAPTER ONE

Memory work

The Subject of Research – a Process

Our object in this book is women's capacity – or incapacity – for action and for happiness. It involves a study of the structures, the relations within which women live and the ways in which they gain a grip on them. We are interested in the process whereby individual women become part of society – a process usually defined as 'female socialization'. The concept coyly circumvents the active participation of individuals in their formation as social beings. Since we are opposed to tolerating conditions that produce suffering – we argue instead for change, for active intervention – our attention will be focused here primarily on the process whereby individuals construct themselves into existing social relations. The question we want to raise is thus an empirical one; it is the 'how' of lived feminine practice.

According to Karl Marx, 'the organization of society and of the State evolves continuously out of the life processes of particular individuals'.[1] Our attempt to study the process of development of 'feminine sexuality' confronted us with the problem of the very constitution of a separate sphere of 'sexuality'. The difficulties we encountered in developing our thoughts along these lines arose from the virtual absence of solid evidence. What we required of ourselves was that we consider and investigate both the production of a specifically feminine sexuality and, alongside this, the constitution of the sexual itself as the process that produces the insertion of women into, and their subordination within, determinate social practices. Complicated as this may at first sound, it has in fact made our work on and with our own memories – the empirical element of our research – considerably easier. Had our questions been formulated within the more familiar framework of 'sexual socialization', our work would have been limited to two possible approaches: studying sex education in terms of the dearth or surplus of information it provides, or studying the sexual training of our bodies in terms of a dearth or surplus of *technique*. In each case, we would have been left with the uneasy feeling of having arrived too late; of having to assume a knowledge which in fact we do not have; of being called upon to choose between unsatisfactory alternatives that do not even touch on the question of our fulfilment and discontent, or of oppression versus liberation. It is not simply some lack of information or technical facility that bars our route to fulfilment, but in some mysterious way, it is we ourselves, our bodies, our relationship to our bodies and, again, ourselves as whole persons in relation to the world, that demand to be taken into account in relation to questions of human happiness, up to and including happiness in the sexual domain.

What we formulated, then, as an empirical and lived question, was the question of how sexuality is constituted as a separate sphere of existence. What this led us to investigate was the process whereby our bodies become sexualized. We used our own memories to review the ways in which individual parts of the body are linked with sexuality, the way gender is expressed through the body, the routines that have drilled us in a particular relationship to our bodies, and the ways in which all of this is knotted into social structures and social relations between the sexes. Our aim, then, was to counter heteronomy with autonomy, unhappiness with a struggle for the capacity to be happy.

Memory-Work as Social-Scientific Method

It has been suggested that, 'with the development of rationally structured academic disciplines in the transition to the modern age, scientific knowledge became irrevocably divorced from everyday experience'.[2] In challenging this kind of separation, we are clearly disrupting not only a whole academic canon; we also require enormous quantities of individual disrespect, if we are to demand the right to use experience as a basis of knowledge. The very notion that our own past experience may offer some insight into the ways in which individuals construct themselves into existing relations, thereby themselves reproducing a social formation, itself contains an implicit argument for a particular methodology. If we refuse to understand ourselves simply as a bundle of reactions to all-powerful structures, or to the social relations within which we have formed us, if we search instead for possible indications of how we have participated actively in the formation of our own past experience, then the usual mode of social-scientific research, in which individuals figure exclusively as objects of the process of research, has to be abandoned. For too long, empirical research has approached human beings from the point of view of their controllability, the predictability of their actions. Character traits and modes of behaviour have thus been catalogued as fixed elements within human subjectivity. Since however we are concerned here with the possible means whereby human beings may themselves assume control,[3] and thus with the potential prospect of liberation, our research itself must be seen as an intervention into existing practices. It could not leave character traits or modes of behaviour unchanged. Indeed memory-work is only possible if the subject and object of research are one and the same person. Even notions of 'subject' and 'object' had to be problematized in our work, amongst other reasons because they posit both as fixed and knowable entities, neither of which is subject to change. Since what interests us is the human potential for liberation, we conceived of human beings in collective and co-operative terms. However enchanted we may have been by princes and other fairytale heroes whose great deeds – often no more than a kiss at the right moment – release the spellbound from their chains we were nonetheless determined to strip these dreams of their tempting character, and instead to rehearse the painful lesson that liberation is dependent upon liberation of the self. Our intervention is itself an act of liberation.

Our suggestion that an account of the process of development of the separate sphere of sexuality, of the sexualization of the body, be pieced together out of our own experience, carried with it a requirement that the object of research herself become the researcher. Human history has involved a gradual process not merely of socialization, but at the same time of individualization, atomization. Individualization takes place most particularly within the institutions of the State. It is not a group, nor a family, but each individual who becomes a citizen, responsible – in different ways according to gender – for his or her own actions. The process whereby individuals subordinate themselves to social and legal conventions also works to a large extent through the body, by its insertion into the prevailing order in the specific ways discussed below.[4]

Our analysis begins from the assumption that we are likely to encounter significant examples of practices of subjugation in our studies of the sexualization of female bodies, since the ordering of women into sexual categories is intimately bound up with female subordination. The particular difficulty we encountered in our work was the taken-for-grantedness of many of our observations; we have until now simply accepted certain modes of behaviour without question, or seen them as typically feminine. Our chosen field of study turned out to be a walled garden of inner secrets, intimacies and idiosyncrasies; at the same time the language at our disposal was one that (like the object itself) prolonged our containment within these walls. Or rather, in calling upon ourselves to record the evocation of desire, we found ourselves speaking, thinking and experiencing ourselves with the perception of men, without ever having discovered what our aims as *human beings* might be. To be (and to become) a woman is in itself to be the polar opposite and object both of masculinity and masculine subjects. Our research therefore focused on individuals who, having submitted already to their own subordination, had no access to any alternative language, nor to any possible means of conceptualizing alternative action. And yet they shared one strength in common. Those who suffer in their subordination – however inarticulate that suffering may be – are many: potentially, they include all women. Thus our work began not only from the premiss that the subject and object of research were one; our second premiss was that research itself should be a collective process. It was as a collective that we recorded and analysed our personal memories.

Writing and the Problem of Literature

Writing is a transgression of boundaries, an exploration of new territory. It involves making public the events of our lives, wriggling free of the constraints of purely private and individual experiences. From a state of modest insignificance we enter a space in which we can take ourselves seriously. As an alternative to accepting everyday events mindlessly, we recalled them in writing, in an attempt to identify points in the past where we succeeded in defending ourselves against the encroachments of others.

Ya van desplumadas.

Our writing is at the same time 'destructive of culture'. The dominant culture deprives us of power in two ways. Meanings generated within it, as well as its way of life, are doubly alien to us: derived from the culture of agents of domination, they arise by extension from the culture of men. Women's relation to language and modes of thought, emotions and attitudes, is one of subordination. In setting out to write, we must in this sense become involved in the 'destruction of culture'.[5]

Writing also transports us across another boundary: it begins to break down the division of labour between literature as creative writing, and everyday language as a means of communication. Down the centuries, the separation of one from another through specialization has on the one hand furthered the art of writing, making it the domain of men; on the other, it has perpetuated femininity's colonization in the realm of language and symbol. 'A true art for all cannot be developed by extending the audience of art to include all humanity, but conversely, by a process whereby the capacity for constructing and organizing the raw material of art (a capacity which has been particularly characteristic of specialists in art) is appropriated by all.'[6] Even if we do not go as far as rejecting the professional practice of literature, it seems to us important to eradicate the harmful effects of the division of labour in writing, since they affect our capacity for conscious intervention in thought or action, or for sensual pleasure at any level.[7] What is more, the simultaneous elevation and degradation of femininity in art, which in effect excludes women from artistic practice, seem to us to make it all the more important for female practice to be given a place in language, and thus woven into the lived relations of society in general.

Women have come to share the reservations of artists on the value of everyday writing. We see writing as an impossibility, since there is nothing to write about. The things we experience seem unimportant and uninteresting; they are banal. This posing of the question of 'theme' reproduces the division of labour between authors and writers. The only way we feel we can become potential subjects of a readable text is by attaining some world-historical significance, perhaps as determined fighters or as victims of tragic exploitation. It seems then that we require more than a little disrespect for all norms and values, if we are to enter the world as conscious participants; a disrespect amongst other things for traditional uses of language, for divisions of labour and theme, for certain modes of thought and behaviour.

Since our aim is to reach a point at which we no longer see ourselves through the eyes of others, we have to take the risk of being seen to make mistakes. In our particular field, the weapon of defence we have chosen is writing.

The Subjectivity of Memory and the Problem of Identity.

Women gained practical experience through consciousness-raising groups of retrieving from everyday life itself the means of transcending the everyday. It clearly boosted self-confidence to know that we were not alone in any of our various modes of experience; and yet there came a point at which we could progress no further. Telling stories became a circular process; no one wanted to listen any more. Hauling ourselves out of the water taught us nothing about flying, but a lot about gravity. As long as our experience was encased within obstinately repetitive gestures, it was impossible – since we had not yet begun to remember *collectively* – to say anything of any consequence about the practices of femininity, whose nature could not be deduced from any known body of laws. It was for this reason that we first proposed to work with and to theorize memory and the everyday, in an attempt to mobilize our pleasure in past experience, to harness it for the arduous labour of theoretical analysis. We found much that it was necessary to change: language, perception, logic, emotions. We had to re-evaluate, to question what we had always taken for granted. Yet it became clear early on that our conceptions of the everyday as pleasurable, and of theory as arduous, were themselves founded on prejudice. In our discussions of sexuality and the body in particular, not simply in relation to anything we might describe as immediately sexual, but even in thinking about hair, clothes, the presentation of the self in general – the work of analysis was fraught with difficulties and obstacles, and theoretical discussion appeared as a convenient escape route. Ultimately, it seemed, our intention to rethink either ourselves or our position in the world had been less than serious. Just as Reynard the Fox disclaimed any interest in the grapes still left hanging on the tree, we too were tempted at an early stage to concur with those of our predecessors who claimed that experience could never be used as a source of knowledge, that experience was too subjective, that individuals did not give objective accounts of themselves. Surely, we argued, it was necessary to insist on objectivity, even if our inclination was to take individual factors into account and thus to set up our work in opposition to academic science in general. It is commonly argued that the lack of objective validity in subjective experience arises from an individual propensity to twist and turn, reinterpret and falsify, forget and repress events, pursuing what is in fact no more than an ideological construction of individuality, giving oneself an identity for the present to which the contents of the past are subordinated. It is therefore assumed that individuals' accounts of themselves and their analyses of the world are not to be trusted; they are coloured by subjectivity.

In our research, by contrast, we were concerned precisely with the ways in which individuals construct their identity, the things that become subjectively significant to them. We were interested in the 'how' and the 'why' of the individual's relationship to the 'givens' of her everyday life, in the way in which she grows into the structures of society. We started from the premiss that human beings, in the process of their socialization, work at restructuring the given elements of their lives, until such time as their existence becomes relatively uncontradictory: in other words, until social action becomes a possibility. Given that there is however no such thing as an existence without contradictions – certainly not within social relations as they exist today, and above all not for women – we had to assume that the absence of contradictions in our self-interpretations will to a large extent be constructed by us; contradictions are forgotten and omitted, left unperceived. While to a degree, it is our use of such constructions that enables us to get by in the world, they ultimately prevent us from gaining a proper grip on reality. At every point where we have indulged in self-delusion, refused to confront issues face to face, avoided conflicts, refuted connections and so on, we have in so doing by-passed, or at least failed to perceive, a certain kind of potential for our future life.

We set out to investigate, then, the processes through which we have formed ourselves as personalities, rather than the way things 'really' – objectively – were. We therefore focused our attention on the way individuals continuously reproduce society as a whole: the way they enter into pre-given structures, within which they produce both themselves, and the categories of society. The example we chose was the domain of sexuality, which women produce and in which they produce themselves in what we will later call 'slavegirlish' subordination.

Our use of the term 'subjective' might perhaps suggest that we view subjective appropriations of social structures as being entirely at the discretion of the individual. This is not the case. The day-to-day struggle over the hearts and minds of human subjects is located not only within social structures, the pre-given forms into which individuals work themselves, but also in the *process* whereby they perceive any given situation, approve or validate it, assess its goals as proper and worthy, repugnant or reprehensible. What emerged in our analysis as a particular way of processing the social world, as its appropriation by individuals, has to be seen as a field of conflict between dominant cultural values and oppositional attempts to wrest cultural meaning and pleasure from life.[8] It is a *compromise*.

On this basis, we also assumed that there is no such thing as a unitary human being. Experience has taught us that we ourselves possess a whole range of insights which we find both attractive and repugnant. We are weighted with emotions that seem to emerge from some point in the past; rationally, we refuse to acknowledge them. The aim of our research was not simply to oppose reason to emotion, but to examine both together, in an attempt perhaps ultimately to change both. We did not intend simply to call upon ourselves to accept what we are, as a means of overcoming our own inner discord; instead, we hoped to find ways of freeing ourselves from the diffuseness of suffering, by embarking on a structuring intervention. Our collective empirical work set itself the high-flown task of identifying the ways in which individuals construct themselves into existing structures, and are thereby themselves formed; the way in which they reconstruct social structures; the points at which change is possible, the points where our chains chafe most, the points where accommodations have been made. The fact that the difficult task of transforming the self-constructed prisons of everyday life can be undertaken successfully has been emphatically demonstrated by the Women's Movement. Here cultural forms once new and shocking are now taken for granted; illegitimacy is no longer grounds for suicide; in many areas of life, restrictive sartorial conventions no longer apply. The attitude we therefore adopted towards ourselves and to the world was one of dissent, of discontent – an attitude we will maintain until such time as we are able fully to develop the human and sensual potential we possess.

In attempting to identify the ways in which we ourselves participate in our socialization, we aimed not only to expand our potential for intervention into and transformation of the world around us. Our work is at the same time directed against a widespread assumption in social theory, according to which human beings are no more than the bearers of roles, the passive agents of norms and expectations. We start by contrast from the assumption that human beings do not simply fulfil norms, nor conform in some uncomplicated way; that identities are not formed through imitation, nor through any simple reproduction of predetermined patterns, but that the human capacity for action also leads individuals to attempt to live their own meanings and find self-fulfilment, albeit within a predetermined social space. Thus experience may be seen as lived practice in the memory of a self-constructed identity. It is structured, by expectations, norms and values, in short by the dominant culture; and yet it still contains an element of resistance, a germ of oppositional cultural activity. It is this intertwining of processes of self-fulfilment with the fulfilment of cultural expectations that is responsible for example for the fixity with which notions of morality become established in our minds. A weakening of the dominant morality within us always involves a simultaneous weakening of our own oppositional potential, since this has developed in and through our appropriation of morality. Take for example the dominant moral precept according to which women are still required to remain monogamous, faithful until their life's end and so on – independently of whether they are passionately in love with their husbands or bored to tears by them. There is an element of emotional resistance in the process whereby we make this morality our own. What makes the morality of monogamy bearable is the assumption that we – every individual one of us – will be exceptional in feeling the lifelong love on which it is founded. We channel that assumption into our desires and dreams, it colours the conclusions we draw from our suffering and joy. Both morality itself, and the way in which we appropriate it, prevent us from even contemplating possible alternatives to the precepts it outlines. On the other hand, we find ourselves similarly debilitated if we simply opt for promiscuity, or demand of ourselves that we live our lives differently – for along with our chains, we also relinquish the hopes we have hitherto invested in the possibility of lifelong love and faithfulness. This dilemma makes collective efforts to strengthen the resistance already contained within our identities so necessary. There is an element of resistance in our demand that love survive lifelong monogamy – since only love can make it liveable. Giving up our hopes along with the constraints upon us takes the ground from under the feet of resistance. If we are to develop new modes of oppositional living, we need to find potential ways of rupturing the unity of hope and constraint. Or to put it another way: our goal must be to find ways of articulating the personal sphere in political terms. In our opinion, such an articulation is particularly important for women, since women have no immediate access to the conceptual building blocks that would help them to come to terms with their everyday lives; thus women tend generally to control no more than half their lives. Story-writing in our view allows the author to arrive at a perception of self capable of understanding lived femininity without appearing inadequate alongside a view of the world centred on notions of 'career' and personal advancement. Instead of stuttering shamefacedly over the inadequacy of our lives, we were able, through story-writing, to give an account of the things we have actually done. We no longer had to judge ourselves by the criteria of an alien culture.

The General and the Particular

The question that concerns us is the way individuals live social relations. We sought in our research to identify the ways in which human beings reproduce social structures by constructing themselves into those structures. We do not assume individuals to be the blind effects of economic relations. In our view, the form that individual life-processes take can neither be predicted, nor can it be deduced from economic laws; it is itself a question for empirical investigation. The experiences of any given individual, the decisions s/he makes for her or himself, the means whereby s/he deals with conflicts, desires and emotions: all of these constitute particular modes of appropriation of pre-existing structures. They differ according to different epochs and cultures, according to class, stratum, gender – they are *personal* ways of negotiating given structures. In challenging each other and ourselves to work with our memories, we were confronted with the problem of the uniqueness or singularity of any given experience. Since it is as individuals that we interpret and suffer our lives, our experiences appear unique and thus of no value for scientific analysis. The mass character of social processes is obliterated within the concept of individuality. Yet we believe that the notion of the uniqueness of experience and of the various ways in which it is consciously assessed is a fiction. The number of possibilities for action open to us is radically limited. We live according to a whole series of imperatives: social pressures, natural limitations, the imperative of economic survival, the given conditions of history and culture. Human beings produce their lives collectively. It is within the domain of collective production that individual experience becomes possible. If therefore a given experience is possible, it is also subject to universalization. What we perceive as 'personal' ways of adapting to the social are also potentially generalizable modes of appropriation. Using our experience – in a positive as well as a negative sense – as an empirical base for our work thus offered the possibility of studying each individual mode of appropriation in detail. Our work derived its impetus from our recognition of the human potential to expand a capacity for action, to develop new possibilities, to enjoy diverse sensual pleasures; this was what led us to investigate the conditions of production of these pleasures, and to press for their universalization. Equally, we considered it vitally important to recognize recurrent forms of suffering in their specificity, in order to avoid reproducing them in the future.

In view of the above considerations, we feel it is necessary to question the way in which scientific analysis disregards individual experience. It is, however, certainly possible to explore actual lived experience within social relations with a view to reaching generalizable conclusions. On the other hand, if research limits itself to the general and ignores the particular, it will be impossible ever to discover the conditions of production of universal human phenomena. If we are to advance down the pathway of liberation, we have to study the ways in which we have set traps for ourselves, as well as to identify the means we have used to sweep aside obstacles in the past. Individual modes of appropriation of the social are frequently conceived as personally unique; in our view, this involves an underestimation of the sociality of human beings. For our purposes, however, a simple recognition of sociality also remains too imprecise. Instead, we chose to work with a more precise notion: what individuals feel to be appropriate to and useful for their personal needs is pre-given in the form of dominant cultural values. In their efforts to make their lives meaningful, individuals attempt to resist the encumbrances of the dominant culture.[9] It is however virtually impossible for them entirely to abandon traditional norms and expectations. On the other hand they can – and indeed do – find compromise solutions that extend the limits of their capacity for action. Thus we witness individuals searching for a meaning to life within pre-existing structures, by engaging with those structures, yet at the same time negating them. Individuals are always active. At the same time, the range of activities accessible to any given individual can be examined as generally available choices. In our own work, our focus of interest was not unique personalities, but rather general modes of appropriation of the social.

We do not, then, conceive of ourselves as fixed, given, unchangeable. As our brief discussion of love and monogamy should have indicated, we feel this allows us to develop collective modes of existence, to reorganize the effects of hitherto existing cultural formations. Our recognition of the necessity to come to our own terms with the social world and to make this, in turn, the object of theoretical discussion, as a prerequisite for research into the appropriation of wider structures, had a dual effect on our work. The first — familiar from consciousness–raising — was the comforting recognition that we were actually not alone in having developed modes of behaviour we had hitherto considered unique, and that the apparently personal and intimate experiences buried within us were in fact more or less generalizable. The second was the insecurity that this questioning of ourselves provoked, from the task we set ourselves of exposing breaks, discontinuities, repressed guilt and painstakingly concealed memories. At an early stage, this aspect of our research led to tensions in group dynamics and to personality problems, both of which carried the danger of renewed isolation – this being the normal response to conflicts. The disruptive and destabilizing effect of memory-work demands conscious collective counter-strategies that we had not yet adequately developed. We have much more work to do in this area. One particular difficulty related to the fact that developing a relationship with our own bodies, subordinating them to prevailing standards, is a painful process within any social group. Thus the immediate problem encountered in any attempt to develop oppositional strategies by entering a different group is the fact that we reproduce our past perceptions of groups in themselves as setters of norms, and thus come to see individual struggle as the most appropriate form of resistance. In attempting to tackle this problem, we came a few steps closer to the construction of a wider collectivity – a project usually obstructed by the antagonistic relations that characterize traditional social groups (with the possible exception of groups within the women's movement, which has gone some way towards forging this kind of collectivity).[10]

In an attempt to recast the problem of destabilization into a form that renders it capable of resolution we studied our own past actions as though in the life of a third person. However important it may be for women to speak and write of themselves as 'I' and thereby to register a protest against the pressures on them to leave their own selves out of account – to attempt, that is, to find a place for themselves within the categories of abstract and impersonal thinking – we believe it is nonetheless essential to use the third person in memory-work. Writing about past events is almost impossible, unless we have some way of distancing ourselves. The very fact that we learn not to take ourselves and our own interests into account has the effect, in memory-work, of reducing the time and trouble spent in writing about ourselves; large portions of experience are neglected, or motives and desires are attributed to our past selves that we would find inadequate as explanations for the actions of others. By translating our own experiences into the third person, we were enabled to be more attentive to our selves. Thus the gaze we cast today on our selves of yesterday becomes the gaze cast by one stranger on another.

Memory as History: the Problem of Ideology

It would be superfluous here to stress the necessity for an historical study of the constructed nature of feminine sexuality. In the case of our particular project, the most obvious method of historical research to choose seemed to be autobiography: the writing of history as a pathway to the present. In reality, however, we believe an approach of this kind to be doomed to failure. Although it appears as a structuring intervention into the chaos of remembered experiences, the autobiographical method is in fact based on a theoretically untenable presupposition. To view childhood and adolescence simply as causal phases of today's person is to assume that actions follow one another logically, that adult human beings are more or less contained within children, that external events produce little more than minor modifications. It also assumes that the factors determining the life of the individual always remain the same. I sound out my life in retrospect from the point of view of an understanding of the determinations acting upon me today. Many of our own biographies work, for example, by ordering our perceptions of childhood experience to accord with our present view of ourselves as handicapped learners. Diversity is compressed and presented as unified evidence that we have 'always' been hindered in our development by this or that person, this or that circumstance. It was a worthwhile exercise to submit the kind of individual and personal history produced by autobiographical viewpoint to more stringent analysis.[11] For a story of the auto-biographical kind represents the sum total of all the social judgments and prejudices, semi-scientific theories, everyday opinions and so on we carry around in our heads and which serve – usually implicitly – as models for our interpretation of the world today. In relation to historical experience those judgments serve most often as solid buttresses to shore up the ruptures in our own construction of ourselves. As dominant norms and values sediment in our minds, they form and inform our spontaneous observations of our own actions and, more particularly, of the actions of others (a process that demands examination from the point of view of a theory of ideology). In the same way, it is possible to study the process whereby we have become the person we are as a sedimentation of different levels of 'working over' of the social. If for example we write down and scrutinize any given memory from childhood, we find ourselves confronted with a diverse number of apparently fixed and given opinions, actions, attitudes, motives and desires, which in themselves demand explication.

Once we have begun to disentangle the knots, the process becomes endless. As we attempt to extricate some clarity from the confusion, the path of analysis leads ever further into the past. Our aim however is to make the process itself, whereby we work our way through and into ideology, the object of our discussions. We need therefore to train our eyes to see this process, and events in the past, in new and more or less unprejudiced ways. The obvious objection here is that it is impossible to divest ourselves of prejudice. Yet since we believe an unprejudiced way of seeing to be essential, we have sought to identify strategies to prepare the ground for its development. One possible approach we have identified involves concentrating on one particular situation, rather than on life in its entirety. Once we have begun to rediscover a given situation – its smells, sounds, emotions, thoughts, attitudes – the situation itself draws us back into the past, freeing us for a time from notions of our present superiority over our past selves; it allows us to become once again the child – a stranger – whom we once were. With some astonishment, we find ourselves discerning linkages never perceived before: forgotten traces, abandoned intentions, lost desires and so on. By spotlighting one situation alone, we learn to recall and to reassess history. We may not always be successful

– but success has become a possibility. It is not so much a question of 'having a good memory', as of practising it. The longer we work with and on ourselves, the more adept we become at retrieving forgotten history. Stepping back into the past, we embark upon a form of archaeology. We discover fragments of an architecture which we then begin to reconstruct.[12] Since we are accustomed to using rapid repression, obliteration and forgetting, to maintain our equilibrium, this attempt to step back into the past, to make the unconscious conscious, both calls into question our normal ways of working over events in consciousness, and threatens our stability as people.

It is necessary to be aware of this danger to the person as an ever-present possibility in memory-work, such is the power of past images to assert a strong pressure on our present life. In questioning the foundations of those images, in making conscious the material out of which we have made ourselves, we are however not only undermining our own stability; at the same time, we are creating conditions for a more resilient fabric for our lives.

We are not assuming that human beings live according to plan, or in continuities, nor that they are always determined by the same consistent factors. On the contrary, phases in the lives of women in particular are lived in a more or less unplanned way; equally, there are changes in the factors that determine their lives. Continuities are manufactured retrospectively in the mind. If this is not carried out as a conscious strategy for liberation we remain at the mercy of everyday images and opinions, which in turn are the result of class struggles in which our liberation as women may very well never have been at issue. From the viewpoint dictated by social norms, forms of resistance ultimately appear as forms of sustained social failure; on the other hand, these norms allow the life story of an individual to be narrated and understood in terms of continuous progress, even if it has in fact been characterized by increasing isolation or deepening poverty. The way our culture represents the reproductive role of women – for example in literature or folktales — turns them into mere objects. It is for this reason that women in particular have only fragments from which to piece together their own past memories. If we were to follow the normal avenues of interpretation, we would end up accepting the kinds of pronouncements women make on the determining factors in their lives in which, for example, they claim always (or even never) to have 'wanted' to be a housewife. Yet in accepting propositions of this kind, we eradicate any possibility of establishing how thoughts and desires arise in the first place. The fact of not being included in history as active participants encourages women ultimately to accept themselves as 'pieces of nature' – which leaves them at the mercy of the dominant culture. Only through their own histori-cization can they retrieve from the dominant culture elements of a new image of themselves, on the basis of which they may possibly be able to construct alternatives for the future.

The Chaos of the Everyday: the Problem of Perception

Once we determined to make our memories the objects as well as the instruments of our research, the very constructed-ness of the social, and thus of ourselves within it, confronted us with a particular dilemma. The much-celebrated unity of subject and object in memory research contains its own pitfalls. We are not used to looking at social forms of perception carefully; our choices of particular analytic focal points are in themselves a product of ideology. In our work, we demanded of ourselves that we question, or overturn, conventional social judgments, that we extricate ourselves from our entanglement within them. In at-tempting to do so, we were forced to resort to the Münchhausen method: pulling ourselves up by the roots of our hair. Unlike Münchhausen, however, we were many; with mutual support, our project might succeed.

In our story-telling, we attempted both to denaturalize exis-ting value-judgments, by describing our memories down to the very last detail, independently of whether or not we consider every element essential, and to disobey the precepts they embody. Our initial aim was to use collective discussions to make it possible to uncover new relations and important traces of evidence within our chosen field of study. Once we began to note down exactly even the most inconsequential detail, we came to recognize the enormous constraints hitherto placed on us by the use of criteria of 'relevance', censoring and restricting our imag-ination and our memory. In subjecting this and other criteria to newly–conscious scrutiny, we began to see how we could criticize dominant orthodoxies on socialization processes, mother-child relations and so on. Any new models of theoretical understand-ing which we then developed in the group were always tested against our stories, and adjusted accordingly. At the same time, they were used alongside the other tools of knowledge at our disposal to shed a critical light on the very practice our stories reconstructed. It was this striving toward theorization that differentiated our project most sharply from consciousness-raising groups. Having made ourselves the objects of our own research, we felt it to be more necessary than ever to use the most highly developed analytical tools available. Theory is often seen as useless to us: why? It seems to us quite possible to focus our attention on theory, and simultaneously to channel our energies in any number of other directions.

Our research has shown that the development of a loving attention to detail is the first prerequisite for a training in social perception. But concentrating on a single situation and describing it in minute detail also had a different significance. Accustomed as we were to being guided by the leading strings of the dominant culture, we tended to formulate new demands on the basis of our questioning of our own ideological socialization. These were the guidelines to which we were to adhere in the process of remembering. We looked everywhere for traces of situations in which we had either voluntarily submitted to our own subordination, or, conversely, in which we had developed early forms of lived resistance. Our memories were thus produced as evidence to support pre-formulated theories. Yet this could teach us nothing new about the ways in which we had worked over our own past experience. In response to this problem, we attempted in our work to approach the events of our childhood with an attitude of more or less undogmatic disrespect. Our basic premiss was that anything and everything remembered constitutes a relevant trace — precisely because it is remembered — for the formation of identity. We therefore decoded the details of our stories as written signs of the relations within which identity is formed.

Living Historically — Writing It Down

What do we actually mean by 'living historically'? Without wishing to take up the cudgels for rationality, or to claim that we need only to recognize the issues at stake for all problems to become soluble, we would still contend that an attempt to free ourselves from dependence and subordination demands that we ourselves live our lives more consciously. In this sense, 'living historically' should be taken to mean a refusal to accept ourselves as 'pieces of nature', given and unquestioned, and a determination to see ourselves as subjects who have *become* what they are, and who are therefore subject to change.[13] In particular, we use the term 'living historically' to signal our desire to change our constricting conditions to make the world a more habitable place. In couching our aims in these terms, however, we may appear to have rewritten our history as a smooth path. We are all familiar with personal recollections in which we appear to have 'resisted' our fate from our earliest childhood. There is little to be said for continuities of this kind. On the contrary, we considered it important to uncover points of disjuncture between our stories of childhood and the way of life we mark out for ourselves today. Our inhibitions about active intervention, fear of conflict, cowardice, evasiveness, debilitating melancholy: all of these may be connected with breaks in our biographies that we continue to live, unconsciously. If we allow ourselves to subject our past to dispassionate scrutiny, we may perhaps be able to effect some change in the present. The very fact that childhood situations were not identical with the image we have hitherto formed of them may allow them to be linked, not only with our as-yet-unremembered past, but also with a future we have not yet consciously thought through. At the very least, a perception of dissonance may be a lever facilitating the transformation of our lives. In our experience of writing these personal histories, that perception often arises out of an individual wishing to write about a particular conflict or problem, then returning to the group with a completely different story, a completely different problem for collective discussion. In order for the group not to react simply with a familiar note of censure – 'this is irrelevant' – we found it necessary not only to take pains to resist our own orthodoxies, but also to use a good deal of imagination, and to attempt to understand displacements of this kind as a challenge to rethink in potentially enriching ways.

The censorship we practise on others is no more or less extreme than that which we practise on ourselves. One of the main obstacles we had to overcome in our writing was our habit of submitting everything to immediate value-judgement. Alongside a few fragments of popular theory, traces of our half-hearted attempts at opposition – most often in the form of some kind of enlightened liberalism – it is possible to identify in spontaneous judgements of this kind the results of our accommodations to dominant morality. Such adaptations obstruct our attempt to use our own past practices to reveal how these judgements themselves have become fixed in our minds. To this extent, the question of whether or not the process of writing itself can begin to effect some change depends on our remaining true to our aim of viewing past situations dispassionately. What will become clear in the course of this book is that focusing precisely on images and emphases, presenting complex interrelations, the very process of putting memory into language, are in themselves enormously taxing.

One final obstacle we had to confront in our writing was our own sense that there is no more to be said, that we know it all already. Particularly since we tend to conceptualize what we already know as the result of causal relations – a conception that cannot do justice to the complex fabric of our memories – an attitude of this kind makes new discoveries impossible. Women's narratives are, very often, interlinked stories. The thread is spun out endlessly; almost from the outset we are led off at all kinds of tangents; it is no longer even remotely possible to imagine the ending of the story with which we began. In putting together written mosaics of our childhood, we found that our narrative mode corresponded closely to actual life as it is lived by women. What we uncover in our story-writing are patterns from the fabric of life, rather than any pre-planned coherence. Indeed the lives of women are not determined according to plans of this kind. Thus writing itself became a practice of active change, the initial step away from an attitude of suffering and resignation, the first attempt to acquire knowledge by bringing to light our memories and displaying them to others. Writing forced us to develop a more consistent approach to our perception of ourselves.

The Problematic

In setting out to study the way in which human beings construct themselves into the world, we may trace the threads of that development and their points of interconnection in our memories; in so doing we discover ourselves, and gain insight into our part in making these connections. We have already seen how everything we remember is relevant to our identity. Yet in so far as we tried to work as a collective, it was impossible for us to discuss, or write about everything that arose; unrestrained storytellers are prone to excess. It was therefore necessary to agree on a theme that could provide a common focus in the work of a project like ours. In our case, the theme we chose was the formation of women as 'sexual beings'. A number of preliminary questions were outlined, each of which involved making an implicit supposition about its context and thus an initial assumption as to what the answers were likely to be. The art of research lies in drawing up the right questions. We had heard of a number of groups working on the theme of sexuality, who had simply taken that theme and outlined a series of classificatory sub-questions, such as: when did you have your first sexual experience, and what was it like? It did not seem at all surprising to us that these groups had written few stories – or none at all – and that their own questions left them feeling discouraged and resigned. For these questions themselves presupposed all kinds of theoretical background knowledge on the part of the questioner, a knowledge of what sexuality can or does mean, a restriction of its meaning to the sexual act alone, a hope that the first sexual act may constitute a definitive origin, or a primary emotional source, which it will not be difficult to trace. Groups of this kind found themselves competing, albeit against their will, against the massive number of pornographic texts in which there is anything but a shortage of words to describe the scene they wish to recall – including the attendant feelings and thoughts each participant is alleged to share. Small wonder then that they were rarely able to avoid the pitfalls confronting anyone entering this particularly well-trodden terrain. The questions initially posed by such groups suggest that they may in actual fact have had quite different goals in mind when they began research, but that the avenues they were to explore had never been outlined with any clarity. The actual focus of their initial interest was not 'sexuality', but 'loss of virginity' – a focus implying that defloration is a decisive event in one's sexual life-history. Hand in hand with that assumption went a whole range of suppositions, theories, prejudices. Analysing these would have been an important first step in the construction of a problematic by these groups, since this would have made it possible for new thoughts and insights to emerge.

We may therefore assume that any set of ready-made questions is likely to be firmly rooted in popular prejudice; the problematic it outlines will be more likely to diminish than to increase our understanding. Our initial proposal, then, was that theoretical questions should only be discussed in the context of the stories themselves if and when they formulated a new and unfamiliar social relation. This may sound arbitrary and puzzling; yet it proved fruitful once work had actually begun. The theme we chose was one that weighed heavily on all of us. In expressing a collective interest in the theme of 'sexualization', we acknowledged each other as experts on everyday life, rather than as scene-stealing rivals. In our identification of that theme, we located one of the points at which we bound ourselves into society. Since our life process is always a process of socialization, that binding into society should not in itself be seen as restrictive. It should on the other hand be made conscious, since this makes clear the process whereby we have absorbed existing social scientific theories, ideologies and everyday opinions. The terrain of investigation into which we enter is not uninhabited; other settlers have been here before us. There may be some advantages in this; existing theoretical knowledge may be seen in terms of a productive force that we can put to our own use in memory-work. Thus our own project for example involved us in a study of a large number of texts on sexuality in general, particularly texts by women, as well as books on sex education and related areas. Yet the advantages were more or less outweighed by the disadvantages; our perception was channelled into colonized forms. Our gaze was, as it were, no longer innocent – if indeed it ever was. In order to reinstate a less predetermined way of seeing, we tried in our own work to formulate an initial problematic by combining together the key elements both of our own prior practical knowledge, and of the theoretical knowledge we had hitherto acquired; it was only after this preparatory stage that we began to write the stories of our own memories.

Insofar as these stories focused on a detailed representation of past events, described as if in a multi-dimensional film made from the point of view of a visitor to a foreign country, to whom every small detail seems essential, since s/he has as yet no criteria to determine what should be considered essential; insofar then as it was possible to 'remember' in the true sense of that word, we could expect to find ourselves tracing a number of linkages that appeared new and exciting, even strange, yet which were immediately recognized by the group as credible, since they formed part of all our memories.

We believe it is necessary to pursue these connections, using them as a basis for the elaboration of a research problematic, as well as for historical research whenever possible: writing new stories around them, drawing on existing theory for their partial elucidation. (This point will be developed at a later stage in relation to specific examples.) This is one way of learning from experience, from the empirical. The principal effect of such a procedure is a *displacement* of the problem of 'the sexual'.

In focusing on the weight of individual distress, or on what individuals feel to have been the most important events in their past, as the starting-point of our research, we forged a connection in our work between the research process and its practical 'effects' on the individual. In studying the way our field of research is colonized by existing theories, explanations, value-judgements and so on, we were simultaneously exposing to scrutiny the structure of our own judgement, as well as the present state of debates and ideological struggles within that field. Existing theory and ideology were tested, therefore, out of practical interest. In taking as our point of departure theoretical questions deriving from our own interests, then setting about writing stories on this basis, while attempting nonetheless (equipped now with an awareness of prevailing forms of judgement) to examine our own past as the past of a stranger, we were placing ourselves in a position from which we could perceive linkages unrepresented in current theory and opinion. These revelations may or may not be fundamental or revolutionary in nature; whatever the case, they certainly represent parts of our lives to which we had hitherto paid little attention. And without doubt, studying them constitutes not only an enrichment of our practical and theoretical lives; it may possibly also bring to light relations initially obliterated from memory for structural reasons – either because they provided the unconscious foundation for the building of existing structures, or because they represented lost bastions of resistance. Whatever the reason, it was certainly worthwhile to pursue these linkages further in our stories.

In the course of our work, we elaborated a theoretical problematic that raised questions about the formation of the sexualized female body as a product of socialization. Our aim was to investigate the organization of bodily activities; the ways in which the body itself and the feelings in and around it have arisen historically; and the ways in which this relates to our insertion into society as a whole. This was the first stage in our reformulation of the relationship between sexuality and domination in general.

Analysis – The Collective – The Comparison

Up to this point, our assumptions as to why our memory-work should be collective have remained implicit; we should now make them explicit. Some of them were purely pragmatic; an individual on her own is not well placed to work through the vast number of theories, opinions, value judgements and so on, that currently cluster around the theme of sexuality. In collective work, on the other hand, individuals can complement each other, in terms of their knowledge of our chosen theme, as well as in terms of workload. Our very choice of theme must also be made collectively, to guarantee that it is generalizable, and that it is significant for the socialization of wider groups. Thus the collective can be seen to militate here against sectarian individualism.

Nor is analysis conceivable in the absence of a collective. In our case spontaneous discussions of any story began with an implicit *comparison*, in which one experience was pitted against another. This was an initial corrective focusing discussion on the credibility of a situation as well as its typicality. Questioning points at which the events described seemed incommensurable with any others was an initial exploration of the conditions under which such events first become possible. Comparison demands of memory exactitude and plausibility. In attempting to produce compatible accounts, we were at the same time demanding explanations, searching for an understanding of our own actions.

The first draft of a story was usually full of inconsistencies, gaps, interpretations whose logic was unclear, breaks and idiosyncrasies. As the story was discussed in the group, spontaneous value judgements, undigested theories and so–called 'scientific' insights began once again to intrude into the relationships described in it; discussions became ever more vehement, since the topics discussed were bound up intimately with our own lives. The aim of group discussion was to uncover new linkages, and to give encouragement to the writer to remember more precisely, to redraft the story. A number of different resistances were encountered here. Queries, expressions of surprise or of incomprehension all too easily convey a note of criticism, demands that the writer make good past mistakes. It was all too easy for group discussions to threaten the very person of the writer, with questions like – 'how could you have done such a thing'? Vulgar psycho-analytic models of interpretation, in particular, are so much a part of our everyday jargon that sophisticated strategies had to be developed to combat the kind of glib reasoning that claims — for example — 'it's obvious you were forced to identify with your mother here'. Faced with this sort of thing the writer would instinctively go on the defensive.

Yet is is above all from within memory itself that resistances arose. Everything of significance was seen to have been written down in the story. In every case, an infringement of the boundaries of the forgotten and the repressed created a psychically difficult situation. Since the aim of our collective research was to retrace in memory the patterns whereby individuals have worked their way into the social world, and since therefore our object was the process of women's socialization, this kind of slipping into amateur psychotherapy clearly undermined our project. One possible way of avoiding it was not to try to overcome resistances in every case but to curtail analysis and to allow others whose personal stability did not seem to be endangered by specific memories to take up the threads. A further suggestion, which we took from the writer Ruth Rehmann, was to ask the collective to complete the rough sketches our memories proved to be. This allowed substantial insights into the ways in which individuals within the collective worked through social material; what is more, the original writer, shocked at what appeared to her the incomprehensible logic of these continuities, would come to recognise the points at which she had not made herself understood, and the reasons why; by then writing *against* the interpretations of others, she could combine a process of self-examination with the first faltering attempts to make herself comprehensible to others. The group thus became a means of transforming what had been up to then a form of communicative incompetence.

Empathy, by and large, proved unsuitable as a method; it stood in the way of knowledge. This was particularly clear in the case of conflicting interests. Many of the strategies by which those in power secure dominance depend on making exploitation comprehensible through empathy. Is the factory owner not forced to take up the position of a father and head of the family, if he wants to keep a grip on his affairs? Does the entrepreneur not have to save money – just like the housewife? And so on.[14] In our attempts to discuss questions related to our own feelings and values, an attitude of empathy could only lead us up the blind alleys of vulgar psychoanalysis as we have already mentioned. What was instead necessary was that we adopt temporarily the same standpoint as the writer; this was the first prerequisite of any comparison with our own ways of processing experience. If even this failed to produce an understanding of others' modes of behaviour, then our surprise at least might lead to further questioning; thus group consensus on the meaning of particular experiences was in every case challenged by accounts of different experiences deriving from similar contexts. For we were not in search of normative guidelines in recalling experience; their content was on the contrary to be presented for discussion (thus for example the fact that we found frequent correspondences between accounts dwelling on the inadequacy of our vital statistics, and their significance for our actions, irrespective of how thin or fat, large or small we might actually be, highlighted the necessity for research into the origins of these internalized norms).

As we adopted the standpoint of others, we came to know ourselves and each other as historical contemporaries engaged in reconstructing the mosaic of experiences by which we were trained to enter society. Admittedly, we learned nothing if we did not pause to reflect on the attitude of each individual to her place within the social whole. Reflection made it possible to reinterpret those taken-for-granted aspects of our lives which we could not focus merely by stepping into the shoes of others. To this extent, story-writing served to 'denaturalize' ourselves and our actions, thoughts and feelings. In collective studies of the same object in different accounts, there evolved a collective subject capable of resisting some of the harmful consequences of traditional divisions of labour. Individual practices contain a number of different patterns of thought, different means of interpreting the self in the world. As long as those different models remain atomized and divided from each other, society will be capable of infinitely reproducing itself in its present form.

By relating these different patterns of thought and interpretation to each other through a process of comparison, it was possible to begin to combat the fragmented inter-relations of human subjects in relation to each other. (This was a first step towards the construction of a collective subject.) Thus the more diverse the backgrounds and present occupations of members of the collective, the more far-reaching the insights gained into socialization in general. (One extreme case of differences in practices and patterns of interpretation is the separation of mental from manual labour, whose contribution to class division and its maintenance has been the object of extensive research.[15] Our work begins, then, from the premiss that the differences in our various areas of experience will have produced and will carry with them specific and distinct boundaries and separations, and that our collective work will make it possible to soften the edges of those rigid boundaries. In other words, we assume that there is an element of socialization in the drawing of boundaries and the delineation of particular domains, for example in the delineation of the sexual.)[16]

The Constraints of Subjectification – The Project

The concept of subjectification can be understood as the process by which individuals work themselves into social structures they themselves do not consciously determine, but to which they subordinate themselves. The concept allows for the active participation of individuals in heteronomy. It is the fact of our active participation that gives social structures their solidity; they are more solid than prison walls. Externally, we are bound to a particular social location. Since we have at our disposal a whole range of interpretations for rationalizing this, we are blind to our shackles. In the stories we wrote about ourselves, that blindness appeared initially as a general indecisiveness. It seemed initially that everything was relevant, possible, random, impervious to analysis. As indicated above, initial discussions of the stories yielded little more than a repetition of the interpretations demanded by our different positions within the social hierarchy. Our strategy was to make necessity the mother of invention, in other words to view the initial discussion process as a peeling away of the layers of material sedimented in our minds – and to make that process a systematic one. The first step in analysis thus involved all members of the group expressing their opinions and judgements; in addition, they studied the theories, popular sayings, images and so on that already surrounded their object: in other words, the way in which the field was already colonized. We encountered evidence of a huge discrepancy between what we normally take to be our theoretically well-founded, enlightened and radical way of thinking, and our spontaneous judgements and feelings on the events of our childhood. This seems to indicate – to put the case somewhat extremely – that our emotions, in contrast to our thoughts, are spontaneously reactionary. A particularly productive stage of our work was thus the phase in which we analyzed the way in which our consciousness becomes ideologized, through noting down all the interpretative models, feelings, thoughts, snippets of popular wisdom, judgements, that we and others might bring to each story.

In our attempts to analyse the process of production of the domain of the sexual, we found that project work is without doubt the most fruitful form of research. It allows not only our own experience to become a source of knowledge, but also for the examination of anything from historical documents, old and new doctrines and dogma, images and fairytales, proverbs and newspaper articles. It slashes through the horizontal seams that traditionally keep domains of experience separate and parallel, allowing us to forge collectively new connections between separate elements of our stories – connections that are then more relevant to the specific questions we want to raise. The task is admittedly an arduous one: but the pleasure it affords is equally great – the pleasure for example of making direct connections between the great cultural artefacts of history, and our own lives (as for example when we look at the representation of the female body in the Fine Art tradition, or when we rediscover the elements within fairytales we had passed over, unconcerned, as children – the fact for example that girls very often have to marry the most repugnant of men, for whom in turn marriage represents little more than a means of ridding themselves of their hedgehog skin, their disguise as dragon or as horse).

If we are to outline strategies for liberation within patterns of thought drilled into us by others, then it seems to us essential to record the mental traces of those traditional patterns, to make conscious the ways in which we have hitherto unconsciously interpreted the world, and to develop resistances against this 'normality'. Only then will it become possible for us to identify the points at which our morality hinders the development of our thinking, the points at which images from the past reassert their hold on us in the present; the feelings we live as productions of our own.

The power of traditional images within us derives in part from our isolation. By making the research process collective, we at the same time make it possible to draw general conclusions. Again, we may assume that women's experiences are colonized in a particular way by dominant patterns of thought, and by interpretations that organize our subordination. Writing against the grain always requires of women that they unburden themselves of the patterns of thought prevailing in what we have called 'everyday theory'. In the normal run of things, everyday theory bundles the experiences of individuals together like so many disparate sheets of paper. Anything that fits the theory is used as evidence; incongruities are disguised or discarded. Our task then is to construct a different order of things.

One further effect of writing down our spontaneous interpretations of the events in any given story was to demonstrate how we customarily experience and assess a particular event simultaneously. Our morality, then, is no more unitary than we are ourselves. The alien and contradictory qualities of our society have been transported by us into our very selves.

Discussion in the group further enabled us to recognize that the fixity of certain value judgements stems from their grounding in a context, or rather to see that value judgements hold only because they are invisible within the different contexts in which they are nonetheless operative. A particular stance — for example, an attitude of sacrifice or universal goodwill, a willingness to suppress one's own interests — may be entirely justified in the context of the family (or at least, it may not appear entirely intolerable); the same attitude in the world of social production, of class struggle, congeals in the form of opportunism. Collective experiments with the many different attitudes that surfaced in our work were a source of great pleasure; transposing them into different areas, seeing how they looked in different contexts; reversing them, trying to invert them, in short, by translating the stories out of the sphere of the purportedly 'natural' into that of the 'manufactured'.

Language

Language is a slippery instrument. The language of science in particular floats far above our everyday consciousness; abstracted from the concrete, it pretends to neutral objectivity. It is therefore particularly important to establish precisely what is being abstracted from, whose interests are being represented, whose side is being taken, under the cloak of 'scientific' generalization. If I speak in scientific terms of 'strata', I remain silent on the question of class; if I speak of class, I ignore gender, and so on. The language of science is, then, in no sense neutral. On the other hand, everyday or colloquial language is hardly our unambiguous ally. That particular events and feelings are expressed is not in and of itself an advantage. On the contrary, everyday language is packed with preconceived opinions and value judgements that act as obstacles to understanding. We only have to look at a few well known proverbs – which, after all are part of day-to-day speech – to see for example how the impression is created that individual advancement is merely a matter of personal effort ('If at first you don't succeed try, try and try again'; or, 'Rome wasn't built in a day').

Language gains power over us when it is spoken by others, or when we have no control over the language at our disposal. In an earlier section on literature and writing we referred to the relationship between artistry in language, and that lack of linguistic competence which both derives from the social division of labour and produces lack of self-consciousness in our actions. Elsewhere, we suggested that scientific theory as yet simply provides no concepts for, and thus no means of understanding the diverse practices of women.[17] In relation to the language of the everyday, we also indicated the ideological character of objects formed in language. Thus an analysis of our stories in terms of the language they employed could afford us new knowledge and insights.

The first point to arise in the work of the group was our awareness of a lack of language. This lack was made manifest in the stories as a paucity of expression, and a related incapacity to communicate. Queries from the group about the precise nature of the events narrated – how we felt, what disturbed us, what we had aimed to achieve – invariably encountered the same prison bars denying us any expressive capacity to mark out a route either for our desires or our disabilities. This lack of an adequate language is not simply a function of the fact that not everyone can be a great writer; it is an obstacle to liberation. Women's emergence of self-conscious from the shadows of prehistory – their movement into politics in particular – demands a conscious appraisal of our lives, it demands that experience be transformed into theory: it demands, in short, a language. One important task for the collective was to act as a kind of language school which, unlike traditional schools, sought out words familiar from our own experience that might equip us for active social intervention.

The cliché was the most common form in which memories were verbalized – a form which might also be defined as the linguistic means by which we are socialized into heteronomy. Lack of language was not the problem here: cliché is characterized by volubility. To the extent that the use of cliché assumes a consensus, it acts as an obstacle to thought and understanding. 'He looked deep into her eyes'; 'she felt her heart flutter'; 'a sob rose in her throat'; 'the blood drained from her face'; the world of female emotion seems to be colonized by imperialist cliché. Cliché defines like a corset the contours of 'appropriate' female feelings and desires. A. E. Rauter's definition of cliché seems particularly apposite here; speaking in cliché is, for him, like 'biting on a plumstone which someone else has spat out, rather than the plum itself'.[18] In using cliché, we are to an extent passing sentence on ourselves; the cliché condemns us to walk on the well-trodden path of that which should be. The cliché debilitates; it acts as an obstacle to understanding.

Thus for example one woman from our group wrote the following on her participation in her own degradation to slavish femininity: 'I realized how fashionable my hair had become; long and curly, it attracted everyone's attention.' Doris Lessing, by contrast, writes of the same complex 'hair' – always so significant for women – that the hairdresser 'sent her out with a very dark red haircut so that it felt like a weight of heavy silk dangling against her cheeks as she turned her head'.[19]

The difference between these two formulations is not simply one of literary competence; it implies also two different kinds of practical political action. While Lessing illuminates the sensuous and erotic element in the sensation of hair brushing against her cheek – a description we are able to understand only because it describes feelings of which we too are all capable – the version written by the amateur writer seems to suggest that her relationship to her hair is determined purely by fashion and the attention of others. In her use of ready-made assemblages of words, which appear credible to her to the extent that they fit with familiar everyday theories, the writer condemns herself anew to subordination. Here, the words that present themselves so readily to us as adequate expressions of experience in fact direct us away from sensual pleasure and bodily feeling. The path to 'liberating' action they mark out leads only to defiant attempts to make ourselves independent of fashion, or of the opinions of others – attempts limited to gestures of refusal, whereas Lessing's use of language enables us to opt for the sensual pleasure.

Language can serve either as a prison house, or as the material of liberation. It is not always easy to bear this in mind. Our linguistic sensibility spans a whole range of images of model virtues which we identify firmly as expressions of commendation or uniqueness. Thus for example we consider a disrespectful attitude reprehensible, whereas in fact it is a necessary precondition for knowledge itself. We use the concept of power as an insult, as something to which we never aspire (mild and gentle as we are); and so we continue to live in a state of powerlessness. We talk of the hard-edged quality of competitiveness, of the immense rigidity it produces in human beings; and yet we our-

selves are barely capable of standing firm in the face of even the
smallest of conflicts. It can therefore only be beneficial to us both
to scrutinize the models given to us by language,[20] and to develop
a language of our own. Contrary to reputation, our everyday
language is more than a little *abstract*: it suppresses the con-
creteness of feelings, thoughts and experiences, speaking of
them only from a distance. Hence the enormous effort involved
in translating female experience into narrative. Much of this
experience surfaces only in passing phrases; thus one trade
unionist in the group wrote, for example: 'he was able to make
numerous contacts in the course of his work for the union, all of
which came in useful when he applied for a very much higher
position'. No words for, nor any understanding of the way in
which contacts are made. What is the price he pays for this
forging of contacts? Whose pocket does 'he' now live in? To
whom is his outspokenness no longer a source of aggravation?
Who has become the object of his flattery? Would she herself be
able to nurture such contacts without placing herself in a position
of extreme ambiguity? And finally; what is a 'very much higher
position', and why does he need it? Questions such as these
became 'askable' in the group. Indeed, after a while it became
something of a game, vying with each other in picking up the
traces of events encased or, as one woman put it, 'ensnared'
within the words we use.

Language is not usually perceived as a malleable material in
and through which we live our lives, a material which we mould,
and through which we ourselves are moulded. From our earliest
school days, we learn to write 'about' the world, rather than to
find a language for the forms *within* which we live. We neither
express the feelings we experience, nor, by extension, do we
have any means of reassessing or questioning them. We simply
reproduce the perceptions we have heard spoken by others, from
whose experience they are equally far removed. One particularly
forceful memory of my own involves an early experience of my
daughter at school. One day, quite nonchalantly, she presented
me with her new creations for Mothers' Day. The text, an essay
for her German class, was saturated with such poignant expressions as, 'day and night you scrub the floor on your knees': 'by
night your tired hands darn our worn-out socks by the dim light
of an old lamp': 'your hands are soft from the eternal round of
washing up . . .', and so on. My response, the outrage of a
modern mother: 'how can you bring yourself to write such
things? I've never darned socks in my life – and what about the

washing up machine? Our floors have wall-to-wall carpeting – and besides, what's happened to the typewriter which takes up so many hours of my day?' Her matter-of-fact answer: 'you know I can't write that – what sort of marks do you think I'd get for *German behaviour*'? This was the one phrase she had coined from her own experience: 'German behaviour'. To me it seems to sum up perfectly the relationship between language and ideology, or rather between the way language is used and the modes of behaviour that instil dominant values in us. Our relationship with language becomes strangely artificial. Even as we write, we have little faith in the words we use; how can we take ourselves seriously when our mouths form words which are and yet are not our own. These are the teeth of our argument; what if they turn out to be false?

Absences – Silences – Breaks

Writing and analysing stories is amongst other things a way of gaining self-confidence. For reasons of emotional survival, we have become accustomed to seeing ourselves in the terms laid down for us, and from a position marked out for us by society. For women, that position is hardly expansive. Memories of early childhood reveal the extent to which our modes of experience, our designs and desires, have become impoverished. By excavating traces of the motives for our past actions, and comparing these with our present lives, we are able to expand the range of our demands and competences. Admittedly, this is not as easy as it sounds. Our stories are expressed in the language we use today. Buried or abandoned memories do not speak loudly; on the contrary we can expect them to meet us with obdurate silence. In recognition of this, we must adopt some method of analysis suited to the resolution of a key question for women; a method that seeks out the un-named, the silent and the absent.[21] Here too, our experience of education maps out a ready-made path of analysis; we have been taught to content ourselves with decoding texts, with searching for truth in textual analysis, complemented at best by the author's own analysis ('what did the poet mean by this'?). 'Re-learning' in this context means seeing what is *not* said as interesting, and the fact that it was not said as important; it involves a huge methodological leap, and demands more than a little imagination. In the group these lessons could be learned. The search for omissions, for the unnamed, became a

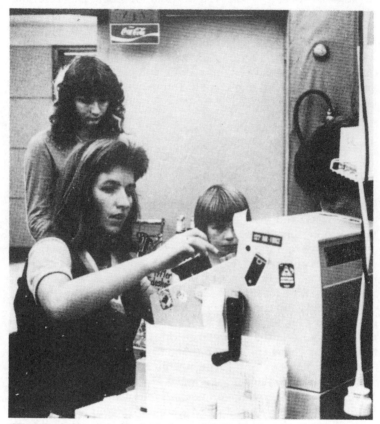

'Working in the supermarket', from *Arbeiterfotografie,* S.208

'A worker photographing his wife', from *Arbeiterfotografie*,
S.207

collective one. Once it had become clear that women, extra-ordinarily, were neither linguistically present in our vocabulary, nor present personally in numerous everyday notions of work and society at large, nor theoretically, in the language of science, our research took on the excitement of a detective novel; we began to develop skills in following clues and uncovering scandals as a preliminary to future transformation. (A study of the changes this produces is illuminating. Twenty years ago, I myself, had no doubts whatsoever as to their validity; indeed, I pursued them with an attitude of reverent thirsting for know-ledge. After reading Irigaray's critique of Freud – which does little more than expose his analysis of femininity as a series of restatements of the fact that women are not men, that they 'lack' something in relation to men and so on – I now find it impossible to read the old texts without laughing out loud: a true release. My awareness dawned late: but it was a great step forward). Along-side omissions, absences and the unnamed, it is still possible to reconstruct past events in the cracks between the echoes of our silence.

Contradiction and the Need for Harmony

There are points in our stories where we break off, to take up the threads at a different point in the narrative. The margins of the story mark a border between the remembered and the forgotten. If the group asked for clarification, our strategy was one familiar from our way of dealing with other areas of experience: we fudged the issue. We might have chosen to tell stories that related a series of events peacefully and harmoniously, or produced a set of inconsistent fragments impossible to forge into a whole. There was no easy solution to this dilemma. It seemed likely that many stories would simply have to be abandoned as 'unproductive'. One method of story analysis proved in our experience to be fruitful, namely the tracing of contradictions. These appeared most often as no more than hairline cracks; at first glance, we seemed to be dealing with a harmonious whole. Yet under the surface, confusion reigned; here polarities are conceivable.[22]

At different points in the same stories, we might impute to ourselves any of a whole range of different motives and attitudes: 'we always wanted to learn', 'we have always been forced to learn', 'we despised others because they learned', and so on.

Transposing these motives into linguistic form made visible the contradictions between them. Since however these were not simply contradictions in language, it was impossible to resolve them on the level of language; we took them instead as a challenge to work on what we now recognized to be real contradictions in our lives, to sharpen our perception of them in language, and to seek to identify further connections still obscured by ('linguistic') ambiguities.

Our perceived need for harmony is particularly detrimental to the expansion of our knowledge. Like wishful thinking, the need for harmony ornaments ugly inconsistencies, plasters over the cracks. The price we pay for the elimination of contradictions is acquiescence in a kind of narrow-mindedness that conflicts at every turn with the level of knowledge we have actually attained. It makes our parents appear to us for example as villains pure and simple; it invites us not only to see conflicts as irresolvable, but also focuses effort on energetic attempts to produce evidence of their irresolvability. How then can we make visible the unconscious structure that underlies this fantasized harmony? Every one of us knows and can give examples of women's descriptions of the daily labour of looking after the husband: 'he's never there. I have to get food for the children. Then they never come home. I only live for the children. They'll leave home for good in the end. My husband likes me to be at home in the evenings. He always goes out on his own.' What we perceive here is an underlying fear of thinking all these things at the same time. The actions of which women speak in this way retain their consistency by maintaining the separation between individual events. When stories of this kind were told in the group, by contrast, the group acted as a corrective to any harmonizing of contradictions. There was at least one member of the group who could give an account of contrasting experiences. In group work, it was also possible (even in the face of resistances that threatened to distort context and structure) to produce a new set of questions, and ultimately to reach a point such that contradictions which had appeared insoluble – and had generated a desire for harmonization – appeared less intractable once translated into a different set of social dynamics. Memory-work must, then, contain an element of practical questioning; it is not concerned purely and simply with a search for new insights.

Interests and Character Traits

Many of our stories derive their initial plausibility from the apparent incomprehensibility of the actions of others. Just as in fairytales the plot is carried forward by the actions of the good and bad fairies, we too view the character traits of others as decisive in directing our lives – even though we have long since stopped 'believing' in fairytales. People act in particular ways, we say, because they are 'evil'; intrinsically 'bad'; mothers are petty, schoolfriends envious and hateful, and so on. In depicting others in this way, we are however likely to be disguising our own contradictions – or at least attempting to construct them into some sort of unity. Ideas of this kind paralyze us in our daily lives. In analysing our stories, we therefore found it necessary to provide detailed descriptions of other protagonists, to represent their actions from the point of view of their own interests and motives. Just as we became capable of producing a complete description of ourselves by virtue of a simple process of distancing (writing in the third person), it was equally simple to write credible motives for the actions of others into the revised versions of our stories. The transformation this effected was no more or less than revolutionary and what we learned from it is incalculable.[23]

Method as Culture

Our project involved individual groups of women working for almost two years on stories of their everyday lives. The individual analytic stages outlined above developed out of these groups' continuous work with their own stories; they were not formulated prior to nor in abstraction from the questions evoked by the stories themselves. In our experience, new modes of analysis suggest themselves continuously – for example it seems to us that it might be worthwhile to investigate the reasons for the appearance at simultaneous points in any story of elements whose relation to each other is by no means 'natural' (to ask for example why clothes are mentioned in relation to conflict, Christmas in relation to an unnamed presence, money). The diversity of our methods, the numerous objections raised in the course of our work with the stories, and the varied nature of our attempts at resolution, seemed to suggest that there might well be no single, 'true' method that is alone appropriate to this kind of work. What we need is imagination. We can, perhaps, say quite decisively that the very heterogeneity of everyday life demands similarly heterogeneous methods if it is to be understood.

Despite our own experience of bottlenecks, dead ends and running on the spot, we would nonetheless plead, in conclusion, that this form of story-writing is a solid method. Writing stories is fun. More than this, it expands our knowledge enormously, sharpens our social perception, improves our use of language, changes our attitude to others and to ourselves. It is a politically necessary form of cultural labour. It makes us live our lives more consciously.

Postscript – Tools of Remembering

How do I set about writing the story of an event from my early childhood? My aim is to gain from past feelings and connections some knowledge of the way we work ourselves into the social world. One of the difficulties is that past feelings and thoughts may be distorted by present-day value-judgements; I have to try to remember as precisely as possible. I attempt then to develop a method which can be applied generally to such memories. For the scene I want to reproduce, I look for a key image, in other words for a tableau, often no more than a fleeting glimpse of a moment from the past, which I have since kept stored in my memory. An example: the furious expression on my father's face as he sweeps aside the personal bric-a-brac I keep on the window-sill in his angry attempts to open the window. The image presents itself to me clearly now. I then recall every detail of my surroundings at that moment: in this case, my bedroom, a room which I still remember as if I were a diminutive 1m30 tall. I myself am standing by my bed, my face turned towards this furious figure of a man. Up to this point, I have used a number of universally understood details (the arrangement of my room, my height) as props to the process of remembering. But now I feel my fists clench involuntarily, I sense feelings of defiance and anger rising within me. Aha. . . my feelings are remembering. Or at least, they are reacting by duplicating past emotions. My anger is strong enough, uncontrolled enough to allow me to feel once again as I did the first time I cast my customary cowardice to the winds and protested, I can see the china cat shattering once again, my little cactus being bent in the middle, it hurts, I cry and scream and storm towards him to hurt him in return, to avenge myself, I want to hit him, bite him, pinch him, kick him.

In searching for a graphically descriptive vocabulary, I begin to feel a definite distance. Although I can now remember the precise details of my struggle with myself – a struggle that was a necessary first step towards undermining my respect for authority, as well as towards overcoming my cowardice in the face of threatened punishment, if only for a few brief seconds – I can now also begin to order both thoughts and feelings. The scene unfolds as I write, searching for the appropriate words; detail after detail surfaces out of the memories that still strive to find expression in language.

It seems, regrettably, that this method of exploring past feelings does not work in every case. Some members of the group had extreme difficulties with it. It cannot moreover be applied at random to any given topic. If we want to extend its range of application, we may perhaps take as an essential point of departure, not an image, but a smell perhaps, a colour, sounds or music; smells in particular are especially evocative for me – the way that every house has its own special smell, instantly recognizable: or the particularly intense smell of spring in the air after heavy March rains. . .

CHAPTER TWO

Displacements of the Problem

Introduction to the Projects

Big Brother

She, a girl barely seven years of age, tossing incessantly and turning from side to side, incapable of sleep. Over and over again, the horror-film she had been through played itself out before her eyes. Her first experience . . . how was she to behave from now on towards the brother who was nine years her senior? Why had he wanted to lie naked in bed with her? He hadn't seemed to notice how it had shocked her, how unpleasant and embarrassing she found it when his thing swelled and stiffened, when he used it to stroke her between the legs – she was still only a child! A little girl who still paid no more than passing attention to sexuality. Besides, her mother had always told her never to let any men touch her between the legs; mother had even disapproved of her touching herself down there. And yet she had been completely defence-less . . . But then again, why 'defend'? After all, her brother hadn't forced her, he had asked her affectionately. Oh, if only her parents had been at home. Her brother wouldn't have dared to do it – as it was, she'd been afraid the whole time they'd be caught, and at one point grandma had come downstairs . . . what would have happened if they hadn't heard her in time? . . . And now it had happened a second time. She felt helpless! Every day the same thoughts plagued her, on the long journey to school and in the evenings before she dropped off to sleep. What on earth was she to do? She respected her brother and was pleased that he now accepted her; that he no longer grumbled at her as he had always done until now, out of irritation at her occasional outbursts of exuberance. And now of all times, when they were getting on so well, he had confronted her with the unpleasant necessity of denying an express wish of his. She couldn't allow it to happen again. What was she to do . . . she couldn't see it through on her own. . . only Mother could now help her . . . tomorrow she would pluck up all her courage to tell her mother about it . . . Mother was sure to put things right again.

This was one of the first stories we wrote on the theme of 'sexuality'. The kind of story we might have expected: sexuality is seen to be directly to do with sex, it begins in the family and is at the same time persecuted within the family, the man is active, women and girls have no sexuality of their own, they are stroked, subjugated, raped. These stories speak a language with which we are thoroughly familiar; they are located at the centre of the discourse in which what we understand as sexuality is produced.[1] At the point at which we wrote these stories, we had not yet turned our attention to the way in which sexuality itself is constructed. Writing and discussing stories of this kind left us with a feeling of helplessness; how were we to identify means of defending ourselves against the forms of oppression they described? No matter how far back they went, these stories always depicted the results of an already existing repression of sexuality. Examining the notion of sexuality more closely, we found it to be represented and lived as oppression at the very moment of its emergence; thus its suppression could not be assumed, as we had hitherto believed, to consist solely in a prohibition of the sexual. But then, what is 'the sexual'? In the first instance it seems clear that it is something that happens with our bodies. In an attempt then to discover the origins of our deficiencies and our discontents in the domain of the sexual, we decided at an early point in our research to focus our study on our relationships to our bodies and to their development. How had we learned to live in our bodies? We set up what we called body projects; initially for all parts of the body (feet, legs, stomach, hips, waist, buttocks, breasts, neck, arms, hands, hair, eyes, mouth, nose and so on). There was no single area which seemed not to represent a problem for one or other of us. Of all projects, we were able to carry only a handful to their conclusion: the slavegirl project, the body, legs and hair. Of the many possible approaches we outlined in the initial stages, we were able to put only a handful to the test. We wrote stories, analysed a small number of proverbs and sayings,[2] studied the changing images of women in the Fine Arts,[3] examined a number of the ways in which the insertion of women into social structures of authority and power occurs across the body.

Legs

. . . . The photo shows my sister, one of my brothers, and me. He and I are sitting "like two young louts", my mother says. My sister, quite proper, chaste, obedient, sits with her legs closed, carefully placed one beside the other. I still have a clear memory of the moment when the picture was taken – I was barely five years old – and the sense of triumphant defiance when, at the very last moment before the photo was taken, I could no longer be prevented from sitting with my legs spreadeagled, the image of this unseemly behaviour captured forever on film. Nowadays I realize that this feeling, this attitude of the body, of the legs, cannot so easily be expressed in the way I felt it then, as proof of independence, as a refusal of obedience, as resistance to the way I had been brought up to behave. Language refuses to render what I intend it to. Whatever I say about my legs – that they are spreadeagled, spread apart, not closed – has an aftertaste of something disreputable, something obscene, it is coloured with sexual overtones. If I want to avoid this I have to talk, not of legs, but of a whole person, whom I describe as loutish or boorish . . . and yet I know very well that everything began with my legs.

Not that my mother taught us idiocies such as to take care during visits to strangers to sit only on the front edge of the chair; on the contrary, we all agreed on the repressiveness of this kind of upbringing. But now that we (my sister and I) were old enough, and above all tall enough for our legs no longer to lift off the ground and dangle in mid-air whenever we sat down, now was the time to talk to us about correct posture. Legs were to be placed neatly alongside each other, one knee touching the other. Anything other than this makes a bad impression, smacks of bad upbringing; it's slovenly, its not what pretty girls do. I did my best. My legs went independent. Whenever my attention wandered for a second, there I was sitting legs astraddle again. I pressed my knees together. Immediate discomfort. The points where they touched became unbearably hot. I felt a familiar nervousness – like the feelings I had when I clenched my hands grimly around the scissors to cut my nails. I got cramp in my legs. Slackening slightly . . . impossible, my legs fell open. I tipped off-balance when they lay like this, in a straight line one against the other. Pressing my knees together gave me some support, and at the same time a little control. And yet – here it was again, this dreadful feeling, as if a piece of wood, a sharp-edged one, was clasped between my limbs. I take my heels off the ground, rock a little on my toes. "Stop fidgeting about," says my mother, "Do you need to go to the toilet?" – "She always goes too late," she confides in passing to her friend. Not that too, why does she have to tell everyone that? She shouldn't have betrayed me. The blue sky on the horizon of this scene, the chance to get up – the toilet was an excuse – and then not to come back. But the blue sky has gone. Only if I stay here, if I don't go out at all, can I disprove the allegation that I never go to the toilet on time. I shift in closer to the table. I'm rigid with tension. The tablecloth mercifully hides my legs as they begin to creep apart again. Why can't I do it? My sister can. She can do everything. No wonder my mother is so fond of her. She tells her secrets. I look across at her peevishly. There you are! She's not sitting with her legs together at all – she's crossed one over the other, the right one over the left one. It looks funny, it can't possibly be right. I call out loud – she's not sitting right either! My mother, accustomed to these outbursts of jealous tale-telling from me, glances up for just a moment, says, "That's not particularly nice either, but it's much better than the way you sit."

Now that I have interrupted the conversation, I am no longer reprimanded for leaving the room. I go to the room that I share with my sister, and decide to practice sitting with my legs crossed. It's not as bad as sitting with them wide apart, and it's not too goody-goody. I decide it works well, and feel grown-up. Only in retrospect do I see that this was the cheapest possible form of protest, submitting to order whatever the cost, for even today I cannot perceive women who don't sit with their legs together as anything but somehow obscene – it embarrasses me, recognizing as I do in all those women an image of myself as I knot my legs one, two, three times or more in my struggle to keep my balance on the chair.'

In our stories, we attempted to recover what we call 'linkages'. By this we mean feelings, attitudes towards other people and towards the world, which have some connection with the body. In the story above, the legs are 'linked-in' to attitudes and emotions in a number of different ways. Sitting with the legs apart is an attitude of resistance. But what happens to the relationship between ourselves and our bodies when they become the focal point of actions of a social nature, means to an end – that of producing a relationship to other human beings? Is the body not liable to become a means of securing our insertion into the prevailing order? This is certainly what happens in our story; the legs are crossed in imitation of the pose of the sister, who is in every way the mother's favourite. Thus our story teller, though she fails to fulfil the requirements of ideal posture, nonetheless manages to emulate the sister her mother adores; in this respect at least she is as good as her sister. Her resistance to the imposition of a prescribed leg position may be seen as slotting her into a position within the family hierarchy. This then raises the question of the connections between resistance and conformity to order or, more extremely, the question of the ways in which we impose order on ourselves by practising particular forms of resistance. There is a further linkage here, namely that between requirements on the writer to keep her legs together and 'growing up'. In the first instance, she has to be tall enough for her feet to have stopped dangling in mid-air before she can be required to keep her legs together. At first she does so simply in response to comments from others; in the end these responses are transformed into a desire on her own part to be able to do what is required of her. The desire for that ability is then linked with competition for the mother's favour.

Ultimately, then, the story raises the question of why this particular position should have been imposed on girls in the first place. The social relations which made it necessary can be deduced retrospectively on the basis of the effect it has produced. Even today, the sister finds it obscene to stand or sit with legs apart. Clearly, then, something 'sexual' is being signified through leg posture. In expending such large amounts of energy on keeping our legs together, we begin to feel there is something we must keep hidden, something which would otherwise be revealed to public view. It is through the activity of concealment that meaning is generated. Leg posture may be seen therefore to acquire sexual significance through being linked with a sexual organ to which it alludes in the act of concealing it. 'Sexualization' is acquired without sexuality itself ever being mentioned. Instead orderliness is stressed in the training of leg posture; emphasis is placed on looking as a pretty girl should and avoiding looking like a 'slag'. Even if a girl has no knowledge of the exact meaning of her parents' pronouncements on leg posture, she is likely to sense from their manner and tone that they are addressing a matter of profound significance. The 'linkages' formed at this point are strong enough to resist all kinds of later insights and enlightenments. In our discussions, for example, the

Die Smo-
kingjacke wurde
einst für Män-
ner gemacht. Heu-
te wird sie von
Mädchen zu Pailiet-
ten-Hot-pants
getragen. Preis:
159 Mark

Stern 8/82

argument was put forward that while 'sexuality' might generally be seen as a social construction, it was surely a matter of *fact* that legs splayed apart were provocative . . . after all they exposed 'it' to general view. But what then of male leg posture? A man of our acquaintance suggested, as an explanation for women's adoption of particular leg postures, that 'women's physical constitution simply makes it easier for them to sit with their legs close together rather than spread apart; it's their anatomy'. Arguments like this condemn the *activities* of women to a perpetual and sustained de-naming.

In our story, leg posture is also 'linked' to personal hygiene. The sister waits too long before going to the toilet, says the mother, much to the embarrassment of the child. In our culture, toilet training (a theme we have been unable to pursue further in this context) is intertwined with the production of our bodies as sexual objects. The shame we feel in relation to our bodily orifices and their secretions or indeed in relation to whole areas of the body, is linked intimately with the sexual significance of those same bodily zones. The goal we set ourselves at this point in our project, therefore, was that of finding out how 'sexualizations' of this kind arose; how parts of the body with no immediate relation to 'sexuality' acquired a sexual meaning. It seemed to us that this could usefully be seen in terms of the sexualization of 'innocent' parts of the body. Our question then was: how do 'innocent' parts of the body become 'guilty'?

In the Manner of Slavegirls

The trade in women as objects is a phenomenon with which we are perfectly familiar – from advertising, pornography or prostitution. The ways in which patriarchy is structured attribute to women no desire of their own.[4] Instead women occupy a hallowed space as objects of male desire. The stimulation of desire is, however, by no means simply a passive process. Posture, external appearance and movement are adjusted by women themselves in their attempts to conform to and reinforce the status quo. There is a name for this female participation in the reinforcement of women's subordinate status: we have called it slavegirl behaviour.

Within the women's movement, attempts have been made to escape from this relationship of subordination, to move beyond the simple reiteration of our complaints against sexist conduct on the part of men. Implicit in the decision to refuse the position of 'sexual object' is a change in our own behaviour. The women's liberation movement has for example nurtured the development of a culture of sartorial resistance to prevailing images of women. Resistance of this kind defines itself in two ways. It is directed against both the gaze and the desires of men, and against the dictates of fashion: short hair, baggy trousers and women's symbols have come to denote *feminist* women.

In our group, the question of the ways in which women constitute themselves as slavegirls was discussed initially in a seminar in Hamburg. At this stage we were still contemplating the process of subjection simply in terms of women's display of their bodies, in other words in terms of what seemed to us to constitute unambiguously sexual invitations – the wearing of short skirts, or see-through blouses for example. It seemed relatively easy to place ourselves at a distance from such things; we ourselves already dress differently in any case – in jeans and jumpers for the most part. Yet we invariably encountered a whole series of resistances and contradictions; after all there is enjoyment to be had in wearing clothes that look good, in taking

ACCES SORIES

pleasure in our appearance. If at the same time we are making ourselves attractive to men who then express their attraction in ways that we find unpleasant, then surely this is no concern of ours; their responses are their own affair. Are we to impose restraints on ourselves, merely in response to the reactions of men? It seemed to us that making ourselves look good did not automatically place us in the slavegirl position. We had the option of developing self-confidence in our bodies, not having to conceal them at every turn; what could possibly be wrong with this?

We see these arguments now as attempts to set ourselves apart from the slavegirl image, to repudiate any suggestion that we might be beautifying or displaying ourselves for the benefit of others, to defend our actions as sources of pleasure and self-confidence. Women in the Women's Liberation Movement have suggested, rightly, that enjoyment, pleasure, women's own desires should be seen as offering the prospect of a potential future liberation.[5] Here enjoyment and pleasure are implicitly assumed to be extra-historical quantities standing in eternal opposition to oppression. In our stories, by contrast, we have detected a connection between pleasure and subjugation; or to put it another way, we saw ourselves taking pleasure in the very process of being trained into particular dominant structures rather than feeling tyrannized by them.[6] Our work in the following pages is based therefore on the hypothesis of an intimate association between the subordinate status of women, and female pleasure. The question we will be asking is one that relates to our potential for liberation: what social relations – by which we mean both objective structures and their subjective apppropriation – must prevail if we are to dismantle the edifice of domination, while at the same time rescuing its pleasures for ourselves?

Our aim in these stories has been to investigate the ways we move within the dominant social order, the points at which we submit to our subjection and oppression. The first stories we wrote on women's attempts to impress others by their external appearance revolved almost without exception around clothes; it was here that submission and voluntary servitude seemed to us to express themselves most clearly.

A Carefully Staged Moderation

They had arranged to meet that evening. She spent the whole day in a state of nervous excitement, and the closer it came to the appointed time, the more agitated she became, like a young girl on her first date. Tonight's meeting though, was of a different kind. True she had fallen head-over-heels in love, but she knew that the attitude of the other towards her was of extreme ambivalence and caution. She knew that the other didn't think of her as gay, only eccentric – an impression she had to dispel at all costs. After all, she had other qualities. So what on earth was she to wear? She had to look as self-effacing as possible, she mused, the other showed a demonstrative lack of concern for her external appearance. More or less everything she had to hand for this evening seemed overly brash. She decided on jeans. The rest would have to come to her after her shower. Body odour was something she wanted to avoid at all costs, although she was likely to get clammy hands at the mere approach of the other. The question of what she was to wear on top now simply had to be resolved. She decided on a man's vest, white, under a blue lambswool pullover. A further problem – shoes! She had nothing that showed the right amount of classical discretion; her boots were too pointed. Her brown suede boots would surely do; they were nice and chunky, if a little high. No doubt the other considered her too tall anyway; for the first time in a long time, this 'superiority' of hers became a source of discomfiture. Never mind, the shoes would have to do, now what about the hair? Maybe she ought to have it cut after all? She could tie it back in a plait, then at least it wouldn't look tarty. But the plait just wouldn't stay in place this evening – all it did was emphasise her prominent ears. She tried to smoothe her hair down against her head but was only minimally successful. As for her face, she did no more than attempt to cover her spots – the other had none and, like all women with clear skins, was bound to find spots disgusting. She was now to all intents and purposes ready; if not exactly confident. On the spur of the moment, she changed the light blue pullover for a dark blue one which looked less fussy, grabbed a grey scarf and the old trench coat (which the other would surely not object to) and set off.

The most immediately obvious feature of this story is the fact that it is not for a man that the woman mobilizes her competence as slavegirl, but for another woman. Are relationships between women thus structured in exactly the same ways as relationships between the sexes? Does the only difference consist in a reversal of the standards by which appearance is assessed? In the story the primary concern of the writer is to produce an external appearance that conveys particular meanings relating to herself as a person. She hopes in so doing to show that she also possesses other 'inner qualities'. It remains unclear what those qualities are. It does, however, seem possible for her to convey them by making herself appear in a particular light. The qualities she is after clearly do not relate exclusively to the body; she does not define them for example in terms of a specific waist measurement or a sexy leg. The expressions she uses to describe the relationship between clothing and social meaning are clichés familiar from the jargon of fashion: 'discreet' and 'classical'. The context in which they occur is, however, an unusual one. The writer's concern is not, for example with discretion for the sake of 'elegance' but with a kind of discretion designed to create the impression that she attaches no importance to external appearance. Despite the displacement of context, meanings generated within the dominant culture are in operation here; the writer's use of 'discreet elegance' both demonstratively silences any reference to 'money', and at the same time signifies that she has no need to 'bother' excessively about dress. But in the subcultural context, her 'restraint' produces similar meanings to those 'outside' it: her clothes convey a sense of her personality as founded on something 'other' than external appearance, on her character. So tenacious is the connection between clothing and personality in our culture that we remain imprisoned within the dominant structures it produces, even as we set about resisting them. It is only the solidity of the connection between dazzlingly smart shoes and the importance attached by the wearer to her appearance, which makes it possible to perceive a reversal of the association as similarly unambiguous.

In an attempt to gain a clearer understanding of the effects on women of their training in 'slavegirlishness', we propose to pursue the question of the association between clothing and personality through two stories on further aspects of the body.

The Body

The response of most members of the group to the pictures accompanying the following story was laughter: 'You mean to say this was how you used to look?' They all found the girl's

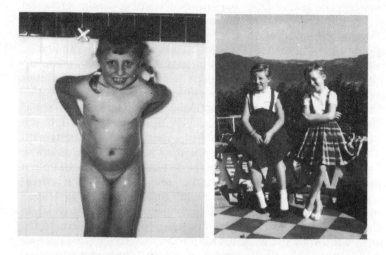

appearance comical, her tummy quite clearly excessively podgy. As women we 'know' how we are supposed to look; we know what remains within the bounds of acceptability and what goes too far. The term we have found for this in the group is a knowledge of the proper 'standards'.[7] While on the one hand it may be possible to increase our self-confidence by meeting these standards, it is on the other hand impossible to match up to them in reality. Erving Goffman, in his book *Stigma* gives the following example of this: 'For example, in an important sense there is only one complete unblushing male in America: a young, married, white, urban, northern, heterosexual Protestant father of college education, fully employed, of good complexion, weight and height and a recent record in sports.'[8]

For Goffman, then, men are defined as acceptable according to racist and sexist standards; the question of class meanwhile is rendered more or less unrecognizable by its incorporation into standards relating to education and full employment. For reasons of time and energy, we have limited our investigation into the standards operative in our context to only one of all their different dimensions. As standard requirements for the external appearance of man, Goffman notes 'good looks' and 'normal weight'. For women, these are merely the points of departure for more final differentiated requirements: there is a precisely determined relation between chest, waist and hip measurement, there are such things as ideal measurements, an ideal height, an ideal weight, each with its own method of calculation. (I myself remember one particularly 'precise' method. I had to multiply my chest measurement taken at mid-breast by my height, then divide the total by 240. By then dividing my actual weight by the ideal weight thus calculated, I arrived at a number against which I could gauge the extent to which I was overweight. The numbers corresponded to four categories, 1.10 to 1.25 indicating slight plumpness, over 1.5 indicating extreme obesity.) A woman has recourse to particular methods to establish whether and in what way she is defective. There is a particular position which her breasts, for example, are supposed to occupy. The question of whether she has sagging breasts or not is not merely a question of the way she appears; it is verifiable by the pencil test. If a pencil stays put when placed under the breasts, then they sag; if not – she's in luck, one more point in her favour. It is the unattainability of standards such as these that makes them so effective and which lays the foundation for women's lifelong pre-occupation with their bodies. Our work in the group has been based on the assumption that our concern with standards cannot be seen simply as a superficial veneer; the clear waters of theoretical insight will not necessarily wash us clean. This is not to say that we ourselves have always avoided the pitfalls of pseudo-enlightenment. When shown the above photograph of the little fat girl, one woman in the group exclaimed, 'I can't see what all the fuss is about; she looks perfectly normal to me.' Her attitude was one of 'pseudo-enlightenment', in the sense that it fostered the impression that the standards we adhere to can be neutralized through knowledge, whereas in fact they are an integral part of our personalities. Knowledge alone is an inadequate means of escape from their formative power. How then do these evaluative standards become part of our personality and with what needs and interests are they associated?

The Story

The father is an amateur photographer. He works in his dark-room, developing films. The assembled family sits looking at the photos he has taken. 'You ought to watch your daughter, her tummy's too fat.' 'Oh come on, she's only a child, it's puppy fat. It'll disappear of its own accord when she gets older.'

What passes through the mind of the child in the course of the conversation? – Perhaps: 'There he goes again, finding fault with me: does she have to be so noisy, she disturbs him on Sundays

*when he's trying to sleep off Saturday excesses, what's more she's a
girl, something he never wanted (so her mother says), and now to
cap it all her tummy's too fat – after all, she is a girl,' he has said.
She doesn't care, of course. Her 'strength' is in her position at
school – 'strength' in the literal sense. She has a friend, too, who is
clearly in awe of her. Both of them used to have long plaits, she cut
hers off and her friend followed suit. Her friend is pretty and
dainty. She tyrannizes her.*

*She enjoys the fights she often gets into with boys. They've made
it into a game in which points are awarded for victories and
defeats. Her points total places her in the top third. One day she
managed to get one boy on the floor. She held his legs high against
her chest so as to be able to kick his behind. He kicked out at her
chest. She felt a sudden searing pain, like nothing she'd ever felt
before. She kept going, emerged the victor once again, then went
on her way and – burst out crying. It was over. She was turning
into a girl. No longer would she be stronger than the boys, she was
turning into a weakling, becoming girlish. No different from all
the stupid cry-babies, dirty fighters who scratched and bit and
pulled your hair! She began to pick fights with girls who annoyed
her; one who couldn't speak German, whose skirts were too long –
facts to which the boys had been indifferent. At some point in this
period she must also have begun to look at herself more often in
the mirror and to see that she was simply overweight. Above all, it
was her stomach that was too fat.*

The story reads like a weather forecast. Bright at first,
clouding over later. The first part transmits a sense of the
normality of everyday disruptions A series of different moods,
meanings and value judgements float through the girl's life,
disparate and unconnected as clouds in a mackerel sky. Then in
the second part, unexpected and unannounced, the storm
breaks. A catastrophe has broken; the writer is turning into a
girl.

Strange the tricks our memories play. Events are etched on
our memory as the triggers of change; we see our socialization
and the construction of our identity, in retrospect, marked by
twists and turns, breaks and fractures. We would not wish to
claim that *memories* of this kind are simply fallacious, a
retrospective exaggeration of quite insignificant events. Yet it
does seem to us problematic that this kind of remembering of
crisis–points veils the normality and the petty, everyday
character of our socialization — making it impossible to perceive

it as a problem. In an endeavour to portray crisis as extraordinary, we make it seem as if the rest of life proceeds quietly on
its way, free of crises, harmoniously – and that decisive changes
occur as the result of catastrophe. Instead of this, we should
perhaps begin from the premiss that all developments contain an
element of crisis and thus that crisis itself has an everyday
quality; that the catastrophe is prepared well in advance, and is
itself the result of a general training in the normality of
heteronomy.

The first part of the story presented above is written in an
almost deliberately understated way — the calm before the
storm. We learn little of the girl's own feelings when her father
talks of finding her tummy too fat. Her observation that this
represents only one of the many paternal rejections she has
experienced gives only a distant inkling of her hatred of her
father in the everyday life of the family. Her somewhat forced
unconcern is hastily suppressed by references to her popularity at
school, and to her possession of a friend. Her description of her
indifference to the fatness of her stomach contrasts sharply with
her body posture and facial expression in the pictures. For the
group, this contrast raised the question of the kinds of diversionary manoeuvres and tactics of deflection with which women
responded to bodily 'stigmas'. These may range from 'wardrobe
engineering' (stripes to accentuate our best features), through
sartorial torture (corsets) to self-deception within strategies of
displacement and desensitization: my mother's liberal use of
proverbs — 'Beauty is more than skin deep' — for my consola-
tion. In the next breath she was quite capable of saying, 'Stand up
straight, you'll never find a husband that way.' Perhaps, then, we
are simply incapable of living with our anxiety over the fulfilment
of bodily standards, without comforting ourselves with a notion
that the true core of our personality will remain impervious to
superficialities. At the same time, the use of these diversionary
tactics and strategies is experienced as a destabilizing influence
on the person of the woman in question; for she is aware of her
own deceit, she knows that she is someone other than the person
she would have others believe her to be. It is the fear of being
found out that causes her insecurity. And insecurity in turn
prepares the ground on which strategies of domination can take
root, securing her willing submission to subjugation, to
normality.

The question we set out to research in our body project was
formulated in terms of our internalization of the standards that

our bodies are to reproduce. In posing this question, or rather in working on memories associated with it, we hoped also to gain a better insight into the origins of our feelings in relation to our bodies, into the things we did and did not take for granted, and into the ways in which this contributed to our integration into the prevailing order of social relations. The way our bodies are to be is determined not only by behaviour directly related to the body (such as diet, sport, concealment or exposure of various parts of the body). In accepting certain 'standards', we acquiesce also in a particular relationship to others, to the identity offered us by those relationships. The history of female socialization as the centring of women around the body has yet to be written; our work here represents no more than an initial step in this direction. Massive difficulties arose in the process of our writing and remembering. After all, in a way that we are more willing to deny than to acknowledge, we ourselves, our bodies, are that of which we write. At the same time, the body is also alien to us; and it is in our sense of its strangeness that awareness begins to dawn of the heteronomous structures that enclose it, and in which the body becomes the medium through which we are inserted into the prevailing social order.

Hair

Hair has unique characteristics. We aren't stuck with our hair as we are with our bodies. Ultimately, it can be cut off, shaved, removed, dyed or otherwise transformed. In the initial stages of our project, while we certainly acknowledged the weight of symbolic significance accorded to hair as sinful, functional, seductive and so on, we considered it unlikely that writing and research on hair would be as emotionally disruptive as writing on other subjects. It would be something to be enjoyed – or so we thought initially. In the following, we have reproduced the first story written on the complex of relations around 'hair'.

On fluff and what it can become

The lights were red. She waited at the crossroads on her bike. Beside her another bike rider waited for the lights to turn green. He seemed to be inspecting her profile. In retrospect, it seems almost unimaginable that a passing remark from him – 'Did you know you had a beard?' – if indeed this was the expression he used –

could have been the cause of a problem which was repeatedly to take possession of her, pressing for change. Could she now reconstruct the individual steps of its development? She was 16, and longing for a boyfriend, when the fluff on her chin first became a problem. She bought a tube of Pilca, then other hair removing creams; they left occasional burn marks on her chin. Wax was another remedy she tried.

At the age of 18 – a man was showing interest in her – she paid a visit to a dermatologist, and asked, curling up inside from shame, if she could remove the small prickly hairs which had now appeared. The doctor, a woman, was surprisingly sympathetic, and seemed immediately prepared to help her. The first appointment was made; it ended in fiasco. The doctor, having examined her chin more closely, refused her treatment. 'That's quite a growth you've got there!'

At some stage, she had taken to using tweezers to pluck them out; from now on, she was careful not to go anywhere without them. It seemed that her boyfriend of the time was unworried by the hairs which she removed so carefully, not only from her chin, but also from her breasts and stomach.

The first letter written to her by her new boyfriend opened with the words, 'My sweet Baby Bear.' She was at once thoroughly alarmed that he had detected 'it', and at the same time relieved to be able to tell him the 'whole truth' this early on. He himself was so good-looking and intelligent; would he still want her now he knew of this stain on her person? She wrote to him; his reaction was cautious. She made an appointment at the hospital for hormone tests. She had also heard that the rate of growth would be slower if she had a baby.

The results of the tests were within the spectrum of the 'normal'. Their parting remark, after all this trouble: 'What on earth do you expect – it's no more than five minutes a day. You should see some of the cases we deal with in here.'

The new Pill they were trying out at the clinic contained only a minimal proportion of male hormones. This was the period when she put on so much weight, she ate like a pig. After six or nine months, her anxieties had abated. She came off the Pill. Later, her boyfriend's reaction to her beard became more or less good-humoured.

Her youngest sister was being treated in hospital for acne. During the treatment, her cosmetic surgeon noticed the excessive hair growth on her chin, which she said was always likely to cause inflammation; she suggested the hair should be removed by electrolysis. Now, one year later, the process is complete. The scars are scarcely visible.

If only she had had her sister's luck at the same age. At the moment she is considering embarking on the treatment herself. She has no boyfriend at present.

The writer cried when she read us this story. She is now over thirty, successful in her work, well liked. We were stunned. At first, in our initial encounters with the subject of hair, we had forgotten that it is not only visible in decorative ways; that hair is not only something femininity 'permits' women to wear. We were certainly conscious of the linkage made between hair and gender – after all, we were all familiar with the hatred of respectable burghers for long-haired male protesters or for the cropped hair of their young female counterparts. Our historical deliberations on the subject of hair led us initially to focus on the social embedding of changing fashions in hair, as well as on the relationship between hair length and status or gender positioning. But we had given no thought to the depth of feeling likely to be evoked by the relationship between hair and gender identity; we had not seen it, as this one writer did, as structuring her activities, her relationships, her consciousness of self. Nonetheless, even on a first reading of this story, we saw our own selves reflected in many of its finer details. Tweezers and depilatory creams, visits to the doctor, reactions to the Pill, subterfuge and disclosure; all of these were practices known to us from our own day-to-day lives. Even if we ourselves no longer practised these activities, they remained operative as repressed doubts in relation to our earlier selves.

And once again we were left with the impression that the extraordinary condensation taking place in the story, the writer's obvious unhappiness, must surely have arisen out of some barely-perceived, ordered daily training in normality. We decided then, to appoint to the group working on the 'hair' project the express task of drawing up a social biography relating specifically to 'proper' hairstyles and 'decency'. Our aide-mémoire for this purpose was a photo album. The memories it brought to the surface on the theme of 'one girl and her hair' were so extensive that we were again forced at an early stage to summarize and shorten our conclusions. Apparently there is no single phenomenon that cannot be made to act as an ordering force in the process of socialization. Or, at least this holds for the female body and its constitution.

The Hair Project

A Hair-Raising Story of Socialization

I remember people in our street saying, 'Such a shame it had to be the boy and not the girl that had naturally curly hair. It doesn't matter so much for a boy, but the girl could have been saved so much work and money when she got older.'

It is important for girls to have curls in their hair. If they don't have them naturally, they have to manufacture them. But the reasons for doing so and the question of who finds such things important are left unspoken. As is the question of whom their curly locks entangle.

I remember numerous stories being told within the family and for the amusement of all present about the time when my hair started growing. What emerged on these occasions was evidence of my mother having worried for some time that her long-awaited daughter might never grow any hair. After all, my brothers had already had a fine head of hair by the time they reached my age. My mother's solution was an old household remedy. My head was rubbed all over – or at least in the places where hair could be expected to grow – with urine. Supposedly, this stimulated hair growth. At last, to the relief of all, the first wisps of hair appeared.

It seems that even the normal barriers of disgust can be dismantled to allow for activities facilitating the first appearance of hair. Clearly then, we are dealing with something of quite particular importance. In our family, it was not only household remedies of the kind outlined above that were used; my grandmother still adhered to a belief in old country lore, in which the influence of the moon figured largely. To make my mother's hair grow, my grandmother had cut off a lock of it when she was four and buried it at full moon under a willow tree. Later, those beliefs were to be supplanted by the promises of an industry that claimed to hold the key to every type of hair care, and to be able to keep all our hair beautiful and shiny.

The history of my hair can be documented without difficulty

91

*from our family album. With two exceptions, all the photos show
me with my hair neatly arranged. In the years before I started
school, I had short hair, sometimes with a little fringe that left
much of my forehead showing. In a number of the pictures, it is
possible to make out the hairgrip that kept even the shortest of
wisps pinned back from my face. I remember a particular movement of the hand with which grown-ups used to sweep the hair out
of my face and slide the grip hard — though carefully — across my
scalp. The feelings I associate with that memory are more or less
unpleasant; the memory of an assault of sorts, an imposition of
order, which left a bad taste in my mouth — though I made no
attempt to defend myself. On feast days and holidays the place
above my left or sometimes my right temple normally occupied by
the hairgrip was adorned with a taffeta bow to match what I was
wearing at the time. It sat perched on my head like a propellor,
leaving my forehead exposed and emphasizing my big eyes. It
somehow made my head the focus of attention. Occasionally,
velvet ribbons were used instead to keep the hair out of my eyes, or
hairslides. No two slides were exactly the same. I preferred the
brightly coloured ones. For very special occasions, a spray of
flowers – real or imitation – was put in my hair.*

For girls, the years before school represent a period of grace in
which they are permitted to be little and sweet. With the entry
into education, family and school begin to work together to
establish work and play as opposites. The serious business of life
is posed from an early age in contrast to the 'unseriousness' of
infancy. The introductory stage of our integration into 'working
life' is marked by a change of clothing and hair style. The frivolous toddler is replaced by the sensible young girl.

*For my first day in school I pulled my hair back into a tight
ponytail. I had no fringe. The pony-tail bounced up and down
when I jumped around, even when I walked. It was possible to
give it some encouragement, by holding my head higher than
normal, and sticking my nose in the air. I was scolded for doing so
– told to walk 'naturally' and not be so 'affected'. The pony-tail
made me feel taller, even grown-up. But I did feel an occasional
slight pressure on my head, just at the point where the hair was
drawn together. A new hair style had to be found for me; it seemed
the pony-tail made my hair too brittle, it wasn't healthy.*

*My career in plaits began when I was eight. I was to wear
various different sorts of plaits over the next six years. I was told
that it had been 'proved' that plaits made for 'healthy' hair; any-*

body would tell me that plaiting my hair was the best thing anyone
– or rather a girl – could do for her hair. Since a lot of girls at my
primary school wore plaits, I too came to think of them as normal.
'With plaits you are always properly dressed. They keep your hair
under control and stop it falling into your eyes in an untidy mess.'

Once their children have begun school (if not before) mothers
are, or at least feel themselves to be, responsible to the school
and the teachers for their appearance. It is at this point that we
locate the first remembered linkages between hair and order, as
well as hair and health. In the first instance the writer describes
an attempt to establish order in hair by means of the pony-tail.
Yet the pony-tail allows the girl to be flirtatious; she is not being
'natural' enough. A whole series of associations surrounds girls
with pony-tails. The glossy magazines, for instance, have their
own caricatures of silly young girls of excessively curvacious
appearance, whose parted lips and merrily-bobbing pony-tails
create an impression at once naive and frivolous. The possibility
that a girl might develop into such a figure appears as a constant
threat, as something to be avoided at all costs.

The argument mobilized against the pony-tail in the story
above concerns health; yet it must be a less straight-forward issue
than this since what is being forbidden is also the jauntily
bouncing quality of the pony-tail. The health argument speaks in
favour of plaits. But over and above this, plaits are said to be
nice, tidy and orderly; in plaits, girls are 'properly dressed'. This
indicates that hair can also serve to undress, that it can be used to
manufacture a form of nakedness, to present the wearer in an
unequivocal (though not explicitly sexual) way as a woman. An
unkempt appearance is impermissible; as a girl, she is required to
keep herself in order. The fact that hair can be provocative and
therefore dangerous for the woman who wears it may be inferred
from one recommendation we found in an etiquette manual of
1967, which exhorts women to protect their hair when out
walking by tying it up in a head scarf in the traditional manner of
the peasant woman.[1]

The tidiness of my hair in the photos is truly convincing. I never
look as if I might have been careering about on my bike or
practising my skipping for hours at a time. It seems that these
tousled moments were never considered suitable within our family
for pictures that might later be used to present individual members
of the family to public view. Since I certainly remember the

abiding refrain, 'go and comb your hair! You look like a little witch,' there must also have been situations in which I did look different. But when I was nine or ten, it was as unthinkable for me to go to school without my hair in plaits – with my hair not 'done' – as it would have been to walk down the street in pyjamas.

It was not only my own hair that I submitted to the severity of order; I attempted also to impose that order on others. A certain kind of unkemptness disturbed me particularly in older women. I felt there was something sloppy about it. There were times, for example, when my grandmother omitted to tuck her sparse wisps of hair carefully under her hair net at the back. If I pointed this out to her, she would respond with a Swabian phrase used by her late husband, 'Mei Weib, das, Hexle,' ('My wife t'old witch').

The use of the witch-figure recalls a linkage commonly made between hair and sensuality. In many representations of witches, they are portrayed as beautiful women who will not accept the mastery of the prevailing order of their time, but attempt to use their own knowledge to create an order by which they themselves can live.

Externally, witches are clearly recognizable by their long, free-flowing, untamed hair; according to popular wisdom, the witch's hair is red, and straggles and streams behind her as she rides on her broomstick through the air. There are, however, also witches who are ugly; there is both attraction and repulsion in this dual investment of emotion.

Another thing we know about witches is that they are dangerous. To call someone a 'little witch' is to play down the danger she represents, to bring it into a relation with a desire for sensuality of the kind attributed to witches and to make reference to the attraction that lies precisely in danger and adventure.

A final question to be considered in this context is the function of the Church as an important agency in the production of images and of relations between the sexes.[2]

Having my hair parted in the middle, then pinned back with hair grips, one at each temple to begin with, later directly above each of my plaits, allowed me to look and be looked at with ease. Not a single strand of hair fell into my face or my eyes, or threatened to conceal my high forehead. It was a rare feature, I was told, and should therefore be shown to best effect.

It is not merely by its shape and colour that hair can be judged; it is considered as part of the general arrangement of the head and, indeed, of the body. It can conceal parts of the body, such as the forehead, or it can emphasize them. A high forehead, in contrast to its 'low-brow' opposite, is considered noble, beautiful, a sign of intelligence. Some women shave their hair-line to make their forehead appear longer. I remember remarks being made about blacks when I was a child, according to which they were by and large a happy and relatively naive and slow-witted people. Links were made in this context between their low, sloping foreheads, and inferior intelligence. The existence of a related reference to the equally-sloping forehead of neanderthal man, confirmed the idea of blacks as people caught at an inferior stage of development. Biologically distinctive marks, such as the forehead, serve therefore not only to construct criteria of beauty and to consign women to a particular site in society; racism too builds social meanings out of biological distinction.

I slept with my hair in plaits and became quite skilled at plaiting it quickly in the mornings. I did not even have to use a mirror. I could feel in my hands what had to be done with my hair. Very gradually the points where the plaits began, at first obliquely above my ears at the back, slipped downwards. My hair now covered my ears as far as the earlobes, which now marked the point where the plaits began. At first my mother drew my attention to the need to plait my hair more neatly. I ignored her admonitions, and in the end she seemed to accept my decision. I had found a way of making my plaits indicate something special about myself – they were my own personal feature. This development also involved giving up the accurate parting at the back of my head. I felt I now looked less like a child, perhaps more like a Madonna.[3]

To stress that someone is still a proper little girl or looks like a proper child is to note the fact that there are girls of the same age who are different (more advanced?) in their appearance, their interests and needs. What then are the interests which such girls have? They are obviously of a kind from which parents believe it necessary to protect their daughters for as long as possible. The parental retort that there will be plenty of time in future for wearing hair loose points to the supposed inevitability of the linkage between adulthood and sinfulness.

What remains unspoken is the notion that 'girls start to be interested in boys much too early these days'. What is actually said is, 'You are the only one who still looks different and who, we hope, still thinks and feels differently too.' It is by these means that ideas of the special, the unique, come to be associated with the childlike, the innocent. Girls from bourgeois families have to learn at an early age to be something special. Later, when they enter the marriage market, their innocence will be much sought after; it is the source of their value.

At the age of 10 or 11, I found myself observing trends in my class with increasing anxiety. One girl after another came to school with newly-shorn hair. Whereas it had previously been possible to divide the class – at least superficially – into two groups, one grown-up, one more childlike. I was left in the end, at the age of 12, as the only one in plaits, clearly viewed by the whole class as the only remaining child. Yet I was not too much of a child to help out in my parents' shop. I was often admired at the time by customers for my beautiful, healthily gleaming hair – particularly because it was becoming increasingly rare in general for girls still to wear their plaits. I received their admiration with mixed feelings. On the one hand, it did make me an object of attention. I was talked about because I was different, something special. I was still a proper girl. On the other hand, the fact that so much attention was paid to me only confirmed my mother in her resolve to try to keep me a proper child for as long as possible. I often thought at the time of simply going to the hairdressers and coming home with my hair cut. After all, nobody was going to chop my head off for doing so. But my plans never got past the stage of daydreaming. Only occasionally, when the whole family started to go on about how wonderful my plaits were, did I get up and leave the room, crying tears of rage at my inability to have my way.

Even in my memories of my conception of the Madonna, it is not simply the virginal figure of Mary which emerges into view, but at the same time an unspoken seductiveness. The two separate constructions of saint and whore are brought together in the iamge of the Madonna. It is this which constitutes the enormous attraction of a virtuous woman. As popular wisdom has it: 'still waters run deep'.

The first great conflict over my hair took place around my first Communion, on the Sunday after Easter. I was ten years old. For a greater range of choice in dresses we drove specially to the nearest big town, 50 km away. After much to-ing and fro-ing, we bought a dress which 'distinguished itself by its plainness'. After all, I was told, it was for a religious festival, not a fashion show. The question of my hairstyle then had to be addressed. I had been picturing to myself for some time how I wanted my hair to look. Whatever happened, it had to be long and loose. I wanted it to fall across my shoulders in great soft waves or rippling curls. I wanted a diadem too, to be placed among an imagined luxuriance of hair. I wanted to look like a little bride. I rarely asked for anything as a child and I certainly never used tears to try and get my way. Yet in this situation my parents remained adamant and quite uncompromising. After all, they said, there would be plenty of time for me to wear my hair loose when I got older; there was a proper time for everything. On the day of your first Communion, appearance was really quite incidental. I was to wear the same plaits as usual, they said, but coiled up into what they called 'monkey swings'. While the plaits dangled around my ears, the diadem was replaced by the usual garland of flowers. 'You look like a proper little lady. It's not everyone who gets the chance to wear garlands of

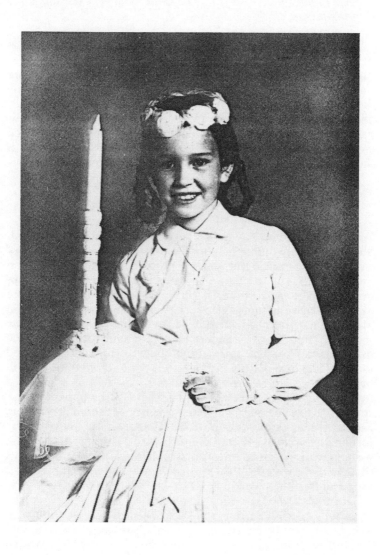

flowers in their hair, like you. They make you very special; really quite exquisite.'

The attitudes we are dealing with here are contradictory; on the one hand a great deal of time and money is expended on preparing for the ceremony, the most diverse activities are undertaken to ensure that everything and everyone is properly equipped for the great day. On the other hand, external appearance is simply asserted not to be of any importance. Yet this particular kind of pure and childlike appearance – paraphrased as 'exquisite', but associated at the time with feelings of 'homeliness' – is in fact endued with extreme significance.

Excursus: Women under National Socialism

When Hitler seized power in 1933, my mother was 21 years old. She was certainly amongst those addressed by the new image of women being carved out under National Socialism. This was an image which was to restore to women the dignity which, supposedly, they had forfeited in the years before 1933. They were to find a place and function in society as mothers and women who put their natural productive capacity at the service of the new society. What, then do the models of femininity ordained by the fascists look like? The hair is usually between medium length and long, woven into plaits which are then twisted round the head in braids, coiled up at the sides into ear plaits. Or it is gathered together tightly in a thick bun. (The same is true of nude representations under fascism.) Some women have their hair waved in careful ridges, kept well in order. The face, and above all the forehead, is always completely exposed. Through the 1930's, women with the more or less masculine-looking, short hair cuts that characterized the 1920's *garçonne* are increasingly rare, as is long and free-flowing hair.

The adoption of an order dictated from above — in which the external ordering of hair may also be included — cannot be explained simply in terms of compulsion amd domination. Instead, it is necessary to examine the ways in which existing needs and desires are harnessed by a given social order. It seems fair to assume that women, by living their lives in particular ways, participated in the formation of the space conceded to them within the fascist order, and that the desires and hopes bound up with that order continue to exist in continually re-modelled

From Berthold Hinz, *Die Malerei im deutschen Faschismus,*
Carl Hanser Verlag, Munich 1974

forms today. Not only did fascism sketch out the contours of new images of women; it also created cultures specifically for girls – the League of German Maidens (*Bund Deutscher Mädel*), for example. Though she might have left the *BdM* behind her a long time ago, my mother could certainly have drawn a part of her ideals of beauty and order from that earlier period.

Her relatively distant sympathies for young girls' culture under National Socialism were encouraged by an 18-year-old girl who spent her year of National Service with us during the war. She more or less took over responsibility for the upbringing of four children in our family. 'Other girls would be glad to have hair as nice as yours,' she would say in one of many attempts to generate enthusiasm for the 'specialness' of my plaits.

The more disparaging variant of her rejection of my wish for a different hairstyle ran along the lines of, 'You're the kind of girl who throws herself off a cliff just because everyone else is doing the same.' And yet all I wanted was simply not to have to wear plaits

From Berthold Hinz, *Die Malerei im deutschen Faschismus*

any more, to look the same as everyone else, less childish, more adult and fashionable, and to be attractive to boys too. My parents demanded of me that I be something 'special', that I distinguish myself from other girls. The pressure to be original and the support given to any activity likely to further the process of my individualization sometimes made me afraid of being unable to fulfil all the expectations placed in me.

Stern **13/82**

In the desire to be like others, there is also a search for security, a desire to be inconspicuous. While it may represent a resistance to parental demands, it also facilitates a smooth adjustment and adaptation to the dominant culture. In the case portrayed above, the form of resistance adopted by the writer had the effect of acclimatizing her to what our society knows as normality. It is not only in fairytales (Rapunzel, Snow White) that the seductive power of hair is evoked, nor is it celebrated only in sagas (the tale of the Loreley). In popular wisdom too, hair appears as something at once desirable and dangerous, as something magical and mystically powerful. As the saying goes in Germany, 'A woman's hair pulls stronger than a bell rope,' or 'A woman's hair is stronger than a hempen rope.'

At the same time, the most strenuous efforts are made in reality to nullify this power of attraction. Even today, many nuns for example still cover their hair with a veil, the form of which often recalls long, tumbling hair. In Islamic countries, debates are taking place as to whether women should wear either the veil or headscarves, which allow only the husband the right to gaze upon a woman's hair.

> Were I a hunter riding free
> something approaching a soldier,
> were I a man, if this could be,
> the heavens would lend me succour.
> Yet here I sit, delicate, fine,
> a dutiful child acquiescing.
> My hair I loosen in secret, alone,
> in the wind it flies streaming and flowing.
>   (Annette von Droste-Hülshoff)

The date on which my hair was to be permitted to fall victim to a pair of scissors was decided, not in consultation with me, but with my elder brothers. Ruthlessly, it was decreed that my request be granted on my fourteenth birthday and not a day earlier. The same

*brothers had a way of expressing themselves quite frankly and
directly on the subject of women, admiring them sometimes for
their legs, sometimes for their breasts, or perhaps also for their
hair. They would argue the question of whether a woman with her
hair loose looked racy, gipsy-like or gentle; women with red hair
were judged to be fiery and mercurial. Numbers of women were
pronounced as boring as the way they wore their hair. In talking
together of such things, they would exchange knowing, understanding glances. But neat, healthy hair was never the subject of
their conversations.*

If today I compare the way the men in our family talked about
hair with the way it was discussed by women, the women seem to
me to have set more store by the texture of hair – it was described
as wiry, healthy, bushy or full – and by its grooming (was it well
looked after? glossy? silky? soft?). Certain arrangements of the
hair were considered nice, elegant. While the dying of hair was
taboo, naturalness was by contrast highly valued.

Amongst the male members of the family, hair 'somehow'
always appeared in association with sexuality; allusions were
made and suppositions expressed as to the hidden feminine
qualities (passion, seductiveness) which were seen to be expressed in hair. Hair could be provocative, it was seen to act as a
signal. It was within this sexist discourse of masculinity that it was
possible for my brothers to manufacture the notions of the
wicked woman as sexually attractive, by producing their own
sister as a girl who was pure.

The Aftermath

*My hair was off. The hairdresser held the mirror up to me from
various angles to allow me above all to look at the back of my
head. I had had to put up a fight to stop her puffing it up at the
back. Her objection: 'it isn't properly styled otherwise. I have to
give you a bit of a bouffant.' She picked up a large aerosol can and
shrouded my hair in a hissing cloud of penetrating, sweet-
smelling, sticky spray – a hood made of lacquer. Cautiously I felt
my hair with my hand. I found hardness where before it had felt
soft. I hadn't imagined it would be quite like this. I had wanted a
hairstyle that was somehow casual, or at least one with more 'go'
about it. What I was most looking forward to was hearing what my
brothers would think of it. But this was also what I most feared.
Although it was actually already clear to me by the time I left the*

hairdressing salon what their final judgement would be, I looked to our first meeting at home with a mixture of hope and curiosity. The first brother I met was the one who is eleven years older than me. Momentary astonishment in his eyes; after all I did look different from usual. Then his gaze became more critical, a change which perhaps only I perceived, a slight flicker at the corner of his eye, an almost imperceptible movement of the wrinkles of his forehead. He walked round and round me – he might have been inspecting animals in a cattle market – and said finally with a grin, sensing my unease; 'Not bad.'

I clearly remember the feelings of uncertainty, fear and disappointment I had at the time. It must have been very important to me for my new hairstyle to measure up to male standards and male eyes. After all, I was no longer a child. With the new status of 'young lady' which my hair allowed me, I should have been able to make my brothers look on me as 'woman'. My failure to do so could be inferred from my brother's observation. His 'not bad' was an attempt to express recognition of my efforts to achieve something new. My hairdresser and my mother had agreed that a style shaped to my face suited my type well; after my brother's remarks, I was all the more distrustful of their comments.

Did I feel only relief when my hair was cut? Was my only worry what my brother's opinion would turn out to be? It was here that my memory failed me. As a group, we decided therefore to consider my stories alongside the experiences of other women. The marking of age, of the transition to adulthood, by the cutting of hair is an experience of socialization undergone, to this day, by nearly all women.

A Better Self

Locks of hair were falling on the floor around me. I tried desperately to smile; I don't remember if I succeeded. All that remains is the feeling of grimacing. The thick plait was later packed into a paper bag. Looking at it, I had a sudden feeling of absolute hollowness in my stomach. It looked so alive, or as if it had only stopped living. . . But what I was able to feel was neither sadness nor relief. We left. My mother made something of a fuss about the price; I was only half listening. I kept moving my head from side to side, it felt as if it wasn't sitting properly on my shoulders, there was something missing: the familiar weight of two bouncing pigtails. I looked at myself disbelievingly in the mirror. The same nose as ever, round and snub; the usual pair of glasses; the familiar small mouth, with its pretence at softness – but then, in the place of two plaits ending in corkscrew curls (there had always been a slight fuzziness about the pigtails, from the wisps of hair which escaped here and there); instead of the fringe which had covered my eyebrows, my own familiar face was framed by silky hair, strangely smooth, tapering off just below my ears in a gentle inward curve. It was certainly a hairstyle, it could even be described as chic, but was it for me? I tried to imagine what 'the others' would say – I hoped they'd like it!

There was now no question that I would have to try again to get proper jeans bought for me; if I changed my image totally, then perhaps the others at school wouldn't be able to find a reason to tease me. The only thing I'd have to be careful of was not to wear blue and green together, I'd been slapped down often enough before for doing so, and I wanted so much to be able to belong for once.

The writer attempts here to achieve social recognition – defined as a sense of belonging and being recognized by others – by her insertion into and subordination to the prevailing norms of clothing and hair. The loss of something to which she has

Translation of caption:
look,
if I loved you, it was for your hair
now you are hairless
I love you no more.

become as attached and which is as important in the constitution of her identity as her hair, is not experienced as a renunciation, since the hopes of social approval bound up with her transition to the new are far greater. At the same time, the story gives a sense of how arbitrary and unbounded this pressure for social recognition may be. First it is the hair that is 'normalized', then individual items of clothing, then the writer has to take into account the harmonics of colour and tone – and so it goes on.

At the Hairdressers

One thing I was quite sure of; I wanted it shorter than short. At the moment, it was long and shining, especially just after I'd washed it. I often wore it twisted into a plait. It would have been possible to think of it as beautiful. But I wasn't thinking of that now. I knew only that I wanted to change something. And if I was to do so, my hair had to be short. I avoided looking in the mirror when the hairdresser began cutting. I had barely registered my change of position to a relatively high revolving chair. My body was enveloped in, hidden under, a matching plastic cape. My mind had already moved on from the hairstyles I'd been looking at in the magazines which the hairdresser put out for customers. They had been too perfect for me, too artificial.

It was falling now, my hair. First one great chunk, shoulder-length, to make the rest more manageable. The first cut was perhaps the most serious. It almost hurt. Now it was too late. How long before my hair would be as long as this again? It felt as if a piece of myself was about to be peeled away. I didn't want enough to be enough. I wanted it shorter and shorter, short as matchsticks. I didn't dare look in the mirror at first. I sat there feeling a mixture of grief and triumph, curious as to how I might be looking. I could feel hair at the nape of my neck, the sides of my face and my fringe. It was to be left a little longer here. I felt body-less.

I was brought back abruptly to reality, invited to take a look just once in the large, inviting mirror. I couldn't help but stare, so changed did I look. According to the hairdresser, examining me with the eye of the connoisseur, 'it' looked really very pretty. I wasn't quite sure how I should feel, not even as the wind played through my cropped hair on the way home.

The desire for short hair: a protest against femininity, and an attempt to establish an alternative image. In this context, hair has significance not so much as a means of gaining social recognition from others, but of coming to terms with gender as a social relation. The stories refer allusively to the possibility of an autonomous pleasure which may lie in the wearing of short hair – where it is softly caressed by the wind for example.

More Hair-Raising Memories

Years later, I sold my plaits on impulse in some hairdressers or other for DM2.50, although I didn't tell anyone at home until years after. They all thought I was crazy for having virtually given away something so valuable, instead of having a wig made out of it.

For my seventeenth birthday, I was given a hand-made hairpiece, which could be used to lengthen my own hair or to give it body. It was made from my mother's hair as a child.

Between the ages of seventeen and nineteen, I was given various sorts of hood dryers as presents; I was to have the equivalent of my own home hairdresser. For my twentieth birthday I was presented with a short wig, together with a black leather travelling case and a large polystyrene head on which the wig was to stand when not being worn.

For several years running, my spring carnival costumes were topped by blue, blonde or black wigs. I was taken aback every time by the quite different person I became. Once, in my first term as a student, when I was wearing my wig for the second time, I ran into a male fellow student, who burst into gales of laughter at the sight of me. From that day on, hairpieces, wigs, polystyrene heads and travelling cases lay untouched in my cupboard.

Even today, when I pay my once or twice yearly visit to my parents, my hair is the first thing they comment on – despite the fact that I have lived away from home for fifteen years now. And one thing is always certain; it never corresponds to my parents' ideas of how it should be. It may be too long, too untidy, hanging down in my face like a horse's mane; or it may be too lifeless – it's lost its old sparkle, it makes me look too ordinary.

As a student, I never went to the hairdresser from one end of the year to another. I let my hair grow and let friends trim it from time to time. To my parents, this could not in any way be construed as 'having my hair done'. Even today, my mother still gives me tips on hair care, sends me features on hair from Brigitte *magazine*,*

---

*(Translator's note: *Brigitte* is one of the leading glossies for women in the FRG.)

recommends this or that magazine, to make it easier for me to decide on the kind of hairstyle I want.

The feeling both sides in this long standing argument have shared over the years is that no agreement can be reached on these different notions of what makes hair beautiful. We share an awareness of the likelihood of arousing resistance and defensiveness in each other. With each fresh encounter, the battle lines seem to be drawn anew, to allow the most diverse differences to be fought out.

In the very last phase of completion of this book, my mother called me up to tell me I was to send her two decent passport photos as soon as possible, so she could get me a new identity card as promised. Her first irritated and agitated response to my astonished question as to why she didn't want to use the pictures I had already sent home, was to ask what I could possibly have been thinking of to send off 'those sorts' of pictures 'without thinking'. It seemed the clerk at the Registration Office had asked her if she really wanted to hand in these particular pictures; he knew me from way back . . . I was to get hold of some different ones. My mother suspected his implied comment to be, 'with hair like that she looks like a terrorist'.

The Marking of Deviance

While on the one hand we ourselves demonstrate assent to our rejection of the dominant order through our hair, the agents of domination on the other hand intervene in the order of hair adopted by those they see as deviant, through a process of marking and marginalization. Hair long ago lost its function of mere protection – in which its usefulness was defined in relation to heat and cold – and has become a symbol of femininity and masculinity – of potency, in its association with beauty. In this context, cropping the hair against the will of the person concerned becomes a demonstration of power, a wound to that person's dignity.

Just as hair may be used 'from above' to facilitate the positioning of individuals within society, to make them recognizable or to demonstrate hierarchies (free men under feudalism wore their hair long; in some cultures it is still possible today to tell from a woman's hair whether she is married, single or widowed), so also it may be used 'from below' as a form of resistance and protest. Over the past 15 years all the movements of protest and cultural revolution with which I am familiar have been bound up with changes in the order of hair. Departing from that order has meant at the same time departing from the fixed order of gender. Long hair is no longer the sole province of women, nor short hair that of men. Instead there has been a blurring of the distinctions between women and men, a levelling out of sexual differentiation through hair. In the European women's movement the 'afros' of US blacks fighting for civil rights was seized upon. Much as the slogan 'Black is beautiful' addresses blacks as self-conscious human beings, so also the collective cultures of women's resistance (changes in hair, the wearing of the colour purple), strengthened the protest of individual women. At the same time, however, the artificial production of dis-order (the permanent wave) once again reproduced linkages between femininity and tousled, tumbling curls. In recent years, as the struggle for emancipation has proceeded further, a different form has come increasingly to the fore. Today, punk brush-cuts, even shaved heads,are being worn by women.

From: R Westphal, (ed), *Women in the Political Poster* Berlin 1979

The Body Project

François Boucher (1703-1770)

To contemporary eyes, the women considered models of beauty in the days of Rubens, Titian and Boucher are more likely to appear as candidates for crash diet plans; recommended for psychiatric treatment, targetted as buyers of laxatives, appetite suppressants and so on. Fair enough, in a sense: after all, the notion that standards of 'beauty' and 'grace' are never trans-historical, or eternally valid, is by no means new to us. Yet even our awareness of the possibility of such changes gives us no insight into the ways in which we internalize the standards that do apply today, the ways in which we live both with and within them. The main thing that has changed is our level of expertise. Today, we don't simply know that the Venus in the picture is too fat; we are able to classify the precise type of her obesity. Newly

113

114

schooled in the terminology of 'Psychology Today' (*Psychologie Heute:* see illustrations), I am able to identify her as suffering from 'combination obesity with three causal factors: genetic constitution, excess food consumption and sluggish circulation'.

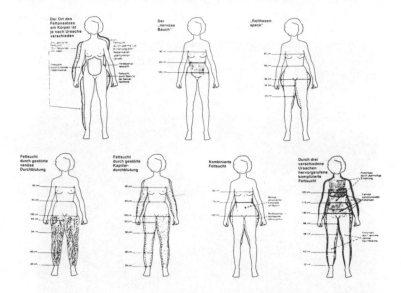

From *Psychologie Heute*, July 1982

When I first came across the schematized figures in the magazine feature reproduced above, my spontaneous reaction was to attribute one of its various forms of obesity to myself, or rather, to slot my own 'obesity' into one of the forms suggested. Is it so-called 'jodphur fat' I suffer from, or am I a victim of 'complex fat syndrome'? Without doubt my stomach is a 'nervous' one. Whatever the case, the diagram alarmed me; for the oh-so-delicately dotted contours, which are clearly meant to portray the ideal figure, in no way corresponded to my own body shape. No matter how much I try to deny it, I find that perception painful. My life would be simpler, if only my figure were as slim as this – or so I believe. I harbour a secret envy of any woman who is slimmer than I. Even of women in the communal flat where I live. They can see no beauty, let alone grace in Boucher's Venus. Their taste inclines them instead towards the slim-trim women depicted in the various women's magazines we flick

through together. The women displayed – or displaying themselves – between the covers of the glossies are called
'mannequin', a term defined in the Oxford English Dictionary as
'a woman who is employed to exhibit to customers the effect of
articles of costume'. What is 'exhibited' is, however not simply
an article of dress, but at the same time, whatever figure is
currently thought of as 'ideal' – the vital statistics of the time. In
measuring ourselves against these, using them as yardsticks of
comparison for the whole, or part of our bodies, we are also
accepting the standards they establish.

What effect does the way in which we live within particular
standards have on our relationship to our bodies, and thus to
other people and the world? Although this question is accorded
primacy throughout this book it is of particular importance for
this chapter. What is the nature of the relations of oppression to
which we consent through our adoption of a given set of standards? And even more fundamentally; by what process have we
absorbed the social standards within which we live so unquestioningly today?

The Legs That Were Too Long

*Her mother has heard of a professor who is researching into
human growth. Not only is he able to establish how long you are
likely to continue to grow, but he is also able to perform particular
operations to lengthen or shorten the period of growth. She is
twelve years old and 1.71m. tall when she visits him with her
mother. She has not bargained for the doctor asking her what is the
maximum height she might like to reach. Her mother is 1.74m.
tall. As tall as she is, or a little taller, would present no problems.
But how much more? Putting a brave face on it, she suggests,
'another ten centimetres'. Her confidence is intended to gloss over
the fact that she already feels too tall. Having now fixed her limit,
she immediately begins to doubt whether it isn't too tall after all.
The result of the doctor's examination: she is going to exceed her
maximum height. The doctor shows her the evidence. He has
X-rayed her wrist. In the negative, it is possible to make out the
individual hinge-joints at the ends of the wrist, the so-called
epiphyseal joints. These grow together in the course of puberty;
when they finally fuse, she will stop growing. The doctor can
gauge from the size of the epiphyseal joints approximately how
long she will continue to grow. He also explains the form remedial
intervention will take. He is to prescribe her female hormones. She*

will then begin having periods. She is to take the tablets for four months, by which time the epiphyseal joints will have closed together.

Her father suggests she might do worse than to join the Outsize Club. They admit women over 1.80m., and men over 1.90m. He imagines it would do wonders for her; she wouldn't always be the tallest woman in the room and it might stop her slouching when she walked – besides which all the men would be taller than she was and she'd have a pretty good chance of finding one to suit her.

After she has stopped growing and her height has stabilized at 1.86m., her father suggests shortening her thigh-bone by three centimetres. Her muscles and other bits and pieces will then grow back of their own accord. Admittedly, her legs will have to be treated one after another rather than together. The process can also be repeated, so that in the end you're six centimetres shorter. But although she would certainly like to be smaller, she has no desire to spend months in hospital for the privilege. Her father is disappointed when she turns down his suggestion. He would have liked to spare her a little pain.

'I must, I must increase my bust . . .'

The first year at secondary school: she comes into the classroom one morning to find a group of girls giggling and whispering secretively to each other. The joke seems to be contained in the bag they're passing around. It opens to reveal a bra. One of the girls in the class has bought it the day before. The newcomer stands aside, wishing she could make herself party to the knowledge that centres around the contents of the bag. She can recall her reaction to a remark made by the most popular girl in the class: 'You don't need that sort of thing, you're underdeveloped anyway . . .' But she remembers only too well the eyes turned in her direction in the changing room when she stood clad only in leotard or swimming costume. The eyes of the others focused on a part of the body which seemed to be linked with the state of being 'developed' or 'underdeveloped'. She could almost feel the glances cast time and time again in her direction: underdeveloped, underdeveloped. . .

The third year: she's been put in a different class, having chosen French as her second foreign language at the beginning of the second year. She now goes around with a gang of four or five girls. Their conversations meander for the most part around clothes, boys, and problems with their figures. Almost all the other girls have developed a bust, or at least wear bras; they think she's lucky to be so slim. She finds it difficult to appreciate their admiration; after all, she wouldn't call herself slim; she's just 'flat as a board'. It hasn't escaped her notice that the first thing boys goggle at is girls' breasts. And that includes the boys she's in love with. They sit in the chemistry and physics labs behind the girls so they can undo their bras in class, or at least reach out and twang their bra straps. The girls they choose titter with pleasure and feigned indignation. She is left out of all of this. The worst experience she remembers from this time is going through Simplizissimus *in a German class. The extract in her German book is called* Simplizissimus and Einsiedel. *The two roles are allotted to members of the class for an exercise in reading aloud. Since she is particularly good at reading, and in fact good at German in general, the teacher selects a part specially for her. She is to read Simplex and a boy will take the part of Einsiedel.*

The man who teaches German is relatively young. As she opens her reader, a thought flashes through her mind; he did it on purpose, he's realized I'm completely flat-chested. He thinks I look more like Simplex than like a girl . . . But she doesn't turn the part down. She answers Einsiedel's enquiry as to her name in the words of Simplex: 'My name is boy,' and hears the suppressed giggles of individuals erupt into howling laughter from the rest of the class at Einsiedel's reply: 'I see you are no maiden. . .' She senses the eyes of all, above all the eyes of the boys fixed on her non-existent breasts, is convinced that every last member of the class must now be aware she's 'flat-chested'; if she could, she would simply run out of the classroom . . .

What is the process whereby we come to adopt prevailing standards of social judgement? We grow into them, internalize them, accommodate ourselves – or at least attempt to do so. Our memories give evidence of phenomena that cannot be represented within available categories; in recalling the feelings or meanings associated with our own past inadequacies, we remember the process whereby standards have been internalized. It is only when I recognize myself as deviating from some norm that the standards on which that norm is founded become truly effective. Memories of the points at which we adopt those standards and make them our own reveal the extent to which we are already subject to their influence, and make their adoption appear as a social catastrophe: 'I am *different*.' Traces of the *processes* through which we grow into particular norms are thereby effaced. Yet surely it is plausible to assume that a sudden recognition of our own incapacities must be preceded by a long process of habituation to 'normality'? Our attention is constantly being drawn to the fact that there is a proper height for girls, a proper time for their chest measurements to reach certain proportions, a proper waist measurement and so on. All this had a place somewhere amongst the images we have of our world. But as long as we remain constituent parts of the social order, fish in its water, swimming with the tide, none of this can become the focus of our attention. Only at points of social marginalization is our attention diverted to the problem of our bodily otherness. Or conversely, it is the failure of the body to acquiesce in the power of the social average that carries social marginalization in its wake.[1] To this extent, a desire to be like the others may be seen as a desire for social integration in the positive sense of the word. To understand this better, it would be necessary to investigate the reasons why notions of the 'average body' amongst members of a social group can come to represent a bond of 'belonging'.

But why should *the body* become a vehicle of socialization? In both the above stories, we may assume that the standards against which the body was judged had been assimilated by the writer over a period of time, that they had become as familiar as images of the streets of her childhood. Living within the standards is experienced as rupture only at the points at which they unfold their full force; the moments at which we fail to meet them.

Both stories are concerned in particular ways with feminine identity. The production of femininity takes place even in questions of body height; the process whereby the biological becomes social is at one and the same time an articulation of the relationship between the sexes. The central problem addressed in our story about height is not the fact that the writer is 'essentially' too tall; she is taller than many other people – but most significantly, she is taller than large numbers of men. She may even be taller than any potential future husband, and difficulties are thus anticipated in her finding a husband in the first place. The salient point is the height of the woman *in relation to that of the man*. Male height is associated with superiority, strength and power, as well as with a protective capacity. It is to women that men's protection is to be afforded. Women are 'beneath' men, in both senses of the word. They shelter under the wings of he who is both larger and more powerful than themselves. In accepting conventions of height, we ourselves then submit to the equation made between men, strength, and protectiveness; or women, weakness, and the state of being protected.

It is around our bodies that we construct our identities; in so doing we simultaneously reproduce femininity within a particular social relation – the relation between the sexes – which, in its present form, is marked by contradiction. Our appropriation of particular social standards thus entails a simultaneous submission to dominant social notions of what it is to be a woman.[2]

'If I didn't have to trail my great broad, square shoulders around with me, if they didn't so obviously invite friendly back-slapping, and equally friendly exchanges of anecdotes on the deformities produced by humping coal, then I might be able to do what Ulrike has done – abandon my responsibilities and get married. . . . As it is – poor unfortunate that I am – I have to take responsibility for my own happiness.'[3]

The extent to which the violence we experience in the process of our development is done to us by ourselves can be shown more clearly by stories of the body than it would be by descriptions of our thoughts, feelings and sensations alone. It is, after all, our bodies that make us unremittingly visible. And it is for this reason that they can be perceived so readily as a reminder of the ever-present need to exert control over the process of our entry into society.

Do we then experience the social standards of the happy medium to be as neutral as the air we breathe? Do they saturate our lives to this extent? In what concrete ways do the agents of our education, parents and school for instance, participate in the imposition of standards? The appearance of father and mother, teacher and classmates in our stories sets them within networks of social relations. In telling our stories, we found ourselves to a large extent lacking in expressions for the way our inner selves are moulded by the painful process whereby our own deviation from social standards forces us to acknowledge them – the very process in which our submission to those standards actually takes place. The very fact that our recognition of our otherness is either represented – as it quite clearly is in the two stories presented here – as a shock to ourselves, or is played down (in the first story, through allusions to the possibility of surgical intervention) makes it difficult to identify the 'normality' of that recognition. We found a clearer focus for our discussions in a scene from a third story entitled 'The Tummy'. There is an *absence* in this story crying out to be worked through further; the absence of the writer's feelings about, and evaluations of references by parents and friends to the danger of developing into someone who is 'different'. Since the story was also accompanied by illustrations, we had evidence to support our own doubts as to whether the writer's fat stomach was felt as a problem only by her father, rather than by the little girl herself. It was also our hope that a process of dispassionate description would safeguard the writer against memories of catastrophe, and thus allow research and analysis to proceed unhampered. We felt the visual material could most fruitfully be used as an aide-mémoire; we suggested therefore to the writer that she begin with an exact description of her photograph. It seemed to us that, in studying not only her own image, but also her positioning in relation to her friend – the photograph shows her presenting herself alongside the writer as a model of girlish daintiness – she might be able to pick up traces of the feelings, actions and judgements on herself which she had experienced at the time.

Description of an Image

Two girls, around eight years old. Girl number one: round-faced and chubby-cheeked, short hair, a boyish haircut. She blinks into the sun, one side of her mouth curving upwards. Her expression recalls film images of the Wild West cowboy at the impending approach of his opponent. For her own opponent, she displays disdain; but she has not managed completely to erase the traces of fear from the crooked grin with which she had hoped to convey an attitude of fearless defiance. Her shoulders droop forwards, her arms encircling a rounded stomach, its rotundity further emphasised by the pleated skirt she wears. The skirt is bunched up on the rail of the patio fence, further reinforcing the impression of roundness. Her legs seem to bear no relation to one another; they are planted side by side with nothing but a large gap between them. However the girl cannot be described in full without comparing her with the friend also shown in the photograph. The stance of the friend, for example, is balletic. She places her weight on one leg, set slightly behind the other; the other leg, which crosses the first, is slightly bent, so that only the tip of her toes touches the ground. Her arms are folded across a waistline which remains nonetheless discernible, while her pleated skirt is nonchalantly draped on the balustrade rather than bunched up around her body. Her head is slightly bowed, she is not looking directly into the sun. Her sweet

smile shows off her dimples and rounds off her cheeks – in stark contrast to the face of girl number one, which is so round as to make dimples an impossibility.

My preference is for the first girl, the ugly one. Her whole body is an expression of resistance. The legs standing any-old-how, the drooping shoulders, the expression on her face, surly, anxious and defiant. She is aware of not being pretty but makes no attempt to become so. She could never be said to be happy in this attitude of defiance; her image is not a contented one. She neither arouses, nor does she seek approval. Her aim is to stop the world from coming too close.

We were taken aback by this new story. The writer chooses words expressing hatred, disgust and anger – her grin is crooked, her shoulders drooping, her stomach round, her skirt bunched up, there is a great gap between her legs – only to confess her love for the figure described in this way. The same defiance that she ascribes to the image of herself as a child was identified in group discussions as characteristic of three further aspects of the story. It is presented in the cry of 'and yet' that her confession of faith in herself implies: in the disdain she expresses (and which she ascribes equally to the little girl she once was) for universally acknowledged standards: and in her disdain for us as a group, for having made her write about this child. This, then, is a story about the writer as she is today; a story of her present disaffection, of her wish to see herself at all costs as ugly and insignificant, while at the same time making it a political matter to stand by those judgements of herself. While for our purposes it may be possible to ignore the writer's contemporary self-appraisal it is however necessary to consider the ways in which she first came to adopt not only this particular attitude toward herself, but also the particular way of constructing herself into the world that still determines her political action today. She described other scenes for us (and for herself) that displayed the same structure as the earlier story.

Strangely enough, the slim, pretty girl liked the fat, ugly girl and allowed herself to be guided by her example. When one day the fat girl had her long blonde plaits cut off, her friend immediately did the same. This is why both of them have the same hairstyle in the photograph. The attitude of the fat girl towards her friend was unfriendly, moody, tyrannical – as it was towards everyone else at school. No one was permitted to swim in 'her' swimming pool unless the games she liked were to be played. The swimming pool gave her a certain amount of power, as did her physical strength – she was also unusually tall for her age. If her anger was roused, she would hit out at things and people. She became, then, the moody child who made everyone around her dance to her own personal tune.

Just like a fairy tale: the assets are equally divided – the goodies are beautiful, the baddies ugly. The ugly fat girl is tyrannical and power-hungry; the slim, pretty girl is forced to submit, to dance to the tune she calls, and so on. In this context, an accord between writer and remembered image can only be lived (if at all) as a massive 'and yet', or else as a retrospective and more or less unconvincing reinterpretation of the writer's own life history as one of resistance.

It was this same resistance, which the writer attributed to all her memories as well as turning it against us as the actualizers of previously existing structures, that thwarted our attempts to discover the little girl she had been. In the analytical phase of our work, even such apparently harmless pictorial memories as those reproduced here triggered the kind of catastrophic spiral that might have led to the failure of our entire project. The searching gaze we turn on the past, while it begins to question the emergent associations between social standards, feelings and attitudes, at the same time undermines much of the self-confidence, identity and forms of relationships we have built up over the years. Our attempt to erase our own insecurity and feelings of inadequacy – since it is those feelings which allow domination to enter our lives – at the same time imperils the consciousness of self that can alone provide a basis for resistance to strategies of power.[4]

Within the body project, collective work offered a solution to the problem of destabilization, insofar as it allowed work on the question of 'the tummy' to be taken over by other members of the group. Our aim was to get a clearer view of the problems involved by *comparing* stories. In an attempt to recapitulate both the process of production, and the various stages by which we came to understand the issues involved, we have printed the stories we wrote as a group in chronological order and without accompanying comments. The conclusions we have drawn from them are then described and developed in a concluding theoretical section.

The Brown Knitted Skirt

It had seams, not at the sides, but in the middle both back and front. Not that this was the only reason why I hated wearing it. The fact of the matter was, it 'crinkled'. It was my mother who spoke of the 'crinkling' in this context. 'Stand up straight and pull your stomach in, your skirt's crinkled.' The thought of the skirt is less than pleasurable: its brownness, the fact that everyone could tell when I wore it what I really looked like, that I had to keep holding my breath, tensing my stomach muscles, pulling my tummy in. Feeling all the time as if I was deceiving everyone around me, concealing from them the truth which this skirt told of my appearance. Whereas in fact something quite different was going on; it wasn't that my tummy was fat, but that I stood sticking it out in front of me. To have a tummy is wicked in itself. The way I stood was typical of me. My sister, a model of virtue, would never let herself go to the same extent. She wasn't as lazy as I was. In my brown skirt, I was recognized for the unworthy character I was: the one who went out of her way to avoid any kind of housework, who was unruly and deceitful, or at least well-equipped with all the right excuses. Photos of me wearing the skirt – I was ten years old at the time and had just started grammar school – show a disconsolate child, ill at ease, skinny, making barely successful efforts to stand up straight. A little girl whose shoulders droop to match the corners of her mouth. Brown doesn't seem to suit me.

The New Dress

Frau W. came every year to sew whatever was necessary for us girls, for mother and for the household. I always looked forward to her visits, and would often stand and watch in the sewing room as my latest dress slowly began to take shape. Frau W. always brought along a pile of magazines with paper patterns in them; I would sift through them carefully in search of a pattern for myself. I was allowed to choose more or less as I wished, although my mother and Frau W. did chime in occasionally with advice. Most of the time I went along with their suggestions. The question of length was always an occasion for laughter, even at the measuring-up stage. Frau W. would say jokingly, 'Well now, we all know the special problems we have with hems – but we'll cross that bridge when we come to it.'

During these trying-on sessions, Frau W. would kneel in front of me to pin up the hem. She measured it with a ruler, exactly the same number of centimetres all the way round. Then she'd stand up, and I'd have to turn around slowly in front of her. The hem was always uneven – a fact she invariably greeted with exclamations of horror. When would I learn not to stick my tummy out so, when I knew very well it wasn't good posture? My mother too would exhort me not to parade my stomach about the place, we'd never get the hem straight this way, I should stand naturally. The fittings always lasted an age. Frau W. would get back on her knees, take off half a centimetre here, add a quarter there, then I'd have to turn round again, and so we'd go on, to-ing and fro-ing, over and over again. . . I put all possible effort into pulling in my stomach, holding my breath at the same time, feeling thoroughly distorted and abnormal. Normally I'd never think of walking around with

my stomach pulled in so tightly – but I had to grin and bear it just this once, or else nothing would ever come of my dress, and quite possibly Frau W. would never make one up for me again – all because of my 'difficult' posture. Grimly, I held my tummy in tight for as long as it took to finish the fitting, wanting at all costs to avoid arousing the displeasure of Frau W. and my mother, both of whom were likely to notice the moment I let go of my stomach. My mind remained fixed all the while on thoughts of the new dress to come.

Tummy in . . .

Between the ages of sixteen and seventeen, she put on vast amounts of weight. Up to then, she had been able to stuff herself with all manner of cakes and sweets without getting fat; now she didn't dare so much as look at them. For her, the worst part of it all was not only the way her face just kept getting rounder and rounder, but the fact people were constantly pointing it out to her. Nor was this the only problem: the apparently uncheckable growth of her breasts, and the fat piling up around her hips, were equally upsetting. Friends who considered themselves too fat saw their 'tummies' as the root of most of their problems. She certainly thought of her own tummy as much too fat, flabby and so on. And yet, unlike faces, hips or breasts, tummies could always be pulled in. You weren't quite so much at the mercy of this part of the body; to a large extent, you yourself could control whether your stomach was pulled in or stuck out. It was this possibility of 'control' that made her stomach less distressing. Is it possible that she's been running around for ten years or more with her stomach perpetually pulled in? When she hears other women complaining about their problems with their tummies, her spontaneous reaction is to think to herself, 'all they have to do is pull it in . . .'

The Park, or The Gymnastics Lesson

Not far from her home in Frankfurt, there was a park called the Palmengarten. *Unlike the Rothschild park, which she often used (although it was further away) because it had a playground, you had to pay a lot of money to get into the* Palmengarten. *It was worth it, though; it had hot, humid glasshouses with carnivorous plants in them, pump-room concerts, gymnastics classes and a much nicer playground with a special kind of swing. It was a long board hanging on four long rods; the board took the weight of about ten children, while two others could stand at the two narrow ends of the seat, holding on to the rods to move the swing backwards and forwards.*

Every Thursday afternoon, the park was open to me for free; I had a special pass to let me in for my gym lesson. My mother had put my name down for the class so I could do something about my weak stomach muscles. She said the only way I could get rid of my tummy at my age was by strengthening the muscles with exercise. In a few years' time, when I was grown up, I'd then be able to deal with it by pulling it in.

Proportions

One day, when she was looking after the shop for her mother, her great aunt looked in on her way home. They got onto the subject of figures, fat ones and thin ones. In the course of the conversation, her grandmother reassured her that her own figure had been just like her's when she was a young girl. Her waist too had always been too short. The child wasn't quite sure whether she was to take this as a slight on her own figure, or a positive judgement on her aunt's appearance as a young girl. Whatever the case, she found the thought of having the same figure as her aunt quite appalling. Not that her aunt was what you'd call fat, and she never ate a lot at parties, but her 'midriff' was certainly quite broad and expansive – or at least, that was how her mother described it. The child saw her as having no dividing line where her waist was supposed to be. Her arms, legs and shoulders, on the other hand, were what might be called narrow.

In what ways is 'having a tummy' discussed in these stories? And how is it that we become immured to the fact that having a fat tummy is impermissible?

1) Let us look first at the expressions used here. 'Don't stick your tummy out', 'pull your tummy in', 'stand up straight', you have to 'strengthen your tummy muscles'. The theme addressed, or rather the problem being manufactured here is not, as it may at first appear, *having* a tummy: to have a tummy is equated instead with a negative deportment of the body. The term 'attitude' should be understood here in both of its two senses; as an attitude of the body, and as a personal attitude of mind. Having a tummy becomes an immoral *act*. It is an expression of bad character – for having a tummy is a sign of having let oneself go. A girl who is not even capable of pulling her tummy in, and thus of exercising self-discipline, is likely to be the kind who doesn't do her homework, goes out of her way to avoid doing housework. . .

2) We become familiar with social standards and make them our own through a process of rearticulation. It is never explicitly stated that 'fat tummies like yours are ugly, you'll never get a man if you look like that', or whatever. Having a tummy is incorporated instead into the notion of a negatively evaluated *activity*. This is what makes it possible to call upon us as subjects to change the existing state of our tummies, through invocations and appeals to our sense of *responsibility*. We are told that we can and must be active in tackling the problem of our own attitude.

3) The decisive issue, then, is that of responsibility: our assumption of responsibility for our bodies. It is assumed that we ourselves determine and have control over our bodies – although we are made 'responsible' to socially predetermined norms. The principle of responsibility relates moreover not only to the tummy, but extends across the body as a whole – a point to which we shall return in a moment.

4) What the 'tummy stories' demonstrate is that we are drilled as children not only in social standards, but also in the methods for dealing with deviations from them. Or to be more precise: in learning the proper way to deal with our 'deviations', we also assimilate the standards from which those deviations take place.

5) The way in which we assimilate and learn to live with particular standards has other effects too. In one story, we read of a young girl feeling that she is 'deceiving everyone around her'. The impression of slimness is a piece of fraudulence which we practise. And yet we have learned to see fraud and deceit as wicked acts. To disguise a tummy is just as impermissible as having one in the first place. The contradiction lies in what we might call the requirements that others make of us – and it is a contradiction whose consequence and dynamic form is a permanently guilty conscience.

6) Having a tummy is at one and the same time our destiny, and our crime (echoes here of original sin?). I am born with shortcomings for which I am responsible; eradicating them becomes my life's work. My very existence in the world becomes the potential source of a guilty conscience.

7) A question that arises from this is the extent to which a guilty conscience produced in this way provides fertile ground, or creates a readiness in us to subordinate ourselves to authority.[5]

8) While the dynamics of the contradiction between opposing requirements have been discussed here in relation to only one part of the body, they could be extended across the body as a whole, or rather across the whole range of its representations. We are able to exert immediate 'control' over the stomach hence the references to 'pulling it in'; yet this does not mean that we are absolved of responsibility for the 'rest' of our bodies.

9) If any deficiency or inadequacy in a different part of our bodies cannot be eradicated immediately, it is compensated for by appropriate forms of *dress*.

10) In their attempts to bring up a child who is both acceptable and accepted, parental agencies reinforce the notion of an identity between bodily attitude and mental attitudes to the world. The requirement that we take responsibility for our bodies is thereby consolidated as a means of exercising control over our social existence, and as a feminine mode of participation in the social totality.

Expressive competence

Women have at their disposal a repertoire of camouflage, concealment, intonations, flattery. . . . As children we assimilate not only bodily standards but also, alongside them, the knowledge we need in order to conceal our own 'deviations'. A necessary part of the 'general knowledge' of femininity is knowing which colours achieve which particular effects (black, for example, 'thins us out'); knowing which patterns (horizontal or vertical stripes), or which particular textile structure (to rib or not to rib) is especially well suited to emphasize or conceal certain parts of our bodies. Besides all this, we know the precise criteria for determining the kinds of clothes, the colours and so on suitable for women of any given age. One example that springs to mind is the scandalized reaction of German visitors to the United States when confronted with the dress habits of older American women.* We are not putting forward any value judgement on that response; it should simply serve as evidence that this knowledge does indeed exist across a broad spectrum of women, and that it orientates itself around precise rules or conventions which it thereby also reproduces.

We would suggest that women's familiarity with the requisite standards, with proportions, with strategies of concealment and emphasis might usefully be termed 'expressive competence'. What we have managed to attain is a competence in non-competence.[6] It is a competence that consists in a skilful manipulation of pre-given standards, an adoption of the most sophisticated tricks in our attempts to meet those standards. It is a necessary form of competence within existing social structures, if

---

*Translator's note: It is still unusual for many older women in the Federal Republic to wear brightly coloured or patterned dresses, skirts etc.; British and American women are somewhat less decorous in this respect!

we are to retain our capacity for action. At the same time, it works to consolidate our social incompetence, insofar as it leads us to acquire expertise in operating within existing standards, and thus both to assimilate and accept those standards, rather than questioning what lies behind them.

Once trapped in a network of prevailing standards, we see no way out. A simple reversal – 'it's fun to be fat', or whatever – merely reinforces the validity of the negative evaluation of fatness in the very act of affirming it. Change cannot be a matter of simple opposition to certain limited standards, nor of living against and in spite of them.

Women who come together in groups united by the common experience of being too tall, too fat and so on, do however constitute a force opposing dominant 'normality'. In tracing pathways around a number of the social constraints they experience, they create 'alternative normalities' within which they are able to channel their energies in new directions, rather than concentrating exclusively on their deficiencies. What we have not found yet are the means that would enable us, collectively, to discover paths away from the road socialization now marks across our bodies.

Große auffallende Muster ... quergestreifte und ...

Auffallende Musterung können sich nur
junge Damen leisten

Large, striking patterns and horizontal stripes should only be worn by the younger ladies amongst us. 'More important than fashion is always good taste', is the title of this chapter from a book entitled *Be beautiful — stay beautiful* by Lilo Aureden, Gütersloh 1955, from the Bertelsmann Readers' Circle series on 'practical advice'.

The Slavegirl Project

Women are not only objects of male desire: they themselves play a part in their creation as such. To see femininity in this way is to identify a subjective aspect within being-as-object, and thus effectively to recognize the inadequacy of the subject-object metaphor for a discussion of the problems addressed in this book. Since women enter the market place as commodities, they are under pressure to make themselves externally presentable – to usc attractive packaging to bump up their market price, or to make themselves saleable in the first place. Implicit in the image of the carefully groomed woman is an assumption that the exchange value of women is open to manipulation, that it may be added to a given use value as an external appendage. Our investigations up to this point seem by contrast to suggest that women's construction of themselves into social relations, and thus into relations of gender, involves the whole of their person. Women's particular mode of socialization centres on the female body, and through it the whole range of women's potential skills and competences unfolds within pre-given constraints. The image that seemed to us best suited to this form of feminine socialization was that of the slavegirl. It allows us both to grasp the relation of structural domination within which femininity is subordinated to masculinity, and at the same time to portray women as active, albeit in the context of given constraints. The image of the slavegirl derives from an historical context in which un-freedom took the form of inequalities enshrined in law; thus it allows us to identify women's position as dissimultaneous with the contemporary situation. At the same time, since society today no longer formally recognizes the existence of slaves, our use of the slavegirl image allows us to tackle the question of how to overcome the forms of behaviour associated with that image. The very anachronism of the image makes our protest all the sharper. Amongst other things, our studies of the capacities, skills and competences of actual slavegirls (in the '*Tales of the*

1001 Nights', for example) made it clear to us that our attempts to use the notion of 'slavegirlishness' as an analytical concept also made it possible to uncover vast areas of historical competence within what is generally conceived as an absence of competence. And finally, we hoped that our use of this term would allow us to describe the behaviour of women in ways that showed them to be at one and the same time subordinate and active; their masters would have to be named, but implicitly. It seemed to us that all of this was contained in the image of the slavegirl. It remained for us to displace the fatalistic connotations of the term 'slavegirlish-ness' – the reduction of the slavegirl to the role of victim – and instead to work out the role it plays in our contemporary context in the maintenance and reproduction of gender as a relation between the dominant and the subordinate.

One of the first things we perceive about the relation between the sexes is not, as Freud assumed, the difference in the sexual organ, but the sartorial differentiations which mark that distinction. 'It is not possible to speak of the human body without posing the question of dress; for as I believe Hegel said . . . dress is the element in which the sensually perceptible acquires meaning, in other words it is through dress that the human body acquires meaning and thus becomes a vehicle of signs, or indeed a sign in its own right.'[1]

'Clothes maketh (wo)man.' We speak of men as being after 'a bit of skirt', we dress in clothes, we ornament ourselves with them, they offer the most diverse opportunities for dressing-up; we may look 'a million dollars' and feel nonetheless 'messy' on the inside (perhaps precisely *because* of the way we look?) We think of dress spontaneously as something added on from the outside, as a form of packaging which encases a true core, an essence – the character, the personality. Dress both buttresses and lends emphasis to the personality, drawing attention to specific attributes or deflecting it from them.

The guidelines for action offered here by morality are contra-dictory: on the one hand, we are called upon not to judge human beings by external appearance, to focus instead on the inner qualities they possess; on the other hand, we are required to keep 'decent' standards of dress. In our work, we pursued this con-ception of dressing a little further. It is founded in the potential we have to be dressed – or undressed – in any way we desire. In the initial stages of our project, the explanation we gave for the apparent existence, despite this, of particular 'types' of women, whose personality (character) is equated with the way they dress, was conceived in terms of habituation; if a woman represented herself over a sufficiently long period of time as a particular type, then that representation, we assumed, took on the character of a habit, and qualities initially taken on from outside became fused with the person.

We were surprised to find that the stories we initially wrote on the dramatic production of femininity had little in common with our existing theoretical presuppositions. They began instead at the point where external clothing, or at least *visible* clothing ended: namely with *knickers*.

Bum-Wiggler

It was getting warmer, spring was coming at last. The time was again approaching when mother could be persuaded to allow her to wear long socks. When one morning the thermometer rose to thirteen degrees, the covetted long socks were put out for the first time alongside the rest of her underwear. But since wearing socks this early in the year was of course nothing short of madness – she remembers her mother's dire warnings of an imminent bout of flu – she was to put on an extra pair of insipid light blue woollen knickers over her underpants. She hated them. They itched constantly and were oh-so babyish. But she gave in to the suggestion for the time being, as long as it brought her closer to the day when her thick tights could be discarded at last. My legs breathing the air again, she thought on her way to school. Most of the girls weren't yet wearing knee-length socks, and she was envied. Wearing socks was taken as a sign of having 'super-duper' parents, whose daughters were able to make them give in to their desires. And then at breaktime the first elastic skipping rope of the year was brought out and energetic battles fought over whose jumps were highest and most complicated. From knee-level upwards, she started to hold down her skirt at the back so that nobody, especially none of the cheekier boys, could see her pale blue underpants. It was an effort. It spared her from teasing, but instantly, it made her make mistakes. In the afternoon she went to town with her grandmother. When they got to the underwear department, she started complaining about how stupid she thought the underpants were. She said she was just going to take them off on her way downstairs before school and not put them on again until she got back to the front door after school. Grandma asked the shop assistant where she could find wollen knickers for the child. Alongside the display of blue knickers – the same familiar colour, perhaps just a little

darker – they found a new line; frilly white knickers in softer-than-soft material with three rows of ruching along the back. They weren't like wool: these knickers were 'easi-wash'. She thought they were wonderful. Her mother's lingerie was made of the same material. She begged and begged, and granny finally capitulated. She was to wear them on Sundays. We'll see, she thought. The next morning, she stuffed her woolly knickers back into the wardrobe and put on the frilly panties, chuckling with delight. She could hardly wait for breaktime, or rather for the moment when the elastic finally reached knee height. Using her arms to gather momentum, she jumped as high as was possibly able. The girls asked where had she got them from, they wanted a pair too, and the boys shouted 'bum-wiggler, bum-wiggler!' Let them shout, this is what grown-ups wear, the boys just don't understand.

It has frequently been suggested that advertising and fashion influence women in what they wear. In this way, it is said, desires are manipulated; or rather, the perpetual creation of new needs leads women to concern themselves with their bodies, their appearance. As far as the activities of the textile industry are concerned, this assumption is clearly to some extent justified. It does not, however, explain why women actually yield to these industries' whispered promises.

What causes consumers to purchase any given product is not real use value, but the aesthetics of the commodity as it impinges upon the sensuality of the purchaser.[2] Advertising is only the promise of use value. Desires, hopes and longings are projected onto the surface of the commodity. The commodity's offers of individualization in fact involve us in a process of typification.[3] This first became clear to us in our work on the ways in which it becomes possible for us to produce ourselves as 'particular' through the appropriation of specific (typical) characteristics – 'womanliness', 'motherliness', 'sexiness' and so on. What aroused our interest were the desires and hopes that are available to be worked on. In the story above, we may identify a number of different desires: the desire for sensual pleasure in the body, for legs that can 'breathe', the desire to be grown-up, the desire to impress others, as well as a wish for winter to come to an end.

Whereas in this story, 'knickers' remained visible, an external sign of integration and freedom, their meaning in other stories coexisted with their invisibility. 'Knickers', we found, had a role to play in different contexts: one writer, whose relatives at a wedding were to be 'charmed and delighted' by her appearance, felt it was necessary to wear her 'favourite underwear – the kind of knickers that don't get stuck in the cracks between the cheeks but are still quite neat and trim'. In another story, a visit from a girlfriend requires 'at the very least an immaculate pair of under-pants', while in another, a pair of 'slightly stretched, worn and yellowing underpants' were a source of anguish to the writer who wore them; they looked like a nappy, they made her into the child she no longer was, they excluded her from the games of other children. In a novel by Helga Novak,[4] the storyteller writes of her shame at her never-to-be-visible knickers: every night she sneaks furtively into the cellar of her boarding school where, under cover and unseen, she can wash a pair of woollen under-pants, the source of her anguish. Knickers are at once the object of discussion and tabooed; much trouble is taken to ensure that they cannot be seen: skirts are made long enough to hide them, trousers not too tight, to stop them showing through. There are no knickers: in part, knickers owe their existence to the art of making them forgotten. Yet despite this, mothers have a range of tactics to make knickers appear as something different from what they are, while at the same time leaving what they 'are' unspoken, forever secret. A good deal of effort is expended on the acquisition of knickers for little girls – frilly ones, with flowery patterns, frivolous in appearance. And moments of resistance amongst the girls surface in the stories: their battle for 'grown-up' knickers and for everything associated with them. That which is not to be shown presents itself and is discussed in these stories as something which *is* to be shown. If we take Roland Barthes's point that the meaning acquired by the body in a given historical situation is assimilated and expressed through clothing, then there still remains the question of why something that cannot be perceived externally should be remembered with such particular intensity, why it should be associated with so many emotions – shame, guilt, resistance, seriousness, unseriousness and so on. Knickers are surrounded by prohibitions, rules of hygiene and moral regulations (we know both what should constitute a 'decent' pair of knickers and what is meant when knickers are said to be 'indecent'). By wearing knickers, it appears that we appropriate and help to produce their meanings. The whole edifice of meaning built up around, across and through 'knickers', as well as the allusions they carry, seem to us to form part of a dynamic of socialization which, though it operates through an external causal relation moving from the outside inwards (social norms and values being taken over by individuals), is lived from the inside outwards. The connotative context of knickers becomes a chunk of morality, so tightly welded to this particular garment that it can no longer appear without it. In putting on a show of being 'nothing more' than knickers, knickers make morality a part of their nature.

Knickers as an Element in Sexual Socialization

The word 'knickers' allows us to speak the unspeakable, rather than simply referring to an article of dress. In using it, then, we are harnessed at an extremely early stage into what is in fact the adult discourse of sexuality. We wear underpants from our earliest infancy; equally, we know from our infancy of their particular status 'down there'. We have an inkling that they are the bearer of a secret, but we do not know the secret ourselves.

I well remember my mother's relief when, from the age of about twelve, I began to change my underpants daily of my own accord, without her having to check permanently whether I had done so. To her, this was a milestone on my pathway to adulthood, something I had grasped at long last. Explicitly, she spoke of me having learned to keep myself 'clean'.

We have already suggested that female socialization takes place essentially through women's insertion into the ordering of the sexual. Knickers function as a key focus in this process. By drawing attention to the fact that they are not to be displayed, knickers function as a sign of the invisible; in seeing them in this way, we learn to acquiesce in the contradictory requirement that we make reference to a core that is 'sexuality' by displaying that which is to be concealed as demonstratively 'non-sexual'. Though we may be motivated by the wish to deny sexuality, the effect on observers is to make them see that which is hidden as that which is most significant, to seek it out, and to deprive it of its ambiguity.

Knickers and Morality

How do we come to know what makes a pair of knickers 'proper' and 'fitting'? Very little girls wear knickers patterned with flowers, cats, frills; older women wear 'long white drawers', usually several sizes too big, long enough to pull up almost to the armpits. We draw meticulous distinctions between underpants (which are unambiguously non-sexual), knickers (whose status is not precisely known) and panties (which are more clearly sexual). Although we may know what makes a pair of knickers 'right', we seldom find ourselves in the happy position of wearing them at the appropriate moment. In public places – the swimming bath or the gym – we have to hide them quickly under the rest of our clothes – once again, there are no knickers (however secure we may feel in the knowledge of having changed them only a short time before). Even in isolation from the body, knickers make reference to sexuality, *are* sexuality. There is as much difference between a pair of knickers and bikini bottoms as there is between being naked and being fully dressed.

Knickers and Security

Every day, we are confronted with new messages from the advertising industry telling us that knickers will no longer suffice to make us feel 'secure' (or rather clean). No problem: the 'panty-slip' will come to our assistance. Every day of the week *even* between periods. The advertisements are sterile and purged of double meanings – despite the fact that the parts of the female

138

body they speak about are decidedly 'unambiguous'. Any connection with 'sexuality' is unthinkable. On the contrary; sexuality is de-named and overlaid (or overdetermined) by the notion of cleanliness, a value through which we are interpellated as 'you who must keep yourself clean down there'. It is perhaps the reference to 'down there' which so unsettles our conscience. We can never be secure in ourselves – where cleanliness is concerned – yet we can be unquestioningly secure in the knowledge of being exhorted to become so.

The Brassière

At the age of 14, I was already relatively big – adults described me as 'fully developed' and my breasts were constantly painful, but they could luckily still pass unnoticed if I was dressed. At last I had a reason for my problems with the horizontal bar, and I now also understood why we girls were left to struggle with two oars in rowing, while the boys simply looped a strap around their chests. I found the whole thing more than a little irritating; at the same time I was also proud of myself, and tried to make my pride evident by playing down this new development. After all, it was an indication that, despite the many faults and deficiencies consistently identified in me, I was still acquiring the normal signs of femininity; though reprimanded for my childishness, I was undisputably becoming a woman.

My sister and I used to sit at the big table in the room we called the hall, because it opened onto all the other rooms and everyone had to pass through it. Enter the boyfriend of our mother we so hated, a kind of guardian who saw our education as his primary responsibility. It was from him that we had learned for the first time to call ourselves deprived children. He approached us with a smile; his index finger passed rapidly down our spines – just checking. Hard to find the words that might describe my feelings as he did so. Describing them as 'turbulent' is inadequate; the word captures neither the direction and source of this 'storm' of emotions nor above all the conflict between its various elements. At first shame, humiliation and anger that this had to happen, at my having to tolerate this kind of inspection, at myself for allowing it to happen. At the same time, a vague awareness that it afforded him some pleasure that placed us in a relationship of involuntary complicity against my mother – a secret she was not to know. Our shared knowledge and the feelings of superiority aroused towards her were coupled with regret at her failure to intervene, with a feeling that it served her right if we kept her in the dark. Then pride, too, of a double kind; for after all, this was a way of detecting whether we were perhaps wearing a bra. The implicit understanding was that we were far enough advanced, our breasts were large enough for it to be possible to make such an assumption; and pride also in the fact that we didn't wear one, didn't use the props that showed you actually needed to, that your breasts were prone to 'sagging' – and which, so he told us, were more than likely to soften our breasts so they'd sag anyway.

The sexualization of 'innocent' parts of the body takes place primarily through the generation of meanings around them, the bundling of signs into a referential system. Female breasts are never innocent, their socialization takes place at the very moment they appear – a moment that also signals the entry into adulthood. Thus sexualization and adulthood occur simultaneously. In the story above, this construction is presented as a process of production. The process by which the woman becomes adult is a system of signs; the references are to the things she already has, or is soon to acquire. The changes she undergoes – which initially become evident as quantitative developments – are objectively verifiable: at some stage, she will reach the point at which body growth stops and sexual characteristics become clearly visible. These biological processes now enter into a social context, or rather it is within this context that they occur in the first place. They are tethered to the meanings through which gender is made. In women, it is at this point that the status of 'being human' is attained. In men, by contrast, sexual characteristics (the first beard) represent one step only in the process of becoming adult; men still have some way to go before they 'get to be somebody'. The writer in our story portrays the process in terms of rupture. Being 'fully developed' – a biological meaning – becomes 'being adult'. Subjectively, the writer experiences it as a source of pain, as an obstacle to her activities. But the positive meaning of being and becoming adult soon becomes dominant – albeit in contradictory ways. It is seen as a mark of *distinction*, of social recognition, something that is not 'natural'. Adulthood is associated with the attainment of sociality and thus with the external presentation of gender. This presentation of gender to the outside world is however also a dissembling of 'something' that has now changed. The change occurs in more than the body – the whole world now relates to the body in a different way and with a different end in view. Massive ruptures are now destined to take place, for example in the social relations within which the writer is placed.

The woman who has just become or is in the process of becoming adult is now neither the 'girl' she once was – she is already worlds away – nor has she yet become what she is 'destined' to be, for, though she is a woman and a sexual being, she has, as yet, no life that is immediately sexual. She does however enter old alliances – with the ordering of hetero-sexuality, for example – in new and different ways. The writer's pride is awakened by the attention she gains from her guardian; the heterosexual order overlays her hatred of him, and her judgement – admittedly a contradictory one – is determined by her sexualization. The unmentionable secret makes the child an adult the moment she is forced to divulge it, or to guard it alone; it is part of the process of individualization – despite the fact that 'it' happens, not to the writer, but to the mother.

The story is also interesting from an historical perspective. It is set in a period that coincides with the early years of the Federal Republic; the guardian has already lived as an adult under fascism. We should note in passing here the fact that each deter-minate ordering of the body represents a subordination within determinate ideologies (in other words, within entire *systems* of norms and values). The fascist discourse of the body was organ-ized around the *will* to health. Illnesses were not seen as problems or disorders of human organs, but as *evil deeds*. An unwillingness on the part of the subject to achieve fitness was taken to signal an unwillingness to be subordinate to the State. In this context, the ideological encroachment by the State on the body seems to us to have occurred quite directly; domination was reproduced through the body. The faint reference in our story to this complex of issues posed a question we have yet to investigate fully, that of how structures of interpellation addressed to women appeared under fascism.

Our stories indicated to us that it would be simplistic to assume that 'slavegirlishness' is a form of behaviour that takes place between human beings – men and women – on a small scale only. It would then also be too simple to assume that the precise methods of the slavegirl are simply 'learnt' in adolescence. 'Learning' would demand no more than finding out what boy-friends were likely to find most appealing, and ornamenting ourselves accordingly. But this is not the origin of the impulse we all feel; that impulse is less purposive, more general, more all-embracing. Knowledge of the effect of particular movements, tones of voice, gestures, ways of dressing, a particular gait: where do we acquire all this, and towards whom is it actually directed? How do we go about making ourselves look sexy? The answer lies, we believe, in the notion of competence.

I recently overheard the following conversation between two couples whose external appearance could be paraphrased as 'fashionable' and 'well-groomed'. One couple was fitted out in various shades of blue, the other in beige. The voice of the blue woman was unpleasantly loud and shrill, her words addressed to the whole of the assembled company; extra stress was put on individual syllables through pointed elongation. Her voice sliced piercingly across the room:
'How anyone could do such a thing!'
'Her legs are fat enough as it is and then she puts on those great thick shoes . . .'
The voice breaks, 'Well I just don't understand it . . . if she wore trousers you wouldn't be able to see her legs and she could wear shoes with a bit of elegance.'
'And then again she has such a sweet face.'
The beige man interrupts her breathless tirade in full flow – with good reason, he may believe, since his subject is the same.
'Well there the two of us were up on the wall, having a marvellous time of course, with the women trying on dresses in this little shop and then coming out and showing themselves to us.'
A venomous interjection from the blue woman: 'All you wanted to do was goggle. But whether what you find attractive really looks any good . . . now that's another story.'
He says: 'I don't know what you're getting so excited about . . .' She says: 'You know as well as I do, the dress you said was stunning looked like nothing on earth.'
She looks for the first time at the beige woman, searching for support, disparaging:
'Men, all you're ever interested in is what's on the outside.'

What sounds like a contradiction – the unseemliness of men judging by appearance alone – appears to us to point towards a possible formulation of the way in which women regulate their external appearance. Women attain competence in this area, not by appealing directly to the desires of particular men, but instead to a free-floating and generalized Masculine (the extent to which men themselves are able to respond to that appeal will not be discussed further here). The detachment of the rules of this particular game from concrete desires makes them diffuse, susceptible to change (albeit across a limited spectrum) at any given moment. At the same time, the competence demanded of women in the observance of rules is so elaborate that the effort and pleasure involved in attaining it conceals the subordinating character of the process whereby women make themselves 'slavegirls'. In our work, we felt that it was useful to study the acquisition of this kind of competence in its most extreme forms. We therefore asked one woman to write a story from a daily working life which is to a certain extent dependent on her presentation of herself for commercial ends: she works as a waitress in a bar.

The Barmaid's Tale

It's a weekend evening – but tonight is going to be a 'one-woman show'. The prospect doesn't worry me in the slightest, quite the reverse, I know I have an interesting evening in front of me and I enjoy the feeling of responsibility for my own actions, the freedom to do as I please. Whenever I'm behind the bar on my own, everything goes like clockwork. The way I divide up my time leaves me plenty of room for improvisation, which contributes to the general entertainment, and makes for a harmonious – but never stagnant – atmosphere in the place. I switch on the coloured lights and the games machines and put up the pumps. I choose the music carefully, something speedy, optimistic, suggestive of cheerfulness to the customers and of movement to me. I choose Stevie Wonder; his music feels to me like acoustic sunshine, full of bubbling rhythms. As I polish the ashtrays, dancing softly to myself, and turn on the washing-up water ready for later, the first customers arrive, lads of the same age as me, whose mood visibly improves when I welcome them by name, with a gleaming smile. They give careful thought to their order, my new poster, 'milk is harmless, DM1.50 a glass' takes its first effect, the grapefruit juice is for me. The rosé is finished, I have to open a new bottle. Although they already know my principle of always dealing with as much as I'm capable of myself, all five offer assistance, which I jokingly refuse, as always. Once they're all taken care of, I nip into the kitchen for a quick check on how I look in the mirror. I have to be spotlessly clean and tidy, of course, otherwise the drinks I prepare by hand have something unappetizing about them. Raising my external attractiveness above this level is risky, but, equally, good for business. The risks begin to become acute if the result of my efforts is overly provocative and sexually stimulating. So for example I have to abstain from mini-skirts, something I don't find difficult, since I can't abide them anyway. For work, the most important thing is for my clothes to be comfortable, with no dangling corners that might trail in the washing-up water, or long, elegant chains that end up taking a bath in the beer glasses. High heels are suicide for eleven hours of standing and running about, besides which I'm not keen on them anyway. I make a point of deciding what I'm going to wear on the basis of how I feel; on warm days, when I generally feel twirly-skippety, well-disposed to the world, talkative, energetic, relaxed and floating, I wear thin, white, loose cotton dresses, let my hair down and go barefoot. When the weather is cooler I feel more serious, more measured, I like to wear boots with sloping clumpety heels, and my preference is for colours of grey and blue, at a pinch turquoise.

For a good relationship with customers, it's definitely more important to have a style which is individual – but not monotonous – than to have a plunging neckline. Most much prefer to look at my face and not my arse; dirty old men really are the exception, and my regulars react much less calmly to drunkards who try and make passes at me than I do. More often than not, they throw them out straight away, as a kind of demonstration that they both accept me as an authority and that they're prepared to support me – so I'm in no sense the image of the waitress as white-aproned sex object! What's more, a woman behind the bar is generally much less exposed to chauvinistic harassment than a woman customer – that is unless she is consciously provocative.

More on my role as woman behind the bar. I play a mixture of manageress, waitress and one-woman entertainer, part-time disc-jockey, occasional healer of souls (yes, even this), a leisure-time friend who just happens to be behind the bar, a favourite partner for a billiard game. I have a reputation as a pretty and very self-confident, lively and eccentric young woman; my customers look for conversational openings with me, they're happy to do me favours, they're charming, and they stay at a respectful distance. Of course the lads do project a certain amount of possessiveness onto me: woe betide anyone who so much as lays a finger on 'our Else'. But this kind of possessiveness isn't the least bit restrictive, not at all. On the contrary, their friendly possession of me allows them to come into contact with each other; it joins them into what might be called communicative communities of interest. This is what makes the atmosphere in the place so pleasant – it's peaceful,

*there's a sense of mutual understanding – and makes it possible to
have more serious conversations. Of course my appearance plays
a part in my popularity, but I'm convinced that my openness and
willingness to communicate are much more decisive, because they
give each individual the feeling of knowing me well and so of
having some claim on my friendship. After all, it is relatively
unusual for every single regular to be a friend of the landlady. I
find the role satisfying, and it fills me full of energy, especially
since I'm learning a whole number of skills in the process – and
after all, who doesn't enjoy being at the centre of a group of people
they like?*

The Competence of the Slavegirl

The first time we read this story, it appeared not to fit with the
question we had posed of how women construct themselves as
'slavegirls'. The impression the writer gave us was one of self-
confidence and proficiency: a liberated woman. She carries out
the tasks allotted to her in the bar with ease, she even enjoys
them. Quite consciously and deliberately, she calculates the
degree to which the effect she has on her (male) customers is
'good for business'. This contradicted the view we had previously
held of the way women 'play their role' as slavegirls. We had
always thought the slavegirl as 'passive', as restricted in her
capacity for action. We had held fast to this notion against our
better theoretical judgement, as well as our practical experience,
both of which pointed to an element of acquiescence in women's
state of oppression. Women are made both supplementary and
subordinate to men, they are abused as objects of sex and pleasure – a fact on which advertising and industry build and from
which they profit by tendering the naked bodies of women alongside commodities for sale. Yet women also know from their
experience that *skill* is involved in conforming to prevailing rules
and orderings. Among other things, we take pleasure in acquiring and endorsing the requisite skills. Our active appropriation
of the rules makes us more self-confident in our activities; in
availing ourselves of the existing order by actively 'exhibiting'
our own bodies, we participate in our own construction as slavegirls. In order fully to grasp the way in which women's sexual
socialization proceeds through the display of their bodies, we
had to think of self-confidence and 'slavegirlishness' as densely
interwoven. An ability to handle given rules with proficiency,

From *Photo*, no. 5, May 1981

and the security that the sense of their general acceptability affords – for example in the games we play with our men, or for the attentions of men in general – give power and strength to individual women. The subjective feelings of happiness and satisfaction accompanying our manipulation of systems of rules are thus more than an illusion, a product of the 'imagination' of individual women; they are a practice through which both sexual ordering, and the oppression within it, are reproduced.

Once we had reached this stage in our deliberations, it was no longer possible to identify women in our stories merely as victims, as the oppressed. Women, it seemed, lived both dominance and subordination in one person, they remained confident and capable of action within relations of heteronomy. Our reluctance to acknowledge this story as one of subordination stemmed from our own incapacity to see two sides at once; for us, women were either victims, or active agents who could never be seen as subordinate. The writer of the story herself demonstrates how familiar women are with the rules of the ordering within which they live. She uses what appears almost as an 'intrinsic' logic to bring the various different elements of the story into mutual association. She is to look functional and smart; her style may be flexible, but only within particular limits; her clothes must be attuned to her own changes of mood, they are not to get in the way of her work, they are to be effective in bumping up sales, and they are to protect the wearer from unwelcome pestering. Thus her knowledge of the ordering consists in a precise knowledge of the *limits* beyond which she must not go. Her awareness of these is lived in the story as competence, and as activity. It is the source of the writer's proficiency, as well as her self-confidence. The fact that she knows up to what point her appearance is good for business, and from what point it puts her at risk, makes her capable of action; it gives her a sense both of having the situation under control and of being at the centre of events. Her 'slave-girlishness' becomes a source of security.

One prerequisite for this kind of thinking within limits is the existence beyond the limits of something threatening and dangerous, as well as something within the limits that is seen to protect us from danger. What is important for individuals is knowing the different gradations and graduations, knowing where the limits lie; this knowledge is what makes them capable of action. In our story, the writer puts herself at a distance from the figure of the barmaid (who is unambiguously an object of desire); she refuses to describe the impression she herself makes on others in terms of sexual arousal, provocation, or whatever. Through the classification of certain kinds of clothes and modes of behaviour as sexual, it becomes possible to define other kinds against them, and to classify these as non-sexual. It is even conceivable that we think spontaneously in terms of a separation between a permissible and a non-permissible form of sexualization; in other words, that we consider it perfectly admissible for women to look inviting, but never 'immodest' nor openly 'provocative'. In the past (and even today) we tended spontaneously to adopt a scale of values, or to draw distinctions allowing us to set ourselves apart, at a distance from the slavegirl. Perhaps the very lack of ambiguity defining particular objects — short skirts, high-heeled shoes, plunging necklines or see-through dresses and blouses, wiggling hips and so on — as sexual and 'provocative' makes it easy for us to distance ourselves from all that, and so to turn our backs on the problem of the slavegirl in ourselves, and of our contribution to her presence there. The order of dress has to be seen, then, as one of the elements – one only amongst many – through which women are drawn into the order of sexuality, and through which they are socialized in the ways of the slavegirl.

A second aspect of the story which we were able to isolate in our analysis sheds light on the forms of behaviour through which women produce associations between men, and bind them together to form 'communicative communities'. Several attempts have been made in feminist theory to outline theoretical approaches to this aspect of femininity. In the work of Heidi Hartmann, for example, patriarchy appears as a relationship between men.[5] Luce Irigaray has taken the same argument further. 'Traditionally, woman is use-value for man, exchange-value between men. Merchandise, therefore. Which makes her care-taker of the material. Whose worth will be valued by the standard of *their* work and their need-desire, by "subjects": workers, merchants, consumers. Women are marked phallically by their fathers, husbands, procurers. And that stamp determines their value in sexual commerce. Woman is always merely the locus of a more or less competitive exchange between two men . . .'[6]

Irigaray sees the exchange of women as the foundation of our culture – men or groups of men are seen to circulate women amongst themselves. At the origin of all societies stands the incest taboo, by which men were originally forbidden to marry their own female kin. Women in primitive societies were therefore hunted down outside the tribe, or exchanged between clans. Women, Irigaray holds, have been 'objects of transaction' between men (since the woman's father or brother received 'payment' for the bride from the future husband). She interprets this in terms of a suppressed male homosexuality, lived out today in the way men shunt women around amongst themselves in order to gain access to each other. Irigaray's ideas are confirmed by the evidence of westerns, or detective films for example, where struggles are frequently played out over a woman, even sometimes a small girl who has either already died, or whose heart has yet to be 'won'. The men's actions revolve around a figure who has no other significance in the film than to make the men into allies or enemies amongst themselves.

Generating communication is as much a skill as knowing the limits beyond which we are not to go. In our story, there is no mention of any interest shared by the individual male customers; this cannot be the reason why they meet together in the bar. The issue arises of how communication can be brought about by women. In the story, the writer is at all her customers' disposal; she takes care of them, provides conversation and entertainment. Is it, then, by the availability of their whole persons that women produce communication between men? The point at which the writer enters into contact with the men is in their display of possessiveness, and the protective role they assume towards her. As the story shows, she does not feel that possessiveness to be in the least restrictive; for her, it is pleasurable, and appropriate to the context, it represents her position as central, and as one of power. In 'The Barmaid's Tale', the limits within which she is contained are drawn by the writer herself, in the justifications she gives for each of her actions. Keeping within the limits makes available a certain space, a certain degree of freedom within her unfreedom.

We asked ourselves at this point how it is that we learn to move within limits, how we are trained in a knowledge of limits, and in a capacity to set them ourselves. Our hope was that we might learn from a new story along precisely what lines our limits actually run. We had in mind a situation in which the writer had done something for which she had been censured, attacked, or 'got at'; we were interested in finding out on what basis she then drew the conclusion that she had gone *too far*.

The Happy Accident

It was Saturday, another scorching day was drawing to an end, though even darkness brought no significant drop in temperature. I had spent the whole day and the previous night serving behind the bar. I had passed my lowest point late in the afternoon; I had taken a shower and put on a clean dress, my favourite, wispy-thin and airy, a robe in white cotton, loose all over except around the waist, the feeling of being dressed in nothing but clouds.

The air in the place was hot and steaming; the lights, tropically colourful but still muted, the hammering-loud beat of the music, muffled and penetrating, the contours of familiar faces veiled in smoke, my own over-tiredness, all of these emphasized my state of ecstatic exhilaration, I raced frantically backwards and forwards across a bar that was barely half-full, unable to relax, but still in the best of spirits and strangely excited, exchanging a word or two with various people here and there; I knew every single customer. I wasn't the only one feeling agitated in this close weather, a number of the customers were standing around, nerves on edge, shirts wide open, visibly ready for action, but stagnating indecisively in their impatience. We exchanged thoughts on the restless tension we all somehow felt – even as we talked, I felt about to burst with nervous energy, looked to hands and feet for assistance, danced perpetually from one foot to another, downing endless ice-cold grape-

From *FAZ*, 15.5.82

fruit juices and shrouding myself in clouds of cigarette smoke. The evening continued, no let-up in the heat, nor in the frantic trembling which shook me all over. Everything in me cried out for movement, someone else was working behind the bar, so I took my place at the stereo; the music I put on was as violent as my emotions. I stepped onto the dance floor and my surroundings faded away, I threw myself into a rippling sea of rhythm, plunged my heated body into the great wailing floods of the guitar as it rose to a scream of joy again, I danced excessively, ecstatically, passionately, the dress clung dripping-wet to my body, the material, paper-thin, made transparent by the wetness, stroked lightly across my skin, exciting me even more. Incapable of stopping even had I wanted to, I danced crazily on to the very last note, shook my body and raced back to the turntable, insatiable, longing for more, paying no attention to, indeed hardly perceiving the fact that all eyes, spellbound, were turned in my direction. (Not a single woman was in the bar that night.) I slipped back out of consciousness and into the music, danced, romped and raged, spinning out all my primitive instincts in movement, then letting the music caress me again, enjoying playing at the feeling of weightlessness, then rising once again to a pitch of primitive emotional frenzy.

Resistance to the Story

Up to the point at which we read this story, our assumption had been that, under capitalist conditions in which the average individual lives in a state of competitive opposition to, rather than coexistence with others, the demarcation of limits was a necessary communal skill. In this story, however, only the writer is present; others surface as surroundings and backdrop, not as active persons, but more or less like the air around her – in a dual sense, as the air she breathes and as an invisible element. It seemed astounding to us that only one person appeared in this new story. So great was our surprise that we attempted to persuade her to rewrite the story, or at least to extend it to a point at which the reactions and feelings of the men, which they themselves had articulated in conversation, became apparent.[7]

Our experience shows that group resistance to a story most commonly arises when what is described disrupts our everyday modes of thought. We have a spontaneous desire to be confirmed in our thoughts and actions, in the intuitive judgements we have grown used to making. In empathizing with and spontaneously affirming a number of the stories told by the group, we not only reinforced each other in our mutual experiences, but also in the preconceptions and simplistic explanatory models they conjured up in our minds. In so doing, we consolidated old assumptions, and made it impossible to question those assumptions in order to gain new knowledge of the issues. In an attempt to break through the barriers to knowledge we ourselves erect, let us try here to identify elements in our story that would otherwise appear 'tangential', or simply taken for granted; this, we hope, will shed new light on the issues we have raised.

'If we want to pass easily through open doors, we should

remember that the frames around them are solid.'[8] The writer of our story occupies a world of her own. Much of what happens takes place in her head – including her account of others' reactions. She writes about herself from an exterior perspective, from the standpoint of a mirror-image of the I; she sees herself through the eyes of others as if looking in a mirror in which she can watch herself dancing. The social world is represented by negation, as a lack of sociality, as isolation and loneliness born of self-imposed censorship. 'Self-imposed', since it is the writer herself who sets the limits within which her 'primitive desires' and a 'seething inner life' are contained. But what does this actually mean for her? In our society, fellow human beings and society as a whole are experienced in terms of limits, restriction and control; thus the attainment of pleasure, happiness and freedom appear to be possible only through liberation *from* other human beings. To withdraw from others, not to have to take them into account for once, just once to be woman through and through – this is how we dream of liberation. We see our 'deepest desires' as abstracted from society – a view that reinforces sociological theories of interaction or interpersonal relationships as much as it does our everyday conception of the human individual standing in opposition to society. In both cases, the individual and society are separate and opposed to each other, the relation between them regulated by roles and symbols that individuals accept, and with which they are called upon to comply (if necessary disregarding what are actually their 'deepest' wishes, needs and desires, in order to avoid deviance or breakdown). In psychoanalysis too, the same notion can be identified: 'The liberty of the individual is no gift of civilization. It was greatest before there was any civilization, though then, it is true, it had for the most part no value, since the individual was scarcely in a position to defend it. The development of civilization imposes restrictions on it, and justice demands that no one shall escape those restrictions.'[9]

The human being is seen here to be divorced from culture: instinctual sacrifices and renunciations must be made for the sake both of culture and of the human individual. The associations established between meanings in our story suggest a similar conclusion. The writer steps outside herself, oversteps all existing limits and dances alone – she is alone. We have chosen to use a concept from interaction theory – social competence – to describe the social relations portrayed in the story. The term is well suited to characterize practice under our contemporary conditions, insofar as it describes the separation of social skills from competences. Since human beings are denied competence, or control over the social conditions underpinning community, their sociality must be acquired and lived as an extra. To this extent, the very existence of a concept such as 'social competence' should be seen as an indictment of a situation in which our individual desires are directed against those of others, and in which relations of competition and antagonistic interests are commonplace. Our capacity to communicate is learned as something extra. It makes its appearance as a competence in being both together with, and at the same time isolated from others, as the knowledge of a system of rules by which we are enabled to move within particular limits. Even communication, or rather the capacity to communicate, appears then as a process of demarcation, as a capacity to draw boundaries between the self and others.

Since our aim is to outline a perspective for the future, we would suggest that liberation should not be seen as the propagation of solitude. Solitude is the strategy put forward, for example, by bourgeois theorists of interaction; or at least, it is the logical conclusion of their analysis. If we follow their example, we come to terms with the world simply by conforming to existing rules, by making ourselves experts in interaction. 'Conformity' derives from 'crying with the wolves'. We are said to find freedom, a momentary capacity to step outside ourselves, in a few brief instants of solitude. But a freedom conceived in this way is based on an absolute separation between individuals and society; society is thought as the sum of a multitude of opposing individual parts. The world comes between human beings as a system of rules which, while on the one hand bearing down on individuals and preventing them from living out their actual desires unchecked, remains at the same time indispensable for their survival.

The Legs Project

'Legs aren't made for walking'

Proverbial legs

In our introduction to these projects, we asked how 'innocent' parts of the body – here, the legs – become 'guilty'. To put the question a different way; how are women's legs articulated within sexual relations? How are female legs harnessed for the production of sexuality?

If in our work we were to recognize the production of sexuality as such, we first had to denaturalize the process whereby female legs become sexualized. We needed to approach our object from the standpoint of a disinterested observer, in order to feel the oddity of our guilt in relation to legs and sexuality, and to reassess both on that basis. The procedures we therefore adopted involved, first, the historicization of the female leg. Our initial step was to visit a museum, where we attempted to identify the ways in which women's legs were represented visually. We left not a great deal the wiser. We had seen countless images of women with bare legs, with legs unclothed or clothed in numerous different ways: women who 'revealed' to the spectator only the tips of their toes, or their feet, or their calves, or their legs to the knee. None of this, however, equipped us to draw conclusions about the meanings generated by legs. We saw only legs, in and of themselves. (The sole peculiarity we noted for future reference was the presentation of male legs during a period when women's legs were entirely concealed from view. Men's legs meanwhile were to be seen emerging from under short skirts, enveloped in coloured silk stockings. To comprehend this phenomenon more fully, it would have been necessary to undertake a whole study of courtly culture.) At a loss as to how to read the images before us, we began instead to interrogate the ways in which legs have been and are spoken about, turning first to a study of *proverbs*. As we sifted through the relevant old sayings, we were at first astonished to discover that women's legs did not figure at all. We found dozens of proverbs on women's hair and feminine beauty (many couched in terms of warnings to

153

men); none, however, concerned with their legs. Instead, most sayings and proverbs position non-gendered human legs (or, in English, 'feet') in relation to social status; or, to be more precise, with human existence in *bourgeois* society. They deal for example with questions of *economic* position; whether one 'stands on one's own two feet', has one's feet 'under someone else's table', or even 'under one's father's table'. The question of whether or not any given mode of existence is happy or unhappy is similarly determined according to the state of legs and feet. Always 'falling on your feet' is positive, as is 'standing (optimally, with 'both feet') firmly on the ground', as opposed to 'tripping over your own feet', or what in German is known as 'getting up with your left foot forward' ('getting out of bed on the wrong side'). Notions of 'pulling the ground out from under someone's feet', or 'tripping them up' seem to be addressing prevailing conceptions of competition. Small wonder then that we finish up on an unfriendly 'footing' with our opposite number . . .

A further linkage we identified was that between power relations in the social division of labour, and legs: workers are told to 'leg it' if they move too slowly, and we then 'put the boot in' if they refuse to comply. The attitude of anyone subject to harassments of this kind is characterized accordingly in terms of their refusal to 'shake a leg'.

Our search led finally to the State itself, to the domain of the military and the judiciary. According to Röhrich, the crossing of one leg over another was originally 'a gesture used by judges as a public signal that the verdict was to be announced'.[1] Thus it would not merely be deemed improper for any lay person to adopt that same pose in court; it would be a usurpation of official prerogative. If the accused then wished to appeal against the verdict, s/he was to 'be upstanding – *stante pede*' before the judge; otherwise the verdict took effect immediately. We speak, too, of getting something 'on its feet', in the sense of bringing it into being; according to Röhrich's dictionary of sayings and proverbs, this particular saying 'seems likely to refer to a mobilizing army rising to its feet'.[2]

And finally, phrases such as 'having one foot in the grave' or 'getting back on one's feet' refer to *biological* existence – although the latter may also be redefined in terms of social relationships, again with reference to notions of economic existence, in such phrases as 'being helped back onto one's feet'.

What basis do these findings offer for future work? In the first instance, we learned that legs are not simply 'innocent' parts of the body that happen to enter a certain ordering of the sexual when attached to women; instead, feet and legs in general have been, and continue to be positioned within a particular order. The one and only proverb relating to legs that carries gender-specific meanings – the notion of the 'ball and chain' that 'ties a person down' – implies different obstacles to freedom for men and women: while men are 'tied down' by their wives and families, a woman's 'ball and chain' is more often than not an illegitimate child.[3]

If the linkage between feet or legs and freedom of movement means different things for woman and men, what implications does this have for other linked pairs: legs and the division of labour, legs and health, legs and economic independence?

The art of showing a leg

Early days

It was around 1909 that the hemlines of skirts and dresses first rose to the ankles. One early reaction from the Catholic clergy was a pastoral letter of 1913, addressed by an archbishop to women at large. 'I feel constrained to address a plea of some urgency to the feminine world. In matters of fashionable dress, I would urge you to observe the limits imposed by moral decency and Christian modesty. Our God-forsaken world grasps every available opportunity for sensual gratification; it surrenders above all to the desires of the flesh. It is to such lasciviousness that the most recent fashions in clothing are devoted.'[4]

Women at the time also spoke out against these developments in fashion; in 1914, Catholic seamstresses complained at having to make up clothes that corresponded neither to 'Christian morality' nor 'propriety'.[5] In the same year, ladies of the Parisian aristocracy were to be found protesting against 'certain excesses in fashion. . . .and in particular against the indecency of those kinds of dresses which expose the whole of the legs to view.'[6] 'Exposing the whole of the legs to view' is synonymous in this context with showing the ankles. In Illinois, USA, there was even a law passed 'for the protection of feminine virtue and in the interests of a propriety which we see as under threat'. Under its terms, women were forbidden by law from wearing 'skirts or petticoats whose hemline is more than six inches distant from the ground when the wearer is standing.'[7]

Within the terms set by Christian morality, the sexual investment of women's actions is said to be *already given*; showing an
ankle is a sign of immorality. The moment women show their
ankles, the Catholic clergy feel bound to respond with a prohibition of what they see as an immoral act, in an attempt to
reestablish traditional moral values. Yet this observation still
gives us no clues as to why legs are invested with sexual meaning
in the first place. Let us look more closely at the constructions in
play here.

In his pastoral letter, the archbishop draws what he assumes to
be naturally given boundaries between morality and immorality.
It was one such boundary which, in his view, was transgressed at
the beginning of the twentieth century by a fashion in clothes that
allowed ankles to be exposed to view. Showing the ankles can be
said to be immoral on the basis of a drawing of boundaries by a
subject the archbishop names as 'Christian modesty'. Who then
is this subject? The exposing of legs was articulated as an
immodest and immoral act in letters penned by bishops of the
Catholic Church, an act likely to instigate lascivious glances, to
promulgate sensual pleasures. Thus it is human beings, operating within a given social agency – the *Church* – who, in the name
of Christian morality, forge the link between the showing of legs
and immorality.

In the second place, we are confronted with a group of *women*
– an Association of Catholic seamstresses. They articulate excessively short skirts as an onslaught on traditional Christian
morality. Meanwhile the women of the Parisian nobility, their
own wish to dress fashionably notwithstanding, define dresses
that expose the feet as 'excessive', as indecent (improper, an
offence to propriety). And finally, the *law*, as an ideological
force sees 'morality' threatened by the new fashion in clothes,
and states the need for a safeguarding of 'feminine virtue'. The
appropriate law is passed 'in the interests of morality'. Thus
morality is made a subject in its own right, with specific interests
attributed to it.

What kind of subject, then, is this 'Christian modesty' or
'morality'? It is not a unitary subject; for as we have seen, it is
produced through the work of human beings within diverse
social agencies, who define the amount of leg women may show if
propriety is to be preserved. As the subject is produced, so also is
morality. While on the one hand boundaries and meanings
become objects of struggle within social agencies, morality is
mediated to individuals in the form of values. What begin as

appeals for individual 'modesty', 'morality' and so on, eventually take shape as regulations imposed from above, to which subordinate individuals may have recourse either as points of reference in relation to which they themselves and others may be called to order, or as the means by which that order is first produced.

The mini skirt

Women show more of their legs these days: does this mean they have become immoral, or are legs no longer invested with sexual meaning? 'As women and girls well know, the sight of a scantily-clad thigh is always provocative: it arouses the instincts!'[8] For the magazine *Szene Hamburg*, it was not however for this reason that women first adopted the mini skirt; instead, this new style is seen to have indicated their refusal to submit to the 'tyranny' to which they had hitherto been subject – they wore mini skirts simply because it 'felt good' to do so. Since the beginning, the mini, it is claimed, has been a 'symbol of equal opportunity and sexual freedom'.[9] Sexual freedom is seen to consist in showing one's legs, *despite* the sexual investment they embody. The question then arises of how they are shown: for legs are not 'purely and simply' bare. Showing them is a highly complex activity – nothing short of an art.

'How to stay fast on your feet'

Our subtitle is a quote from the women's magazine *Brigitte*.[10] The idiom used recalls the sayings we have already quoted – although they did not refer to the legs of women. What does it mean for women to be 'fast on their feet'? Is the phrase purely functional? A hint on how to 'get ahead', or how to 'stand fast' in the world? In the initial stages of our analysis, this supposition seemed to us to be justified. Plenty of exercise is recommended to Ms. Brigitte: the stated reason – 'the more mobile you are, the less noticeable it is that you don't have the legs of a super-woman.'[11] Here mobility is not the origin of 'super legs' but hides the fact that Ms. Brigitte is no superwoman when it comes to her legs. But what kind of legs does Superwoman have? What makes a woman 'fast on her feet'? The necessary qualities are specified only through a statement of what they are not; superwoman legs are never too thin (if they are, they become 'spindly'), neither too short not too fat. The point at which legs become too short, too thin or too fat is never indicated; it is something women simply 'know'. All a woman needs to do is to 'take a critical look at herself'. Measuring herself critically against the 'norm', she recognizes the evil truth: her legs simply don't fit the bill.[12] The woman then criticizes not the norm, but herself and her own bodily form. The advantages which she may hope to accrue through her attempts to adapt her own legs to the relevant norms are made to appear as natural as the norms themselves; in becoming 'fast on her feet', she will also appear more attractive.

What can a woman do to acquire the legs of Superwoman? In the first instance, as we have seen, there is exercise. Secondly there are ways of dressing, clothes that transmute bodily forms: panty girdles that 'smoothe out the lumps at the top of your thighs'.[13] It is important, Ms.Brigitte is told, to check before purchase 'that the girdle isn't too tight. Long support tights in softer nylon are best for that free-and-easy feeling'.[13] Free-and-easy Ms.Brigitte is to slide herself with the greatest of ease into the constraints within which she is to live. Clothes do not simply enable her to mould and form her body, but to 'cheat' as well. Certain colour combinations make it possible to 'stretch' legs that are too short; they can no longer be said to look 'dumpy'. Now she can create the illusion of long-leggedness. There are 'optical illusions' for fat legs too; they disappear, or are 'kept tucked away' underneath brightly-coloured, thigh-length tops or tunics. Pale tights and shoes make excessively thin legs 'appear' less skinny; or they can simply be hidden under long, loose trousers. In short, the diversionary tactics of fashion are many and various.

Through these kinds of deceptions, it seems to us, the foundations for women's perpetual guilty conscience are laid. There is a dual mechanism at work here: the guilt engendered through the identification of a deficiency is overlaid by secondary feelings of guilt at its concealment through trickery and deception. How do women come to terms with these petty deceptions, in a climate where all women are likely to be familiar with some version of the popular warning that 'women's beauty may be only skin deep'?

The art of posture

Legs are feminine first and foremost in relation to posture; this is what is worked on before attempts are made to enhance the beauty of shape and surface with stockings, depilatory creams or hide-and-seek devices. In an attempt to establish why this should

be the case, we set about writing stories and at the same time studying manuals of etiquette on posture.

Etiquette manuals are concerned with the *formal* dimensions of social intercourse, at the centre of which stand bodily postures. Women are drilled in correct posture above all through particular positionings of the legs. Each of us possesses an astonishingly detailed knowledge of what is and is not permissible; in a sitting position, the legs must touch at the knees and be kept parallel from the knee down. When we walk, attention must be paid to the size of the steps we take; 'striding' is to be avoided at all costs. Legs carry other parts of the body in their wake; leg posture in a standing position affects the appearance of the belly, stomach and back, while the crucial areas of interest in walking are hips and behind. There seems to be no escaping what we came in our work to call the *structure of commandments and prohibitions* around legs; for any attempt to avoid error directs us, not towards a vacant field of permissible options for sitting, standing and walking, to any of which we may have recourse as we please. Instead, *everything* carries meaning and appears to be regulated in advance. It is for this reason, for example, that what is 'correct' is by no means always simply the opposite of what is prohibited. 'Proper posture and gait should not be confused with preciousness. Mincing along like a sparrow, or swinging your hips in emulation of some personal heroine will not make you look natural, but affected and even vulgar. The only attractive posture is one that is natural and relaxed.'[14]

How is it that we come to acquiesce in all of this? In the manuals, we find this question answered by a particular *promise*. The book from which the last quotation was taken conveys that promise in the title itself: 'Learning to be liked'. Now any woman who considers herself above such things might like to think back, as we have done, to her past. My own mother's attempts to teach me manners were accompanied, the moment she sensed resistance on my part, by the words, 'You'll be thankful one day!' A whole series of promises were implied here: the promise of independence – 'you will learn to move in the world without me, self-assured and secure no matter where you are, even amongst strangers'. The promise, too, of a superior class position in the social hierarchy – 'you will feel at home and be accepted in refined or distinguished company'. And finally, the promise of femininity – 'you will learn to find yourself a suitable husband'.

Our suspicion, based on a study of these and similar expressions, is that it is not only the order of gender into which we inscribe ourselves through bodily posture, but also the order of class. The notion of the 'ladylike' woman capturing a 'suitable' husband is a signal of that dual inscription and subordination.

Happiness in moderation

How precisely do we know how we are to move – neither too much nor too little – , what is the correct posture to adopt – never exaggerated, affected or artificial, but at the same time never stiff or uncontrolled, or any-old-how? It is, we contend, the idea of 'naturalness' that helps us out when we're stuck.[15] It functions as a point of orientation in our search for a yardstick of appropriateness; countless activities are organized around this one concept.

If our forms of social intercourse are to appear natural, despite the effort it has taken to acquire them, then they cannot be adopted, nor discarded, according to the exigencies of the moment. Instead, they must become *second nature*, perpetually reactivated, even when we are alone. This, as we learn in the first chapter of *Learning to be liked*, is what distinguishes 'poise' from mere superficial 'good form'. (And poise, a naturalized second skin, is the hallmark of the lady.)

Since we never know clearly what is to be the ultimate product of our efforts, we find ourselves using a *value* judgement as an axis of orientation, rather than following some strict and unambiguous convention (along the lines, for example, of the medieval sumptuary laws). Accordingly, we as women become preoccupied permanently with checking our appearance (the sideways glance in the mirror) and attempting to judge whether or not it corresponds to that value. Enough is never enough, the question is never settled once and for all, time and again it must be reassessed and considered, it demands comparisons, adjustments, experiments with our own appearance. Social conventions are thus anchored within ourselves; they organize our action from within, in a dynamic process whereby they move from outside to inside, then outside again. Our constant preoccupation with self-examination is what causes us continually to realign ourselves with the dominant values of femininity.

In our attempts to establish more precisely the nature of the ideas around which we orientate ourselves, we carried out a survey within the group itself. Other members of the collective were asked to note down on paper what they thought constituted

'attractive' legs for women. Our first reaction was one of astonishment at the very detailed ideas each of us had on the subject.
We had of course known what our own preoccupations were, but
for the rest of the group. . . .In almost every contribution to the
discussion, the leg had been further divided into *sub-sections*
(foot, ankle, calf, knee, thigh) which both maintained particular
proportions in relation to each other and were at the same time
required separately to meet particular demands. Each and every
aspect of the leg was included in the descriptions; the *form*
(tapering, slim or rounded, with no gap at the top etc.), the
nature of the *surface* (satiny, hairless, slightly downy, not lumpy,
sculpted, no hard skin), their *consistency* (hard, slightly
muscular), *colour* (bronzed), the *visibility* of what lies beneath
the surface (bones, muscles, tendons, veins, no burst capillaries
or varicose veins). Our next step was to examine the means we
might have at our disposal to meet the requirements described.
One woman's wish was for knees 'whose bones showed', while
another wrote that 'a woman's knee must on no account be
knobbly'. Others found hairless legs, legs covered in soft down,
or slightly hairy legs attractive. If we assume for a moment that it
is the 'masculine' gaze that we turn upon ourselves here –
although we do not yet know how that gaze became our own – we
may perhaps assume that, though such a gaze does not allow us to
satisfy the whole range of possible interests, it does make it
possible for us to satisfy some of them some of the time – leaving
our legs hairy for some men, removing the hair for others. Even
allowing for certain natural limitations, it is at least conceivable
that we might manage, by engaging in certain activities, to satisfy
particular norms at one time or another.[16] On the other hand, as
we realized on closer scrutiny of the descriptions, our principal
difficulty consisted less in conforming to these diverse norms,
than in what we termed the 'not-too-much-and-not-too-little'
structure. Almost without exception, our descriptions of our
own notions of beauty ran along the following lines: feet were to
be delicate and as small as possible – but 'not too tiny' – calves
were to be rounded, but still not overly muscular; they were to
have muscles whose outlines became faintly visible when tensed;
they weren't to be too stumpy – but then the legs of a champion
athlete weren't much coveted either. Thighs were not to be too
fat, but then again not too thin; not too broad, but not scrawny
either. One member of the group then elaborated on the subject:
'there are only a few woman whose thighs are as slim as they
really should be, and even those few are generally too skinny, so

that again there is no nicely continuous curve'.

Not only do none of us have the kinds of legs we described; our attempts to produce our own legs in ways that correspond to the ideal entangle us in endless activities. We find ourselves vacillating permanently between the various different qualities which we wish to approximate (albeit always in moderation). This is how we become involved in a perpetual process of self-adjustment, production, withdrawal, reconstruction and so on, working towards a goal that slips ever further from our grasp, the more closely we approach it.

The next question we asked ourselves was about the nature of the activities dictated by these organizing norms. In the most general way, we had noted what we called a *structure of infinite activity*, which arose from our entanglement within contradictions, and our participation in the production of deviations from the norm. Our interest then focused on concrete activities: what is it that we are called upon to do, how much time is consumed by these activities in our lives, what other pleasures and new potentials are we thereby forced to forgo? We knew from the outset that there were demands on us regularly to retouch our suntans, occasionally to shave our legs, remove hard skin, apply cream from time to time, and do a little sport on the side. In this respect, our survey of the members of our group had revealed little that was new. Yet it was not until we had clear evidence on paper that we could establish what it was that our ideas were defined *against*, what it was that was deemed inadmissible. In the end, it seemed that what was considered impermissible was a narrow emphasis on *work*, for example, on physical labour, or indeed on any other work that left us no time for the necessary activities concerning our legs. We might perhaps feel able to support such notions – we too are opposed to narrow one-sidedness – were they not so immediately elitist. For one of us, this abnegation of work immediately conjured up images of women playing a round of tennis, then spending the rest of their day preening their bodies and window-shopping. In this context, our arguments for work and for the cultivation of more than our external appearance have their basis in conscience, and the morality of production. Work is opposed to pleasure and diversity. As long as our legs can offer us the latter, the exigencies of production will appear dreary by comparison; we will be unwilling to dedicate ourselves wholly to its moral imperatives.

In view of this, we were all the more surprised at a much more significant discovery in the detailed written descriptions, namely that a whole number of sensual pleasures were also deemed inadmissible. The 'one-sidedness' they condemned arose not only from work, hunger and a strenuous existence, but equally as a consequence of pleasures external to production. The norms by which beauty is measured demand of us that we 'practise moderation', refusing to indulge in eating to excess, taking too much exercise, indeed throwing ourselves wholeheartedly into any one thing – either into work or into pleasure. Our enjoyment of whole periods of our lives is simply ruled out as a matter of course; old age is the prime example, for this is the time when the skin begins to sag, when legs become too fat or too thin, curves lose their fullness, and so on. Minor ailments become major catastrophes – what is to be done about varicose veins? Even in the stories of ourselves as object,[17] we continued to maintain that we wore this or that piece of clothing (a transparent cotton dress for example) because we ourselves found it pleasurable, and not because we wished to display ourselves to others, but we found, ourselves robbed even of this tenuous argument at the point where we began to scrutinize our own efforts to conform to the norm; we need only list all the clothes we no longer wear, the pleasures we have renounced – certain movements, nude bathing, gymnastics exercises and so on – simply because they don't make us look good! (Even as we were writing this section during one of our summer work periods in the countryside, one of us felt unable to go swimming during the lunch break because she thought she looked so terrible in a swimming costume.) Thus the norms we adopt place us in opposition not only to working women, to the old, the sick and the poor – a positioning which makes it clear that the discourse of femininity is also a discourse of exclusion (of classes, generations and so on) – but even to our own pleasures. Prevailing norms parade before us a whole tempting display of beauty and happiness, only to reveal themselves as the organizing forces behind the dreariest possible form of self-control: the principle of moderation.

Repressive training and seduction

The Hotel Foyer

At the age of 12, during a holiday with her parents, Barbara was initiated into the art of walking across large open rooms. She hadn't wanted to fetch their newspaper from the other end of the hotel foyer; she felt unsure of herself, not knowing quite where to put her arms, finding it difficult to keep her balance while at the same time trying to put her feet down one in front of the other, instead of alongside each other. Barbara knew the unfortunate truth: she was stiff and angular, she took after her father who, in the words of his mother-in-law, looked 'like someone who's swallowed a pole' when he walked. But her parents suggested that now was the time to forget her inhibitions and walk across the hotel foyer; since at this time of her life, there was no reason to attach any significance to the matter, she wouldn't have to worry about practising now. Later in her life, when all this became more important, she would be appropriately nimble and sure of herself. The hotel foyer was empty; Barbara began practising. Every morning she fetched the paper for her parents, and her mother was proved right; she gradually came to feel more sure of herself, and glowed with pleasure if ever she managed to do the whole thing properly for once.

In attempting to establish what there was to learn from this story, we were confronted initially with a set of received ideas that might well have prevented us from learning anything. Which of us, after all, had not experienced the awfulness of parents who fussed endlessly over our upbringing, jammed books under our arms at mealtimes to make sure we kept them tucked in close to our bodies, or balanced books on our heads to make us stand up straight – parents, in short, who wanted things from us for which we had no desire whatever. In our discussions, then, one of us was always ready with some word of endorsement: 'of course, that's just how it was, that's how they made us into what we have become, how they licked us into 'feminine', or even 'ladylike' shape. . . ' But was this really the way it was? We could have reached the same conclusions without bothering to write a single story, without the painstaking labours of memory-work. A study of the promises held out by the etiquette manuals, on the other hand, suggested an alternative interpretation. Here the process of forming the body is made attractive to us through the setting of very specific goals. Ultimately, we ourselves certainly wish to be able to move with ease as women in the public sphere, to be independent, attractive, sure of ourselves. In scrutinizing the spontaneous ways of thinking that occupy the terrain of 'good posture', we were therefore presented with a first set of contradictions: are we to see ourselves as the objects of a repressive education, or are the goals we pursue in fact created by ourselves?

We now took a second look at Barbara's story, in an attempt to establish whether it offered in itself any resistance to the old familiar ideas it seemed to purvey. The story begins with a familiar moment of coercion – a moment described however with a certain measure of approbation. On what basis, we now asked ourselves, is this attitude of approval founded? The explanation was to be found at the end of the story; here, it is the act of practising itself which becomes a source of pleasure. What is more, that feeling is not generated, as the etiquette manuals would have had us believe, out of any simple desire to attain a specific goal; it arises instead from the activity of learning itself. Thus the story appeared resistant to analysis in the terms we had previously outlined; instead, it was suggestive of a new and hitherto unperceived linkage between *order* and *happiness*, produced through the activity of learning. To put this another way: it seemed to us likely that the pleasure of learning marks out a track along which we are drilled, through bodily posture, to adopt a position within the dominant order of gender and class. Since this hypothesis seemed to us at first both innovative and quite horrifying, we decided to pursue it further; for if the pleasure we take in learning can be harnessed to produce our insertion into and subjection to an order, then we are confronted with a difficult strategic problem in relation to our potential for future liberation. Up to this point, we had sung an uninterrupted song in praise of learning;[18] the process of learning represented to us the primary activity through which we might escape dependency and oppression. Yet clearly it is possible to 'learn' many different things. Is it therefore true that the feelings we experience in acquiring new skills – which make the effort easier to bear – actually blind us to our own ultimate goals?

In our work, we took Barbara's story as a challenge to ourselves to investigate more closely the relationship between learning, pleasure, and the insertion of ourselves into, or our liberation from a given order. Had the theories on which we had based our elaboration of a theory of female socialization ever even posed this question? After examining the responses of critical psychology, and of the 'Project Ideology Theory' to that question, we concluded that, although those theories were fruitful in a whole series of ways,[19] they could not tell us how social relations are lived concretely by individuals, and in particular by us as women. It was for this reason that we turned to memory-work. Yet regrettably, it was in relation to the concrete learning situation that Barbara's story maintained the most obdurate silence. We are told only that 'Barbara began practising. . . .she gradually came to feel more sure of herself, and glowed with pleasure if ever she managed to do it properly for once'. But what *exactly* did she do, what feelings did she have at which particular moments, what constituted becoming more 'sure of herself', in what ways did her parents further the learning process? The questions remain unanswered. What made Barbara begin to practise and learn in the first place, what conception had she formed of a time 'later in life, when all this would become more important'?

Discipline and Independance

The history lesson

When I was still at grammar school, we had a history teacher, a woman of at least fifty. She herself displayed constant self-discipline, and she expected the same from her pupils. The grades she gave had little to do with figures on end-of-term reports, or even with her own sympathies; on the contrary, she was able to demonstrate quite clearly that they were allocated according to the proportion of her subject matter that had taken root in our minds. Whenever she came into the classroom, this coolly self-contained woman (she was not especially tall) was always greeted with complete silence, even before she deposited her huge leather bag on the desk. The same had been true from the very first day; she had never needed so much as to raise her voice in our class, though we were known throughout the school as undisciplined; for unlike the threats of textbooks poised to fling in our direction, or teachers' histrionics, her expert handling of the subject matter, the concentrated energy which she devoted to it – all this combined with an authoritative dignity – made a deep impression on us. At the same time, she could by no means have been described as popular; she was too cold and distanced. But she was respected, held in awe: and she rewarded our respect by presenting her material in ways which were not only skilfully precise, but also bursting with enthusiasm, full of grandiose pathos – all of which added to the excitement of her lessons.

She once explained to us what it was that distinguished a piece of work 'good': precise knowledge of the facts, an impeccable grasp of terminology, and an understanding of the context; a capacity to analyze, and to form our own judgements. At the end of any lesson, she would give out reading material which allowed us to go back over whatever points we had not yet fully understood, so that the lessons themselves could be dealt with at high speed – all of which had very positive consequences for my ability to concentrate. I have a clear memory of the fascination that gripped me as I listened to her talk; for she concentrated, not on the assimilation of facts dictated by the curriculum, but on relations between them, conclusions and insights. With her description of events in my mind's eye, I found myself suddenly able to use what I had learned to identify more generally applicable laws of cause and effect in human history: what had been a dreary subject of schoolwork came to life as a theoretical discipline. Each recognition of familiar patterns of action and events, each conclusion I drew, as those patterns were filled out with knowledge of their background, and of the relations between their different elements, filled me with profound satisfaction, even triumph; for was I not learning things which would allow me to fathom and better to understand the processes I saw at work around me, the mechanisms of politics and social issues; was I not acquiring a skill that would equip me to struggle against hardship, against the criminally corrupt conditions that so often confronted me? Now that I knew where the roots of the evil lay, I could breathe more freely, see more clearly, launch myself headlong, impetuous and intoxicated, into the study which would at last equip me to answer my own questions – rather than simply posing new ones endlessly. Burning with enthusiasm, I studied and debated, barely able to sit still in class with the excitement, eager only to absorb more and more of the feelings of strength inspired in me by this new knowledge and understanding.

Quite clearly, the writer is inspired by and takes pleasure in the activity of learning; her new knowledge is seen to give her strength. In order to gain access to the pleasure of the new, she has to adopt different attitudes from those she practises elsewhere in the school; attitudes of self-discipline and correctness. In the context created by this one teacher, attitudes rejected in an act of resistance by the pupils are themselves repositioned as attitudes of opposition within and against the school. The teacher embodies the spirit of discipline – it is she who demonstrates what it means to act in accordance with that spirit, who 'makes a deep impression' on her pupils, who possesses an authoritative dignity, who keeps the class under control with a minimum of fuss, by herself adhering to the principles she advocates for them. She wins her pupils' approval, not so much as a person but as a personification of particular attitudes; it is, indeed, not so much the teacher who they love, as the knowledge she transmits. Accustomed as they are to living within relations of personal dependency (on parents, other teachers, friends); subject, therefore, to personal antipathies and affections, her pupils cannot but experience the situation this teacher creates as an enormous release from dependence on the incalculable. Their appropriation of knowledge further increases their independence – a process convincingly described here by the writer.

Across and through the teacher in this story, indissoluble connections are forged between knowledge, independence, discipline and rectitude, forming a network of associations within which 'opting' for independence comes to signify an acceptance of discipline – a discipline that is not perceived as arduous, but experienced instead as a source of support. Discipline itself is invested with pleasure.

Beauty and Character

By now, it will have become clear that the sexualization of legs does not occur as *directly* as we had at first assumed. Our first story on the subject was able to show us how legs became sexualized,[20] not by a simple process of prohibition, the linkage of legs to notions of indecency, but rather through silencing, the de-naming of this and other associations. Initially, we had also assumed sexualization to result from some conscious and explicit invocation of sexuality; here too, we had to revise our own hypothesis. The activities in which our legs are involved seem not to be lived as purposive or unambiguous expressions of some sexual imperative. Instead, in the hotel foyer story for example, we saw the writer deriving a form of enjoyment from learning which inspired her to practise and refine a particular attitude and ordering of the body, and thereby at the same time to participate in her own insertion into the order of dominant social relations. In both the stories quoted, sexualization appears more as an effect of diverse practices around the body, than as a consciously sexual act. Can the same also be said of the apparently unambiguous sexual actions through which we attempt to present our legs in a seductive light? And if it can, what kinds of feelings accompany these activities, what hopes and desires do we attach to the presentation of our legs in this way? When we requested a story on this question, one member of the group wrote the following:

The swimming pool

When I was 14, I had a boyfriend, and we went swimming together, me, him and my girlfriend. It would be the first time he'd seen me as I really was. I was scared that from now on he'd prefer my friend to me. Though she was just as fat around the waist as me, her legs were nothing short of gorgeous. Not a flaw from her thighs to the tips of her toes. I was nervous, although at the time I actually didn't like my boyfriend as much as all that. In fact he'd always been the one who had run after me, and my reactions to his advances had been more or less cool. I actually preferred his friend, who I'd also gone out with, though not for very long, and when we split up I was more than happy to respond to Manfred's attentions. But I still didn't find him exactly exciting. And still I was nervous. I took my time getting undressed in the changing rooms. I tried to recall all the sayings we'd learned in German and scripture lessons: it's not looks that count, it's your character that's important. (All well and good, but my friend's character wasn't bad either – in fact mine was probably worse, selfish as I was.) Perhaps I could use the situation to test him; if he didn't now start preferring my friend to me, then his feelings for me would be truly genuine. I couldn't stay forever in the changing-rooms. Unfortunately (or luckily?) there wasn't a mirror there for me to be able to look at all of myself. I couldn't see precisely how awful I looked. I knew what a difference there was between me looking down at myself from above, and someone looking straight at me and seeing all of me. Still. . . . I summoned my courage and went out. Renate and Manfred were already waiting outside and talking. Were they not being excessively friendly, and was Renate not making an incredible display of her long, straight legs – making a real exhibition of herself? We went off to find somewhere to lie down. I hardly spoke a word. Let the two of them get on with enjoying themselves. I wasn't interested anyway in their superficial chatter. Nor did I have any desire to go in the water. I stayed where I was, lying reading a book. From then on, I always let the two of them go off swimming on their own. That summer, they did so frequently, and I had to give up my beloved swimming. Who after all could I now go with? We all remained good friends.

On an initial reading, our response to this story was that it was saying nothing new; legs are assumed to be there to attract men, and it is precisely for this reason that they cause us problems. 'More attractive' legs are viewed with jealousy, since they seem to promise their owners greater sexual fulfilment than ours do us.

It is no wonder that we discover nothing new in this kind of 'content-orientated' reading. As an alternative, we scrutinized the *mode* of speaking and writing employed here. The first identifiable feature is the presence of an almost philosophical character in the text, through its discussion of 'reality' and 'authenticity', 'superficiality' and 'character'. These ideas are in sharp and immediate contrast to the banality of the story's contents; their use invests an everyday situation with the drama of 'true revelation'. Baring one's legs becomes a guarantee of visible 'reality'; the action is lived as a test of the 'authenticity' of another's feelings. The inflated significance attached to this situation could not, we discovered, be explained in terms of its subjective importance for the writer, since she is by no means in love with Manfred. Why does this moment nonetheless assume such importance for her? The contradictions in this particular dramatization of events forced us to search for new and different explanations; it seemed to indicate that the linkage of nakedness to truth might carry more general significance.

In a story that centres on weighty concepts of this kind, it seems necessary to turn to those very concepts as the point of departure for analysis. How do they organize the text's specific understanding of reality, what attitudes to the world do they delineate? A mode of expression that speaks of 'the sight of me as I really was' produces an opposition between true and false appearance; it constitutes something akin to a reality and an unreality of the body. This raises the question of the grounding of this particular distinction in social experience. One possible answer might be that the many guises women assume while changing clothes are lived subjectively as *dis*guises, and in this sense as deceptions.[21] This is true of the 'tips' in *Brigitte* magazine on how to make legs look longer and slimmer for example. The magazine offers a simultaneous questioning of, and a response to the anxiety that deception engenders, in its formulae for 'making the best of your body'. The effectiveness of its recommendations derives perhaps from its ability to appease our guilty conscience, and to safeguard us against exposure. It does not require that we hide away and cover ourselves, but rather that we emphasize our 'true' appearance. Thus we live under the permanent threat of a revelation of the 'truth', a disclosure of the concealed truth of our visual appearance. One day our moment of judgement will come! (For one of us, the immediate possibility of that moment is all too clear first thing in the morning. 'How often I have thought to myself, "My God, if he sees me in bed this morning, I'm lost!" I remember those feelings of anxiety becoming ever more deeply ingrained; once, when I'd lost a lot of weight, I remember being afraid that anyone who fell in love with me at that stage might possibly assume that was how I really looked, when actually I had a terrible figure.') Through the social 'test', what has been constituted as the 'reality' of visual appearance is brought into association with the 'authenticity' of emotions; in this way, the female body is made the touchstone by which the authenticity or inauthenticity of emotions may be determined. A woman who deceives a man through the disguises she adopts, has to face up to the prospect of his deceiving her in turn over his emotions. If the woman drops her mask and reveals her body, then the man will also reveal his authentic feelings, the presence or absence of true love. At the same time, authentic feelings are defined as those that by-pass the body; they are instead directed inwards, towards the character. It is through the relation between character and the body (discussed more fully below) that the body becomes the decisive pivot around which the true self is defined.

We seem to have succeeded, after all, in learning something new from this story. Our legs acquire their weighty (or burdensome) significance, not merely as a result of their potential to attract (or indeed to repel) sexual partners, but also because, in the ways we have outlined, the question of our legs becomes a question of *identity* for us. The sight of legs as they are 'in reality' becomes the sight of *me* as I 'truly' am. It is within a particular ordering of the sexual that we ask ourselves the question, 'who am I?' By demanding that we pose the question of our own identity, that sexual order helps to organize that identity. This is what we term the 'subject-effect' of the discursive order. It allows the sexualization of legs to be lived subjectively in 'non-sexual' ways, in other words, as the production of identity. Though there is nothing new in our recognition of the *fact* that women construct their identity around the body, this story does identify one of the many elements that constitute the *mode* of that construction. The body is positioned in a particular relationship with other, 'weightier' themes; it becomes the pathway to truth. Our reading allows us to appreciate more fully the limitations inherent in this construction of identity. The girl in the story does not experience her body as directly sexual, but as a body that contains another truth: her nature as woman. This is what is incarcerated, deprived of opportunities for development, within the naked and unchanging body.

As a way of illuminating how the body places constraints on female identity, we want finally to look briefly at the ways in which the masculine body forms mens' identity. Neither bodily strength and agility, in sport or in work, nor their concomitant pleasures are reduced to sexual meaning alone – on the contrary, they offer multiple potentials for men's development. Yet in no sense can the discourse that surrounds the male body be seen for this reason as a discourse of liberation. W. F. Haug's analyses of the specific effects produced by the male statues of Arnold Breker — one of the most significant artists to have supported German fascism — and of the role of medicine as an ideological force under fascism,[22] point to the very opposite conclusion, namely the immense importance attached to the masculine body in the production of ideological subjection. Haug demonstrates the ways in which individuals can be 'called to order' across the body, for example through the articulation of health and fitness as the results of particular activities and attitudes within which men construct themselves as orderly citizens of the state. The procedure is more or less as follows: physical fitness, strength and efficiency are stated to be products of self-control, self-restraint, self-discipline (in opposition to self-centredness), of a hardening of the self and of the will to health. Thus sickness and weakness are construed, not as a failure of bodily organs under unfavourable living conditions, but reprehensible *actions*, as signals of an unwillingness to conform.[23] The consequence of this articulation of health to morality is that 'individuals are called upon to become subjectively active in their insertion into the prevailing social order. If they comply, they become the subordinate masters of themselves. . . .subjects who excel at their own private activities within the circumscribed spheres of action mapped out by the dominant order of power relations.'[24]

It could then be said that men subordinate themselves through their bodies to the State, while women subordinate themselves to men, and only via men to the State. The woman as woman owes her body to a man; as a female human being, she owes him her character. A man, as man, looks to her body; as human being, to her character. At this point, we conclude that the question of identity itself may perhaps be the crux of our problem. Why should the girl in our story owe anybody any such thing as her 'true self', whether this manifests itself as body or as character?

And what is the effect of the division marked out here between the body and character? Our investigations have brought to light a complex interplay of connotative relations; the naked body connotes identity, and produces the notion of a unitary gendered self; it says, 'this is what I am as woman'. At the same time, the hope remains that the true self, the female human being, will also be perceived, that the gaze that rests on her will be directed inwards towards her character. Thus the body is complicit in turning the gaze to seek for something that lies within. The body says: 'I am the exterior, something else still lies within'. What, then, is sought on the inside; what is it that is owed from within, and to whom?

In a previous study by the Ideology and Theory Project of the *Argument* collective (PIT), the ways in which individuals participate in their own insertion into power relations have been investigated comprehensively. According to PIT, this process takes the form of an *ideological subjection*, whereby subjects live the relationships of domination and subordination inscribed within those relations as imaginary initiators of those relationships – or, as they put it, 'from the inside outwards'. 'Ideological subjection is brought to bear upon the individual from the outside, as a multifarious network of expectations, presumptions and supposed attributes. Individuals find themselves besieged by expectations which confront them as a normative image of their being. The assumption of particular norms projects a solid core of being into the individual; modes of behaviour which arise as responses to expectations are then interpreted as the pure expressions of that being. The modes of behaviour required are those through which individuals insert themselves into the social order. They are however seen to be traceable back to certain traits of character; it is in the *character* that the marks of individuality are said to be anchored. . . .Individual character is understood in terms of a *debt* which must be paid to society. Concrete modes of behaviour thus become symptoms of a hidden character. They either offer evidence of that character – or they betray lack of character. Thus in the notion of character, the forms in which experience is lived are defined as deriving from a substantive inner self, rather than from accrued experience. A woman who is discontented with her marriage is therefore seen as a woman of discontented character. . . .She owed a debt of contentment of society, and her discontent renders her guilty as debtor. It is thus that individuals are thrown back on their inner selves; lived experience of the social order is individualized, and individuals are arranged into types on the basis of their participation in, or their remaining at odds with that order.[25]

We return now finally from inside to outside. Not only thought and action are read as signs of an underlying character; the body too is read in the same way. Even in our own enlightened times, when we no longer believe in the truth-telling power of palmistry, phrenology or typologies of constitution, we nonetheless all retain a more or less conscious conception of the relationship between external appearance and personality (as Benjamin said, the face of anyone over thirty is their own responsibility). The body is thus harnessed in two ways for the production of the inner self. First the body demands, 'turn your gaze away from me and look within!' Yet at the same time: 'Look at me, and you will know who I am!' The body thus becomes part of the process whereby we build ourselves into the social order, living from the inside outwards. The hope expressed by the girl in one of our stories that her boyfriend might one day look to her inner self, cannot therefore save her. As she herself already partially understands, her inner self is equally incapable of repaying the debt she owes him. . . .

In the course of this section, our discussions have proceeded in a somewhat unexpected spiral; from proverbs 'about legs, we were led to a discussion of notions of citizenship, and not, as we had expected, to sex. We find ourselves now finally at our original point of departure, but on a different level; our story has led us from legs to identity and character, from character as a form of ideological socialization to our relationship with the State – which is conducted through the intermediary of a man. The mode of construction of this relationship, and the meanings that accrue to the body in the process, are topics for further investigation.

Notes on Women's Gymnastics

Not sweating, but glowing . . .

What can gymnastics possibly have to do with the sexualization of the body? Watching women's gymnastics is quite simply aesthetically pleasing; the things the women are able to do, and the control they have over their bodies, are more than worthy of our admiration. And yet one woman in the group persisted in seeing all this as nothing more or less than pornography. Two women in the collective, both of whom had done gymnastics themselves as young girls, found this notion absurd. One man meanwhile (the same one, as it happened, who had defended the sitting posture said to be socially acceptable for women by claiming it to be determined by the distinctive construction of the female abdomen) found the idea nothing short of ridiculous: 'you see the same thing in everything these days'. Initially, I myself belonged to the faction that saw women's gymnastics as simply 'aesthetically pleasing'. Today, my feelings on the subject are more ambiguous. I see women gymnasts as making their bodies appear more malleable than men's, I see their antics as they tumble across the floor as a set of gestures of submission. Among men, by contrast, strength is put on display. I personally find the exercises of the women more pleasing, and would like to be able simply to sit back and enjoy them; yet at the same time, I am aware of the millions of male observers whose gaze makes sex objects of the women I am watching.

In the first place the clothing is very different: while men simply wear long trousers, woman's leotards curve up sharply around the hips, lengthening the appearance of the legs and emphasizing the pubic area. The men's trousers, by contrast, are not tight to the body; they are held taut with straps and braces, allowing the genitals to remain invisible. The men's gym suit is also sleeveless, so that the shoulder and arm muscles are not only revealed, but shown off to their best effect. The woman's leotard has long sleeves that render arm and shoulder muscles more or less invisible.

176

The display of strength is to male gymnastics what the conceal-ment of strength is to its female equivalent. Ever since the 1920s, when women first began to take part in national and inter-national gymnastics tournaments, the question of strength has been a focus of debate; at various times, exercises or apparatus seen to demand too much in terms of physical strength (what constitutes 'too much' is unclear) have been declared unsuitable for women (these include for example the parallel bars, the horse, and rings). Since the 1952 Olympic Games, women's international gymnastics has been governed by a directive according to which four pieces of apparatus are deemed suitable for women: the parallel bars, the beam, floor exercises with musical accompaniment and vaulting over the horse.

In the course of the 1950s, exercises on these four types of apparatus, as well as the development of women's gymnastics internationally, met with vigorous resistance in the Federal Republic. Functionaries responsible for women's gymnastics within the *Deutscher Turnerbund* (Association of German Gymnasts) – who will be referred to from this point on as the women's team leadership – were critical above all of the Soviet Union, whose female gymnastic techniques were beginning at this time to find favour abroad. Disagreement centred on the ways in which women could or should display and move their bodies. Opposition to international gymnastics took its most extreme forms between 1954 and 1960, in a ban, implemented by the women's team leadership, on female participation in the Olympic Games and other world tournaments. There was how-ever nothing that might have been called a consensus in the Federal Republic at the time on the proper model for female gymnastics. The two principal voices in the debate were those of the women's team leadership, which had a section of the press on its side, and a number of gymnastics clubs whose members opposed the condemnation of international gymnastics practices as unfeminine, having themselves adopted such practices by around 1952. In the following, I shall be looking only at the position taken up by the women's team leadership, since the reasons its members give in support of their definition of women's gymnastics are available in particularly detailed form.[1]

Sophie Dapper, a member of the women's team leadership, addressed herself in the following quotation to the differenti-ation between 'masculine' and 'feminine' body movement. 'Ludwigsburg (the location of the Second German Women's Gymnastics Championships in 1951 – Ed.) has once again provided us with the clearest of evidence of the differences between women's and men's gymnastics, proving once again that the former is neither comparable to, nor should it be compared with the latter. The character of women's gymnastics is demonstrated by the greater diversity of its forms and most particularly by the uniquely feminine quality of movements which are lighter and looser, which flow more rhythmically than those of men, making even the most difficult exercises appear as joyful *play*. Rather than attempting to blur this characteristic *difference* between masculine and feminine movement, we should aim instead to emphasize it further, to allow women's gymnastics to become increasingly a genuine expression of the essential physical and spiritual qualities of women'.[2]

Sophie Dapper wanted to 'emphasize' difference in the movements of men and women, in order to allow the 'essential qualities' of each sex to find 'expression'. Yet in positioning particular movements on either side of the opposition feminine/masculine, and calling this polarity between types of movement an 'expression' of 'essential qualities', she herself reproduced that polarization of qualities, and thereby also femininity. If we now look at the ways in which the women's leadership described 'feminine movement', we should be able to determine what they considered to be the specific movements that expressed feminity. In Sophie Dapper's definition of specifically feminine movement even 'difficult exercises' were to appear as 'joyful play'. And, as she said elsewhere, 'despite the strenuous effort often expended in gymnastics, it should retain its character of joyful play, even under competition conditions.'[3] At first glance, the women's leadership appeared to be dissociating itself from hard exertion and the display of strength. But 'difficult exercises' or 'strenuous effort' were not dismissed out of hand; instead, 'difficult exercises' were required to appear playful. Difficult exercises should not look difficult; exertion might be strenuous, but must at the same time be play. Strength is not rejected by the women's leadership, only *visible* strength.

To the eye of the observer, a femininity that fulfils such requirements will seem opposed to exertion, hard work and strain. Women are to make the activity of gymnastics appear effortless – playful weightlessness, a playing that transcends their own physical limitations. What matters is their appearance, not the level of strength which their actions in fact demand. Indeed the woman gymnast is exhorted to expend *additional* energy in order to make her actions appear 'playful'. Womanly movement 'is fluid and rhythmic'.[4] Inge Heuser, another member of the women's team leadership, looked to women gymnasts for 'a sequence of natural and flowing movements'.[5] And Dapper had the following criticism to make of international women's gymnastics: 'for no apparent reason, rhythmic movement is frozen into positions and attitudes that are obviously posed, at times bordering on the flirtatious.'[6] Among the 'posing' figures rejected by the team leadership were for example the scissor jump, the splits and the bridge position.[7] On the one hand, these positions were already invested with sexual meanings; on the other, the rejection itself became complicit in the production of sexualization. Explicitly, the reason put forward for rejecting 'posing' of this kind was that it made excessive demands on the strength of women gymnasts, and that it interrupted the rhythm of movement. 'What we (the team leadership – Ed.) are attempting . . . is to remain true to a particular principle of movement; beyond a certain point, there are forms which do not allow that aim to be fulfilled. Maintaining balance whilst doing the splits on the bar may command respect for the achievement it represents; but the form itself is hardly compatible with the natural flow of sequential movement.'[9]

For Sophie Dapper, the principle of rhythm also had an educative function. 'If physical exercises for women are to be filled with a life that is truly alive, then they can be developed only on the basis of the rhythmic movements of the organism . . . humanity is not made of dead or empty forms . . . but wholly and entirely of *expressively* formed and spiritualized movement.'[10] The new distinction drawn here by the women's team leadership between *empty posing* and *expression* contributed a new element to the construction of women's gymnastics. The initial distinction was between play and visible strength. In the terms laid down by the women's team leadership, female gymnastics was now definable as *expressive play*, as opposed to *empty posing* and *visible strength*.

Inge Heuser made a further distinction. For her, 'acrobatic poses' had a place in 'vaudeville', but not in gymnastics. 'Those who simply imitate or ape the example of others sacrifice their personality in so doing. . . . If Schiller, in his essay on grace and dignity, defines grace as beauty moved from within; if then he recognizes grace as existing only where there is a correspondence between surface appearance and inner self, then we must acknowledge these forms of *decorative gymnastics* and *acrobatic posing* to be often no more than external veneer. I find it mortifying to see how the public at large is no longer able to distinguish between what is false and what is genuine, between a first-class gymnast and a vaudeville star.'[11] Initially, Inge Heuser's argument appeared close to that of Sophie Dapper; she defined 'posing' as simulation, as a set of movements that fail to correspond to the inner self. The woman gymnast who wishes to retain her 'personality' is called upon to use specific kinds of movements; her personality is located in movements that she herself produces. At the same time, Inge Heuser's argument generated a new associative link: 'acrobatic poses' were consigned to the category of 'vaudeville', rather than gymnastics. In general terms, then, the team leadership defined female gymnastics by placing it in a series of *oppositions* to women's gymnastics as practised in the Olympics.

Play (= invisible strength)	– visible strength
Expression (= full posing)	– empty posing
Women's gymnastics	– acrobatics – circus artifice – vaudeville
The experience of movement Lebensfreude (joy in life) Health	– the effect of display on the audience – superficial veneer – the awakening of amazement
genuine	– false, imitative

What was it about circus acrobatics that so disturbed the women's team leadership? What did they see as the specific point of difference between gymnastics and circus? Liesel Niemeyer argues that the gymnast must give priority to the 'experience of movement', as opposed to concentrating on the effect of display.[12] And in one article in *Deutsches Turnen* ('German Gymnastics', the journal of the German Gymnastics Association), gymnasts are exhorted not to play to spectators. 'The goal is that the gymnast herself gain in health and vitality; it is not to provide the spectators with jumped-up dressing-table beauties.'[13]

But what in reality does circus acrobatics set out to achieve? The acrobats' aim is to enrapture their audience through the presentation of their bodies; to make the spectators laugh, to excite and provoke amazement, to entertain the people. They display their bodies for the benefit of the spectators. For a woman gymnast, such conduct is dubbed unseemly. She is called upon to concern herself solely with the experience of her own movement. She is neither permitted to consider the effect she has on the spectators, nor to reveal any potential effect which the spectators may have on her. Does this demonstrative refusal of communication perhaps contribute to the production of a voyeuristic gaze in the spectator, since he is assured of the fact that his gaze will not be returned? The body of the performing gymnast makes visible a soul turned inwards; the soul is 'visible', but not available for communication.

Kicker 1970

I want to return at this point to the two reasons given by the women's team leadership for rejecting 'poses' they considered sexually charged. In the first instance, those poses were said not to correspond to the natural flow of sequential movement; secondly, they were seen to demand too great an expenditure of strength. By around 1960, however, the achievements of gymnasts from the top nations of the world were seen to have 'risen to a level where it has become almost possible to talk of champion performers as having reached perfection. At this level of perfection, movement has become both more *fluid* and more *rhythmic*; the rigidity of the pose has been more or less overcome.'[14]

In 1959, Cläre Akermann of the women's team leadership gave the following account of floor exercises at the Second European Championships. 'Their affinity with ballet becomes ever more clearly evident. Both Russian competitors displayed a precision and *expressive force* in their free floor exercises, a confidence and a playful ease which made it impossible for anyone, ourselves included, to do anything but applaud them. Their performance was no mere simulation; it was *genuine*.'[15] The gymnast Barbara Otto took a similar position on the various converging viewpoints on the subject of movement. 'The fact that the international style has managed satisfactorily to resolve a number of its earlier problems was demonstrated (at the Rome Olympics, 1960) by the degree of harmony achieved in many of the floor sequences. The adoption at intervals of a static but graceful position by the gymnast not only did not interrupt the rhythm of the exercises; it actually reinforced it. The German Gymnastics Association has until now prohibited the static position for German women gymnasts, out of a fear that it might give rise to 'empty posing'. That such a fear is unfounded was demonstrated in Rome by the world's best women gymnasts. Their performance spoke from a heart which allows neither falsity nor emptiness.'[16]

A significant shift: the women's team leadership was now prepared to accept 'posing' as long as it could be seen to flow expressively into the sequence of movement. What kind of movement was it, then, that was acceptably feminine? The splits, executed with fluidity: a scissor-jump, so long as it no more than hints at the opening of legs that are immediately closed again. Is it the essence of femininity that is expressed in movements such as these? And how are such movements perceived by the spectators? Without going into too much detail, we might perhaps mention here the attempts of sports journalists to guide the gaze

of spectators along lines that go some way toward answering these questions. One journalist has described 'Olympia's beautiful daughters' as follows. 'Once upon a time, the women of Olympia were a bitter aperitif. They whetted the appetite, but they were sharp, biting, harsh on the tongue. Sport was the death of beauty. But nowadays, it gives it life.'[17]

The 'appetite' is 'whetted' by women who participate in sport. Whetted for what? The journalist does not make this explicit; but any reader capable of negotiating the discourse of the sexual knows what he means. By 1972, sport can be seen as giving 'life' to 'beauty'. Thus through the association of 'sport' with 'appetite-whetting', the inference can be made that sport produces bodies that arouse desire.

In the illustration above, taken from the *Frankfurter Allgemeine Zeitung* of 6.5.72, a female gymnast is depicted holding a position on the floor. The caption reads: 'A treat in store this weekend for gymnastics fans. A guest performance by some of the world's finest apparatus artistes . . . ' The 'treat' referred to is the inter-state tournament announced in the article – yet could we imagine a male gymnast at the bar in the accompanying photograph? Image and caption are arranged in a way that demands the woman gymnast be read as the 'treat' readers have in store. The sports journalist mediates between gymnast and reader; s/he maps out a way of reading women's gymnastics, by organizing the gaze turned by the spectator on the gymnast in specific ways. Photos and accompanying text together effect a closure on the meanings associated with the activity of the gymnasts; in sexualizing the practice of gymnastics, the journalists produce a lasting association between women's gymnastics and sexuality, and constitute the gymnast as sexual object. Is this perhaps the source of the widespread popularity of women's gymnastics?

CHAPTER THREE

Constructions of the Domain

Sexuality and Power

The repressive hypothesis

In titles of books that express women's resistance to masculine sexual norms – 'The Shame is Over' or 'All this false instruction' –, we may detect reverberations of reproach, echoes of demands for change. These are books of 'shocking revelation'. *My Secret Garden: Women's Sexual Fantasies* (Nancy Friday), *When day embraces night: women's erotic fantasies* (Gudula Lorez), and so on. They offer us a chance to acquaint ourselves with other people's way of doing 'it', with their thoughts and feelings in performing the sexual act. A chance, or perhaps a demand that we measure ourselves against those others, learn something new, uncover sex's secret traces, free ourselves of the constraints of an enforced silence. At first glance, books of this kind do indeed seem to be undermining the injunctions warning us that 'one does not speak of such things'. Their response is: 'We refuse to be part of this "one" of whom you speak, we shall not only speak out, we will shout out loud, we will find words for every last one of those living stirrings of a sexuality which you who have pronounced this prohibition deem outlandish or banal. We shall prove to you that sex is neither to be found in the outlandish nor the banal, but that it belongs to the nature from which we have been alienated; that our subjection to constraints and restrictions denies us the pleasure we are capable of attaining.'

Many of the women who spoke and still speak in this way have been concerned with more than a liberation from prohibitions governing sexuality alone. They demand a society in which there is no longer any necessity for sexuality to be repressed. Surely,

185

they argue, sexuality contains some force that disrupts prevailing conditions, exploitation and oppression – why otherwise should sexuality be a 'forbidden joy', a 'prohibited pleasure'? This seems, they claim, to be the only explanation for the need of any 'one' to see sexuality twisted and trammelled, diminished and perverted.

What then, we ask in return, is the relationship between sexuality and domination, and by what means can that which is repressed – sexuality – become liberated? In recalling our past, we are confronted first with the forest of no-go signs that patterned the suffocatingly narrow horizons – narrow at least in respect of sexuality – of a childhood oriented around petty bourgeois norms. Bodily contact and nakedness were frowned upon. How often did our parents curl up in shame when we burst into the bathroom, to find them 'in the altogether'. The horrendous scenes when we were caught peering through the keyhole at someone undressing on the other side – the embarrassment we felt as keenly as our parents, who in their turn were scarcely able to speak their horror, approaching the topic in roundabout ways, then compensating for their own difficulties by punishing us all the more severely. Those notorious games of doctors and nurses, for which we had to seek out the most secluded spots we could find to avoid being caught. A world where something which was seen in retrospect to be so 'natural' was surrounded by prohibitions and restraints, shrouded in secrecies and obscurity.

With the onset of adulthood, we looked for ways of violating the prohibitions, seeking to identify opportunities where once there had been obstacles, openness in place of secrecy, ways of shedding light on the obscurities.

The common term for this suppression and persecution of sexuality is *repression*. The term is used on the assumption that sexual desire is felt strongly by all individuals. This is the main source of energy in our lives. If, as is the case in our society, that desire is suppressed in action, and subject to a verbal taboo, then this has particular consequences for the development of the human being (whose drives, according to Freud, may for example be channelled into cultural activities, for the sake of which individual happiness is sacrificed).

Among the fathers of those theories, we may count – apart from Freud – authors such as Wilhelm Reich and Herbert Marcuse, later Reimut Reiche and others. There follows a short introduction to these writers, in which we also raise the question of the place accorded in their work to the difference between the sexes – and thus to the oppression of women.

In many of these writings, we find sexuality represented within the constricting framework elaborated by Freud: sexuality is repressed and prohibited by the very family in which it initially emerges. In the first instance, sexuality consists in sexual desire for one of the parents. 'A boy's mother is the first object of his love, and she remains so too during the formation of his Oedipus complex and, in essence, all through his life. For a girl too her first object must be her mother (and the figures of wet-nurses and foster-mothers that merge into her).[1]

Freud saw sexuality as the determining influence on our lives, more or less from the moment of birth. In Reich, meanwhile, we find a careful description and examination of the deformations and constraints imposed on sexuality, and the consequences to which they give rise. 'It is important to make clear that today there are no people with a fully developed, integrated, sex-affirmative structure, because all of us have been influenced by the authoritarian, religious, sex-negating machinery of education.'[2] . . . . 'The child quickly learns that he may neither exhibit his own sexual organs nor look at those of others. As a consequence, he develops two kinds of feelings: first, guilt feelings that develop when he yields to his desire to do something that is strictly forbidden; and second, with the concealment of the genitals and the taboo around them, mystical feelings in connection with everything sexual.'[3]

Reich then draws the following conclusion for progressive pedagogues, teachers, parents, etc. 'Before posing the question of sexual enlightenment at all, one must first decide unequivocally in favor of sex affirmation or sex negation, against or for the prevailing sexual morality. Without such clarification about one's own position on the sexual question any discussion is futile.'[4] At the same time, it is necessary, maintains Reich, to be clear about the fact that 'sexual repression causes diseases, perversions, or lasciviousness.'[5]

Neither Freud nor Reich discusses sexual difference as a relation of domination. The pathways to liberation which they outline do not differ for men and women. In the student movement, it was on the basis of a reading of these theoretical 'fathers' that experiments in a potentially emancipatory praxis were formulated. The work of Wilhelm Reich was particularly influential in a movement that linked the emancipation of sexuality both to the emancipation of the personality and to the development of a capacity for struggle against capitalist exploitation. Out of the repression of this 'primal instinct,' it seemed there arose the authoritarian character that accepted and subordinated itself to repressive force (Marcuse). Yet theoreticians of the student movement were soon confronted with a problem: how were they to explain the new wave of sexual liberation – public demands for the cultivation of sexuality, tips on how to enrich our sex lives and make them more pleasurable (examples range from the 'pathbreaking' films of Oswald Kolle, and Beate Uhse's sex aids, to the more general sexual and commercial exploitation of women). 'The methods of ruling human beings under contemporary capitalism have borrowed in so sophisticated a manner from the sexual revolution that a naïve belief in the self-liberating force of sexuality under such a system is no longer easy.'[6]

For Marcuse, the new sexual freedom was merely illusory; in reality, he argued, it was by its very nature oppressive. Oppression took effect, he said, by a process of 'repressive desublimation'. 'Libido transcends beyond the immediate erotogenic zones – a process of non-repressive sublimation. In contrast, a mechanized environment seems to block such self-transcendence of libido. Striving to extend the field of erotic gratification, libido becomes less 'polymorphous', less capable of eroticism beyond localized sexuality and the *latter* is intensified.'[7] 'Repressive desublimation' consists then in the intensification of a restricted eroticism, in its reduction to (genital) sexuality.

One of the more radical demands of the student movement articulates with brutal clarity a particular relation between the sexes: 'Fuck the Establishment – never fuck the same woman twice'. The women who attempted to live by this motto had to struggle against the guilty conscience that ensued if the 'distortions' of their bourgeois upbringing made them love only one man, or prevented them from taking pleasure in sex with more than one. In the *Sozialistischer Frauenbund* (Socialist Women's Association) for example, we were later to discuss the ways in which this so-called liberation had pandered to male 'sexual appetites', to the women's detriment. It was not until some time after the emergence of the women's movement that women were able to say 'no' without being dubbed 'unliberated'.

The processes by which humanity is theoretically constituted as a masculine category have been examined by Luce Irigaray in her book *Speculum*. In an acute and irreverent reading of Freud, she demonstrates how he takes masculinity as the yardstick against which all objects and actions are assessed, constructing women as deviations from the norm. The world revolves around a single question: 'to have, or not to have a penis?' According to Irigaray, Freud assumes the primary distinction in human beings to be that between 'masculine' and 'feminine': ' . . . yet the question of how remains unspoken and it seems to you [Freud] not to be worth the trouble of pursuing further. Silence then on this unhesitating certainty that protects you from mistaking the sex of a person you might meet at *very first glance*. Most important for you, it seems, is an unerring conviction in your own incapacity to be wrong. And a knowledge that Culture (?) protects, reassures you (has protected, has reassured you) that a discriminating difference is inescapable.'[8]

In her critique of Freud, Irigaray questions our assumption that certain phenomena may be taken for granted as 'sexual', or that they must 'necessarily' be thought in relation to sexuality. In Freud, all infantile activity is examined in terms of the child's future procreative or reproductive capacity. Taking as his starting points the active, potent man and the passively receptive woman, he demonstrates and explains the way in which barriers and obstacles interpose themselves, and are subsequently 'worked over', along *this one particular route*. However despite the radical nature of her critique, Irigaray does not contest the notion, derived from the theory of repression, that sexuality *per se* is repressed. Her aim is to identify the avenues along which women might pursue and attain their own liberation. Yet her references to a properly *feminine sexuality*, to the 'primordial feminine' it is our task to seek, to the 'flowing' to which these pathways may lead us, remain for the most part shrouded in obscurity and mystique.

To recapitulate: the proponents of a theory of repression take as their point of departure a clearly definable domain, which they call 'sexuality'. Since this is conceived as the foundation of all forms of pleasure, we are said to be emancipating ourselves if we interpret all our pleasures as expressions of a long-concealed sexuality. In this context, resistance often takes the form of an affirmation of the status quo; certain emancipatory efforts from within the women's movement, for example, can be seen as reflections of women's perennial reduction to and confinement within the boundaries of sex. In an apparent attempt to preempt claims that 'women have nothing to offer except sex', women are now saying, 'Yes indeed; but do you know what this is, our sex?' Accepting the constraints imposed on their sexuality, they uncover a 'plenitude' within it; or – a different strategy – having perceived that the male categories within which they live fail to embrace their 'true experiences', they then impose categories of their own. On this basis a feminist 'culture of the body' has been able to emerge and flourish. Here the body is nurtured, explored, liberated from its chains. In their simultaneous pursuit of a sexual politics and of a lived female cultural practice, women are said to be avoiding a reduction of femininity to the realm of the sexual. Yet if sexuality is thought and lived as a determining and determinate domain, about which determinate statements are (or can be) made – a domain that exists in clear differentiation from other domains – must we not establish the process by which that domain has been constituted? What determines it, what is its dynamic, what combination of elements within it makes it whole?

If we are to focus attention on the ways in which sexuality is constructed, we must first abstract from lived sexual practices and modes of behaviour, if only in order to avoid reproducing our entanglement within concrete phenomena which are themselves consequences of processes we have yet to investigate.

Sexuality as Production and Social Construction

At this point, we propose to discuss the value and the limitations of theses propounded by Michel Foucault, in terms of their contribution to knowledge and to practical strategies. Foucault is considered here as the representative of a methodology, so-called discourse analysis, whose principal proponents are found in France (although it has also increasingly become the focus of debate in West Germany).[9] Though Foucault may be both difficult and 'obscurantist', his work does introduce a degree of flexibility into solidly encrusted patterns of thought. We propose, then, first to trace and present his theory so that the useful elements of his work may be retained in the subsequent critique.

In questioning the repressive hypothesis, the ideas developed by Foucault run counter to our everyday understanding of sexuality. Not only does he ask, 'what is this sexuality of which we speak?', of what does it consist, what are the modes of its formation — questions which, in these 'enlightened' times, are already bordering on the heretical — he also casts doubt on the notion that sexuality is subject only to consistent repression and enforced self-denial. In his view, the object of sexuality does not belong to any stable order, nor is sexuality a static quantity, eternally unchanging: the contrary is the case. His method consists in traversing the mountains of material that constitute the domain of sexuality as if exploring a foreign language, the origins of whose authority he is attempting to comprehend.[10] In short, he refuses to assume as given the domain whose real constitution he has set out to document; he must first constitute it in theory. Thus rather than working with existing assumptions about, and/or definitions that determine what sexuality is, he asks both how it comes about that a particular set of statements clusters together to form what is then understood as 'sexuality', and also precisely *what* statements are of relevance. The object of his investigation is the *discourse*, which is 'neither a super-structure, nor a specific social field but the form of the constitution of the social.'[11]

Foucault's point of departure is an accumulation of statements within the materials (by which he also means the practices) through which the discourse is constituted. 'Discourse' is a critical concept refusing the supposedly given unity of particular domains of knowledge. In the original Latin, the term 'discourse' (*discurrere*) means 'running around'; in the context in which it is used here, it refers to a system of language, objects and practices. It implies a practice both of speech and action; who, it asks, speaks on a particular object or event and when, where and how? The concept acquires significance for us in the context of Foucault's hypothesis that sexuality exists only within discourse and through its mediations; that it has, then, no stability, but changes instead in accordance with social conditions.

Church confession, for example, is generally cited as a model instance of repression; Foucault maintains the opposite. Confession documents (from the seventeenth century for example) demonstrate the *situation* of confession to be a *site of production* of discourses of sexuality. The fear of speaking 'it', the compulsion to probe every action from the point of view of a prohibited sexuality, the perpetual confrontation with infringements of a law which decrees that 'it' is not to be countenanced in thought or deed – and so on. The powerful agency of the Church decreed that sexual actions were endlessly to be spoken out loud; more, that they were to be expressed in the form of confession. Yet a confession whose necessary accompaniment is a guilty conscience, becomes meaningful only if defined against statements about actions that do not require confession. There are rules and boundaries that delineate one area from another, and sustain ambiguities between them. In the vast grey area which then shrouds all actions, each and every act may be considered a potential subject of confession. Sex becomes a secret whose traces are to be uncovered. All phenomena are assessed according to whether they 'belong' or not in this category, whether or not they contribute to the truth of sex. Entire scientific disciplines are called upon to examine sex, to put us 'in the know'. Foucault demonstrates how statements about sexuality construct is as an 'object'. Investigations into sexuality take the form of particular modes of classification whose development allows the perverse to be distinguished from the normal, the sick from the healthy and so on. From now on, sexuality is susceptible to normalizing judgement, and to therapy. Our first question, then, is as follows: how, and from what point of view, are particular events described, and what ensemble of utterances is bundled together to form 'sexuality as object'?

It seems to us that the example of perversions is particularly well–suited to pinpoint the specificities of Foucault's approach, since we ourselves make a spontaneous association between perversion and its repression. Is it not the case that 'deviant lusts and practices' have been outlawed and persecuted, prohibited and marginalized in favour of sexual morals and norms directed only towards reproduction? 'No', says Foucault; and, as far as the 19th and 20th centuries are concerned, he claims we should speak rather of 'a dispersion of sexualities, a strengthening of their disparate forms, a multiple implantation of perversions'.[12]

Before the 19th century, marriage had been the focal point of interrogation, as an institution bounded by rules and recommendations, forced under examination to speak perpetually of its own deficiencies and misdemeanours. Since marriage functioned as the sole normalizing standard, there was no differentiation amongst any of the other phenomena that emerged outside the conjugal mode and its practices. There was, then, no hierarchization of the punishment reserved for 'outsiders'. 'On the list of grave sins. . . . there appeared debauchery . . . adultery, rape, spiritual or carnal incest, but also sodomy or the mutual caress'.[13] It was not until marriage became a matter of course, the norm, the predominant practice – a stricter one, now that it more or less regulated itself and was no longer governed by judicial proscriptions, but appeared instead as a universal convention, responsibility for which had been entrusted to the individual; not until then did marriage begin to withdraw increasingly into silence. 'The legitimate couple, with its regular sexuality, had a right to more discretion.'[14] From now on, all those previously condemned uniformly as 'deviants' were to be compelled to step forward and speak of their deviation; the notion of 'the unnatural' cut a pathway through the multiplicity of possible deviations, constructing a 'stepladder' of crimes: from now on, adultery and homosexuality were to be differentiated as perversions.

Sexuality versus liberation

Foucault does not set out to examine the degree of repression or tolerance of the state apparatuses. He rejects the very concept of 'repression', on the grounds that it refers exclusively to discipline and the law; in perpetuating the notion of repression as a movement from 'the top' (the agency of repression) downwards, it fails to do justice to power relations as they actually exist.[15] For him, it is the form of 'deployment of power' that is of decisive importance; he sees power, not as a prohibition, but as a force that makes accessible to itself all lived practices and forms. Here Foucault is contesting a model whose point of departure is the legal definition of power (in codes, institutions, prohibitions) or, by extension, its definition in relation to the State (since it is through the State that rules are ordained and laws passed to mark out an initial field of commands, prohibitions and censorship). Foucault instead proposes a strategic model formulated in terms of relations of force. 'And if it is true that the juridical system was useful for representing, albeit in a nonexhaustive way, a power that was centred primarily around deduction (*prélèvement*) and death, it is utterly incongruous with the new methods of power whose operation is not ensured by right but by technique, not by law but by normalization, not by punishment but by control, methods that are employed on all levels and in forms that go beyond the state and its apparatus.'[16]

Earlier, we raised the question of the relationship between sexuality and repression; we now learn that power does not fear sexuality, but rather – in the most extreme formulation of this argument – that power takes effect *through* sexuality. The example of masturbation illustrates this more clearly. At the beginning of the eighteenth century, childhood masturbation was invested with enormous significance; it became the object of constant observation, persecution, punishment. Disputing traditional notions that associate the persecution of infantile onanism with the increasing power of the emergent bourgeoisie, Foucault proposes to investigate the preconditions for, and the effects of what at first appear as 'restrictive' demands. He notes that this was also the period that saw the reorganization of relationships between children and adults, parents or educators, an intensification of internal family relations.[17] Childhood was the missing link in the chain that connected parents and educational institutions to agencies of public hygiene. 'Situated at the point of convergence between body and soul, health and morality, breeding and education, the sex of children became at one and the same time the target and the instrument of power.'[18] This 'network of power across childhood' at the same time *constitutes* the sexuality of children; in focussing the attention of pedagogues and doctors on infantile sexuality, in the effort of the latter to disallow sexuality in any form, they construct their object, the domain of sexuality. At the same time, they make it secret. Knowledge of sexuality is never complete. The commandment, 'thou shalt not masturbate', speaks sexuality, produces an entire discourse around what is known as 'child sex', founds a new domain of knowledge, directs our perception towards the hitherto unknown. Children who we once watched at play with tenderness in our eyes – tender not least because we thought them asexual, 'innocent', never to be brought into association with sexuality – are now scrutinized for any sign of touching themselves 'down there', of transgressing prohibitions, of turning from 'innocence' to 'guilt'. Parents, educators and pedagogues are now exhorted to take responsibility for the prevention, or the detection of crime. At all these points, it is *power* that takes effect, extending its reach, inspecting, expanding and replenishing its field of operation.

The dynamic of sexual repression demonstrated by Foucault proceeds not by concealment and silencing, but through exhibition, observation, classification – here an object is both made available for discussion and, through this very process, constituted as an object. Familiar or hidden pleasures are tracked down, 'abstracted' from the individual, incorporated into rules and schematized systems that appear as structures external to, yet now once again 'implanted within' individuals. The avenues of encroachment upon the body and pleasures are multifarious.[19] Police and schooling, philosopy, the law, psychoanalysis, medicine – one by one, they take the floor, debating and deliberating on the body. There is now no area of life in which the body is not an object of speech. The effect of all these utterances

within institutions and agencies is both to produce and to intensify sexuality; Foucault himself thinks these methods of
encroachment as linked together to form a 'great surface
network' in which 'the stimulation of bodies, the intensification
of pleasures, the incitement to discourse, the formation of
special knowledges, the strengthening of controls and resistances, are linked to one another, in accordance with a few major
strategies of knowledge and power.'[20] Foucault calls this network
the *deployment of sexuality*. It functions through the regulation
of sexuality, marking out the sites on which it may and may not
appear (segregated boarding-school dormitories, the parental
bedroom and so on). Thinking sexuality in this way, as a
network, invests the question we have raised with new meaning:
how can we liberate ourselves from the oppression that has
entered into sexuality? Having assumed initially that our task was
to 'liberate' sexuality itself, we are now led to believe that we
may have to liberate ourselves from sexuality.

The immediate question which arises for our analysis of the
production of sexuality is, 'by whom, then, is it produced?'. We
have cited the Church and the academic sciences as agents of
production; to these should be added the agencies of the State, as
well as the whole sphere of the judiciary. If every one of these
institutions stands on the side of power and domination, then we
are faced with the startling conclusion that what we had conceived of as a 'revolutionary force', and endeavoured to live out,
to proclaim without inhibition, is in fact a construct of the
dominant ideology. Sexuality is on the side of domination; its net
is drawn together ever more tightly, the more voluble and
'candid' we become. Any struggles for liberation of this kind will
simply intensify our subjugation.

The uses of Foucault

We have now introduced three terms: discourse, power and the
deployment of sexuality. What is the interplay between these
three terms; how useful are they in discussing the constitution of
sexuality? The term with the broadest range is the 'deployment
of sexuality'; it refers to the ordering of sexuality that delineates
the framework within which individual behaviour occurs. Its
principal axes are, according to Foucault, the husband-wife relationship and the parent-child relationship, within which the basic
elements for the deployment of sexuality are developed ('the

feminine body, infantile precocity, the regulation of births and . . . the specification of the perverted.'[21]). At the same time, they mark out the family as a site for its operation, whose task is 'to anchor sexuality and provide it with a permanent support'.[22] Within this ordering, something is moving, 'running around': it is discourse. Determined by the development of sexuality, discourse is lived, acted out, spoken by individuals. Yet Foucault never once turns his attention to these human subjects, to their active participation in the appropriation of discourse, for example. It remains a mystery *who* has constructed the sexual order; it is also unclear how its transformation might be effected through human action.[23] Since discourses are everywhere, power too is omnipresent; it is the universal effect that derives from a chain of determinate utterances; it is not bound to any one person or class. Even the notion of interest is abandoned by Foucault. Relations of power may 'serve' as instruments, yet they do not function 'in the service' of some pre-given interest. They are serviceable only if they can be made to become such within strategies. According to Foucault, then, the object of analysis should be, not 'causes', actions identifiable as origins, but the effects produced by these actions in relation to other operations. 'Sexuality' is one (constructed) effect of this kind. The product of combined efforts from diverse sources, it can be made to serve processes of regulation, prescription and so on; yet there is no original association between sexuality and the services it renders. Power thus seems to be an all-embracing presence, whose effects include its own resistance to itself. 'They are the odd terms in relations of power; they are inscribed in the latter as an irreducible opposite.'[24] All objects and human beings exist within relations of power; even those who resist, who set their faces against what appears to be the norm (homosexuals, to take one example), participate in the production of the norm in the very act of opposing it, by allowing the norm to be articulated against its abnormal opposite.

Let us summarize once more. Sexuality is an ordering that operates not in the first instance through prohibition, but rather through the incorporation of increasingly wide areas of knowledge. 'Sexuality' emerges within specific systems of rules, relating not only to the immediately sexual, but also to the body in general, to dress and so on. It is managed and controlled within institutions. The effect thus produced – 'sexuality' – becomes the 'object' of pedagogies, psychologies, criminologies, each of which seeks to identify its truth. The concept of truth is thus implemented as a function of the prevailing sexual order; it acquires meaning only through its implementation. What makes the search for truth necessary is the possibility that there may be untruth.

Our point of departure was the question of the strategies that can or should be adopted to bring about women's liberation from sexual oppression. Since, in Foucault's scheme of things, we are all active within the same ordering, power is omnipresent. Thus for example, the 'object' sexuality is constructed through the knitting together of discourses into a single demand on individuals that they orientate themselves around heterosexuality and monogamy. These are the 'threads' that pattern our lives, the standards against which our life-situation is measured and in relation to which a woman may be said for example to be 'too young by half', 'old enough by now', 'no longer young enough', 'almost a woman': she is a 'ripe young thing' – or its opposite – and so on. We all know the passages in novels where the young hero is reunited after many years with his childhood playmates; and lo and behold, the young girl has blossomed into a not-yet-full-grown woman. (It is worth noting that women's 'ripeness', or otherwise, for marriage usually expresses itself in biological characteristics, whereas for men it is questions of professional qualification and 'social standing' that constitute the relevant criteria. The man's sexual potency is not seen to be at issue, but the degree to which he is locked into a social structure that offers him particular kinds of security – financial security, for example.)

If power is everywhere, there can be no resistance outside of power. Even if we do not behave as 'monogamous heterosexuals', but as 'promiscuous homosexuals', we exist, in other words, merely as deviations, defined against what is 'right and proper'. In this way, we participate in the constitution both of the 'normal' and of the 'abnormal'. Thus individuals and institutions function at one and the same time as reinforcements of, and of resistance to the existing order. The 'pro' is created out of the 'anti'; conversely, the 'pro' (here marriage) itself creates the possibility of disavowal and opposition. This has certain implications for our efforts to liberate ourselves. We may speak loudly or softly of our 'sexuality', we may live it to excess – or not at all; caught eternally in the networks of power, we change nothing of its ordering. Power – without which sexuality cannot be posited – remains deaf to demands for liberation.

We need now to know more about the ordering of sexuality; in the first instance, how is it constructed? What are the linkages within it? And further: what is our point of entry onto its terrain? How do we move within it? With what structures of competence and non-competence does it confront us? What is our own involvement in the construction of those structures? In raising these questions – which relate to social subjects – we are already moving beyond the Foucaultian problematic. At a later stage, we will return to it.

The State and Power

One of the important discoveries we made was our recognition of the part played by the deployment of sexuality in socialization. The body now no longer appears as a 'simple piece of nature', whose secrets we can penetrate, in order to develop a 'natural relationship' with it. We are dealing instead with prescriptions and demands, commandments and prohibitions, a system of rules whose influence takes effect from the outside inwards. Taking Foucault's argument and extending it further, we want to suggest here that there also exists, within that rule-system, a relation of cause and effect from the inside outwards. As rules are assimilated by individuals, they take on a semblance of 'naturalness', and constitute what is known as individual 'character'. This, amongst other things, accounts for their durability and for their consistent reproduction.

Within this system of rules, sexuality functions as the marker of a space, a sign yet to be filled with meaning: 'Don't forget to wash yourself *down there*', '*Don't* put your hands under the bedclothes', 'Take your hands away from *there*', or – a clear reference that still contains as absence – 'if you don't pull your shoulders back, your breasts will start to sag'. We have no difficulty in making the association between what remains unspoken, and 'sexuality': it is in *not* being named that 'it' comes to be understood as implicit. Even 'sagging breasts' are not mentioned in the context of health, but associated instead with a future promise of sexuality; 'breast-sag' is the opposite of beauty, and beauty belongs to the realm of sexual attraction. Potentially sagging breasts are associated with the threat that no man in future will be interested in their owner. In orientating ourselves around notions of this kind, we voluntarily align ourselves with the order to which we are subjected.

Let us reexamine Foucault's conception of power, scrutinizing it now from the point of view of strategies for liberation, of a

Wo der Körper leicht die Form verliert, fehlt meist die richtige Muskelkontur. Auch die Form der weiblichen Brust kann verbessert werden, wenn die unter den Brustdrüsen liegende Muskulatur trainiert wird (der BH unter der Haut!)

Translation of caption:
Some parts of the body tend to flabiness when the muscles are not kept toned. The shape of the female breast can be improved if the muscles underneath are exercised regularly (the bra beneath the skin!)

politics of female opposition to women's sexual oppression. When Foucault speaks of the 'positivity of power',[25] he is referring to the historical transition from authoritarian rule (the rod of iron) to 'mass persuasion'. Modern power is no longer grounded in organized physical violence, but takes effect essentially through ideology (what Lenin termed the spiritual 'rod'[26]). In mediating to the masses a set of values, norms, attitudes, beliefs and so on, ideology cajoles them into 'voluntary' submission. These values are transmitted in forms such as legal commandment and law. The law irons out antagonistic differences (we all enjoy equality before the law), while at the same time creating them; it appears as an organizer of unity, a force for the homogenization of oppositions between classes and genders. This is the ideological power that constitutes individuals as subordinated subjects.

In the juridical concept of subjectification, distinctions are made between responsibility and loss of responsibility, or between sound and unsound mind. Ideology creates a communality not otherwise present in society; it offers us social forms within which it is possible to live class and gender contradictions. No woman is 'forced' these days to live within the restrictive forms of the family – yet more than two-thirds of women do so.[27] In choosing to live exclusively within this private form, they are at the same time acquiescing in restrictions on their acquisition of social competence. This results in women's 'voluntary exclusion' from society – an exclusion that simultaneously reproduces the sexual division of labour. Social responsibility is delegated to the man who works out in the big wide world, while the modest housewife holds sway over the household where she awaits him.

The notion of the positivity of power refers both to the organization of consensus and, historically, of the 'bourgeoisification' of human beings, their acquisition of responsibilities, rights and duties. It refers also to their *individualization*, each individual interpellated as citizen, exhorted to fulfil the relevant duties or to shoulder his or her responsibilities as *pater* or *mater familias*. Individuals are not simply subordinated to some alien power; they absorb it into themselves, living their being-within-the-order as an act of free will. Knowing the system of rights and duties is an ideological competence; conformity to the system brings the reward of being left in peace (by legal institutions for example).

A relevant example here is the following statement by the politician Norbert Blüm. 'To talk of the private relation between parents and children in terms of "power relations" or "coercion" – words which are used to characterize the struggles between the social partners – reveals an ignorance of the distinction between private and public life. It tramples the defences of private life – the four walls into which we withdraw to safeguard ourselves from the intrusions and restraints of the State. It exposes human lives to public scrutiny, exhibiting them remorselessly to the public gaze. Our lives are simply laid bare.'[28]

If Foucault's analysis is less concrete than Blüm's, he is nonetheless equally concerned with the *techniques* of power, here essentially with their function of normalization. His concept of power is immensely problematic, for he quite unceremoniously equates powers with domination. The fact that the notion of domination implies a relation of oppression does not concern Foucault; nor does the fact that the apparent intermingling of power and domination is actually illusory – in reality, they obey different laws. Power can be turned against domination; and it seems to us that it is in the difference between the two that there lies the possibility of liberation.

A second problem – closely linked to the first – arises out of Foucault's explicit lack of attention to the State. Certainly, power relations have a materiality within institutions and apparatuses that – and here we would agree with Foucault – form 'sites of power' extending beyond the State. Yet they still remain within its strategic purview. In our view, it is therefore imperative to make analytical distinctions between the State, power and domination, in order to examine the linkages between them and their effects on the field of research.[29] In that case what can we retain from Foucault, despite this fundamental point of disagreement?

Power appears in the work of Foucault as a system of norms brought to bear on, and thereby producing a particular domain: here, the domain of sexuality. Our interest centres on the way in which individuals individualize themselves (as effects of norms), by using the power of normalization to measure disparities, determine levels, fix specificities and name differences. This is what allows normalizing power to achieve its homogenizing effect; all individuals orientate themselves around the same standards to produce themselves as individuals. Individuality in this context consists in a particular combination of deviations from, and conformities to standards. The problem of individualization is thus closely linked to the possibility of *knowledge* ('knowledge is power'). The more precise knowledge one has of prevailing

FRECH

Hier wurden alle Haare
stramm nach oben
gebürstet und mit
Klemmen zu einem Tuff
auf dem Oberkopf
festgesteckt. Damit der
Tuff so plustrig
wird, die Strähnen antou-
pieren. Ein paar Haar-
spitzen in die Stirn zupfen.
Fotos: Bernd Böhm;
Make-up: Linique

standards – or the better one knows one's object – the more intricate the possibilities for differentiation become.

Although Foucault himself does not discuss the way in which sexual difference is socially constructed, we have been able to identify avenues of investigation leading on from his comments on individualization. There is a mode of individualization specific to women; it operates above all through the field of sexuality. (Whole sectors of industry devote themselves to offers of individualization: a perfume which is one woman's own, the exclusive scent of a certain soap, that 'certain something' of a cigarette made for women only.) In the first instance it is through exhortations to acquire 'exclusivity' that the ordering of sexuality takes effect for women; these domains arise as an effect of, and are instrumental in producing, that ordering. What then emerges from this assemblage of various norms and requirements is a particular 'type' of woman: the 'tomboy', the 'cold fish', the 'unapproachable type', the 'frivolous', the 'maternal', the 'elegant' and so on. These terms attract the appropriate adjectives: 'racy', 'forward', 'sporty', 'cosy', 'lascivious', 'loose', 'stand-offish', 'sexy'. We are all familiar with the fashion magazines urging us to 'make the best of your skin type, hair type, facial type', and so on; the implicit inference here is that a given type is what we *are* – and not, for example, that there are long processes at work through which that type is *made*. When we ourselves claim to belong to a particular type – a statement that amounts to a definition of our essence, a reference to something more or less inherent in us – this represents what we earlier called a relation of cause and effect 'from the inside outwards'. Socially–constituted formations enter into feminine personality structures through a process that we will term here 'auto-naturalization' (*Vereigenschaftung*). Using the concept of auto-naturalization makes it possible to represent social construc-tions, including ideological formations (in the media for example) as phenomena that are 'made' and yet are also inherent within individuals. Use of the term here represents an attempt to grasp the subjective subordination (the ideological subjection) of individuals to the ordering of the sexual as a *process*.[30] The sexualization of a woman's body – a process equivalent to her individualization – represents an inclusion of the female subject in ordering of the sexual.[31] Our hypothesis, to conclude, runs as follows: in girls, the process of individual socialization is synony-mous with the sexualization of the body and its parts.

An Active Ordering or Active Subjects?

We were seeking guidelines for a liberation strategy in the domain of sexuality – or better still, opportunities for active intervention. Our concrete problems with Foucault began here. In his account of the deployment of alliances and – this is of particular interest – the ordering of the sexual, he emphasizes that both will *of necessity* continue; they may be subject to historical adjustment, they may produce different discourses, but they will never entirely disappear. If we examine the source of our dissatisfaction with this conclusion, we come to his under-lying historical assumptions. Human beings who make their own history have no place in Foucault; instead, human beings are the effects of the structure (the 'order') that attains its goals by the most devious means, and remains impervious to willed efforts to change it. To the vital question, 'what is to be done?', we could find only one answer in Foucault: study the deployment of sexuality with care, equip yourselves to move more competently within it, repeat to others the things you have learned, in the hope that they can also be enlightened. Fruitful as it might be, above all in methodological terms, Foucault's approach has a conservative core. He shares with bourgeois sociology an incapacity to think the individual in social terms; society remains a purely external force, the environment merely *surrounding* the individual. Where sociologists see people subject to the influence of existing social relations (stratum, milieu, role), he posits individuals whose actions are determined by the ordering of sexuality. He sees this not as a single mechanism working monocausally (in which case the prohibition of infantile masturbation might produce a sexually repressed adult); instead he sees that mechanism as a perpetual process. Sociality is under perpetual construction. Since he allows neither for active subjects nor for any potential self-determination, both appear dispensable in projects for class and sexual liberation. Thus it is hardly surprising that Foucault is so vague about future prospects. The demands he formulates have already been rendered theoretically untenable. On perspectives for the future, he writes, 'we must not think that by saying yes to sex, one says no to power; on the contrary, one tracks along the course laid down by the general deployment of sexuality. It is the authority of sex that we must break away from, if we aim – through a tactical reversal of the various mechanisms of sexuality – to counter the grips of power with the claims of bodies, pleasures and a range of knowledge, in their multiplicity and their possibility of resistance. The rallying point for the counterattack against the deployment of sexuality ought to be not sexual desire, but bodies and pleasures.'[32]

Are we to understand that there is still something – some core, some essence – into which the otherwise omnipotent ordering of sexuality has failed to penetrate? Have we come full circle; are there two sides to the equation after all: the deployment of sexuality *versus* the body and its pleasures – the only difference being that it is now no longer 'sexuality' that is to be liberated, but the body? There is no resolution to the contradiction implied by the Foucaultian approach; once he has demonstrated that the body has been, and remains, an effect of a process of sexualization, once it has been shown that pleasure is not an ahistorical quantity, we cannot return to the body or to pleasure as the elements of liberation. More drastic reconstructions are required if the positive aspects of Foucault are to be rendered feasible.

Feminist historiography has engaged intensively with approaches to historical research developed in France — Lacan, Althusser and others. Women have looked for ways of using the methodological contributions of these writers in their own work. This has been a particularly fruitful development, for the absence of a female historiography (as well as the disparities between the realms and areas occupied by women and men) has entailed a departure from prevailing historiographical procedures, in which the scholarly sources are reviewed, and a number of divergent interpretations adduced.[33] It is possible to use proposals such as Foucault's to challenge fixed assumptions about fields of knowledge, or emphases within the discipline of 'History'.[34] Yet one key question raised by feminist research relates to the presentation of women. Is research to be focused upon them, or should they themselves bring their actions to bear upon it? An awareness of Foucault's major flaw – the absence of subjects – has led a number of researchers simply to 'append' what seems to be missing link: the woman as subject. Thus whereas women initially appeared as passively suffering victims of social conditions, they are now presented as engaging in active resistance struggles. Since, however, womens' transformation from the victims of historiography into the active agents of history takes place only in the heads of the women historians in question, nothing is changed in the 'real' lives of the women under consideration, and these women do not change either. The following statement has been proffered, for example, as evidence of women's active part in the reduction of femininity to 'the biological' in the nineteenth century. 'Women were anything but disinterested bystanders in this development. The contradiction between the notions of a woman's "job" and "her vocation" was intensified and exploited, but never actually resolved, by women themselves. They themselves pursued the professionalization of their own work to the point of Taylorization, while at the same time celebrating the notion of the family as a compensating value. In the cult of domesticity, they both adopted and further elaborated the existing biological and moralistic components of feminine roles.'[35] Here then, women are seen to be 'passively subversive'.[36]

In this example, the concept of the 'cult of domesticity' is presented as a 'compensating value' and women are viewed as 'active' and 'strong'. They are seen to have held sway within the household and to have made their own of it. The fact that it is women who exercise power seems immediately demonstrable, since they monopolize caring roles within the family. After all, what other member of the family is capable of cooking or sewing buttons; who else knows where the laundry is kept, and so on? Conceivably too, women may participate actively in the construction of that monopoly, by *maintaining* husband and children in a state of noncompetence. And yet we are left with a sense of unease, for surely the *form* within which women become active in this sense, within which they construct themselves as powerful, is one that also causes them suffering and unhappiness? If, however, the activities of women are presented exclusively as practices of resistance, our perception of this very unhappiness becomes distorted. We lose sight of the *form* within which individuals exist; and yet it is the form that prescribes modes of activity, their potential for expansion and their limitations. In the example we have quoted, the form in question is the family, whose private character allows it to be counterposed to society and the wider community and isolates it from social developments. The fact that activities such as cooking, washing, cleaning and so on, insofar as these are organized within the rigid confines of the 'happy home', embody only minimal potential for development, even if they are carried out in oppositional ways, is submerged in any critique concerning itself exclusively with women's personal activities. If Foucault treats human beings as wriggling fish caught in so many nets, in this kind of feminist research the fish are transformed into fisherwomen. To extend the metaphor, what is lacking is a concern with the net that pre-establishes an order for the social whole. We remain ignorant of how the net is woven and cast.

But how might an analysis of form be thought out in conjunction with deployments of power? Or to put the question a different way: how can Foucault's work be made to yield fruitful results for women's liberation?

The Deployment of Sexuality on Firmer Ground

For Foucault, the deployments of alliance and sexuality may be taken as read. He presents them as *necessary* modes of socialization, whose content and structural method are the first possible objects of analytical scrutiny. The 'institution' of that ordering is never called into question. If we follow Foucault in assuming these deployments to be synonymous with 'the social', we risk falling into the same trap of assuming an absence of any future perspective. His theoretical premises foreclose human self-determination as a potential form of socialization. Yet the concepts of self-determination and heteronomy are central to our present investigations.

In what follows, we have therefore attempted to reconceptualize sexual ordering, taking an analysis of ideology as our starting-point, and to see it as the mode in which an ideological socialization into heteronomy takes place. By conceiving the deployment of sexuality not as something more or less 'natural', but as an external ordering located *within* social relations, we can come to understand the ordering itself, not only as susceptible to change, but also – like the State – as capable of transformation. This is its first characteristic. As to its second: out of the hitherto neutral concept of 'deployment', it is possible to construct a critical concept that can be mobilized against the existing coercive socialization process. The ordering of sexuality can then be seen to perform the function of transforming social contradictions into livable social forms. The concept of ideology associates the social form within which individuals are active, and the competences they acquire in that context. In this way it allows self-determination to be seen to be taking place within heteronomous relations, and makes it possible to conceive of the individual and society in terms other than those of mutual exteriority and opposition. We may conclude that sexuality should be viewed as ideology, in other words as a complex system of norms and values, through which individuals socialize themselves from top to bottom.

Structural Method of the Discursive Formation

In our exploration of 'sexuality', we have sought to establish what it is that restricts and oppresses us as women, and to propose possible means of change. There have been women who have changed solely their practice, only to discover that the problem was not an immediately 'practical' one in the sense they had assumed. Since introducing a new kind of 'praxis' into love relations was not sufficient to eradicate domination, the women who attempted to do so were still left with the same feelings of self-consciousness in relation to their bodily pleasures. Through Foucault, we have learned that 'sexuality' cannot be viewed as a fixed, ahistorical, clear and pre-given quantity, elements of which may be denied, or 'simply' enlarged upon, and so on. Our original hope was that we might attain a greater happiness by uncovering a secret which we looked for within sexuality. We have also discussed the rules, the utterances, the linkages which together make up the social construct of sexuality. We have seen our task as one of examining a construct that was manifested in a set of arrangements affecting our lives. In our continued search for ways and means towards liberation, our next aim will be to carve out a space for a conscious autonomy, by investigating the rules to which we have become habituated, asking whether and how they have restricted or incapacitated us.

In any study of the laws which determine a given object of research, there is always a danger that the persons involved will remain imprisoned within those self-same laws, since they are, as yet, unidentified; we have no means of knowing what we are overlooking and what we are taking for granted. Much of what seems 'self-evident' to us derives its obviousness only from perceptions and evaluations which are themselves social. A single word is enough to evoke a whole range of associations: a woman is said to be 'loose', a word made more vivid by its opposite – 'chaste' or 'decent', or perhaps 'virtuous'. 'Virtue' arouses nothing like the same amount of interest as 'looseness'; what lies behind the latter term is a colourful mixture of attraction and repulsion in which 'it' is the determining force. 'Looseness' is also only conceivable in one particular context; it is impossible, for example, to portray a virgin as 'loose', while a voyeur, by contrast, is almost automatically a man of 'loose' morals. The domain of sexuality is particularly loaded with restricted meanings of this kind. The very arrangements which govern sexuality require of us that we become well versed in 'it', that we know what 'it' entails, that the slightest allusion be explicitly recognized for its 'obvious' associations. Like participants in a contest, we are confronted with jokes, overtures, passing glances whose one message is blatantly clear. In this contest, the reward which beckons to the swiftest, the best, the most original amongst us is 'knowledge' – a knowledge which functions in this context as a promise of sexual fulfilment (learn to do it the . . . way!). If we respond by attempting to comprehend and grasp what 'sexuality' is (to place it within some conceptual framework), we find ourselves creating it. What most of us attempt to identify as 'one thing and one only' ('he's only after one thing', but she 'doesn't go the whole way', she denies him 'just one thing') is probably not the only thing. We are diminishing reality by allowing our perceptions to be forcibly confined within the strait-jacket of a restricted view of sexuality, by reducing our judgements and feelings to a single common feature, and by channelling our potential experience in one direction only, subordinating this experience to a 'sexual reductionism' which is certain to cause us suffering.

Pinball

The illustration on this page seems to us to be a particularly 'successful' instance of sexual reductionism. The artist presents himself as a critic of the sexualization of male perceptions, a feminist man who demonstrates how 'filthy' the fantasies of men are.

Edward and Nancy Reddin Kienholz, *The Berlin Women,*
Dibbert Galerie, 1981

So much for the 'filth': but how do we proceed from here? I asked a number of men what they associated with 'pinball machines' and the activity of 'playing pinball'. What did they connect it with? Their answers ranged from 'the fascination of standing in front of the machine, the desire to win at all costs', 'the control over a ball you can't directly touch', 'the thrill and the pleasure of the game', to 'release of tension, getting rid of aggression'. Their first response to the Kienholzian interpretation had been one of stupefaction. But suddenly, it did appear 'possible' to them that playing pinball might perhaps involve something else, that it might be a 'substitute' for sexual deprivation. Is not the excitement of tracking the movements of the pinball in fact ('when it comes down to it') sexual in nature? In the course of our discussions, the connection between pinball and sexuality came to be seen, not as one of a range of possibilities, but as the 'truth' of pinball, which someone had now expressed with irreverent frankness. For men who assumed the 'brutality' revealed here to be their own, what was produced was both a 'guilty conscience' and an (admittedly stunned) acknowledgement that it was indeed their own depravity (or perhaps their potency?) that was on display.

How does Kienholz achieve this reduction? How can he come to count on our sympathy with his indignation – which we may not necessarily share? What he sees is men playing a pinball machine. This is clearly a source of entertainment and pleasure for them. They move and play with their bodies; the sequence of their movements is punctuated by the forward and backward thrusts of their pelvis. They grip the machine with both hands; it is under their control. Their movements are aggressive. Winning brings a sense of 'release'. The language at our disposal to describe this sequence of events is suggestive of another context. Indeed it seems to have originated in this 'other' context, to which the activity of playing pinball must be subordinated. Knowing no terms of its own, having no words to describe itself, pinball resolves itself instead into something 'obviously sexual'. We now have to post the familiar question: are we not dealing with sexuality, rather than with a 'harmless' game? The challenge rings out to men at large: delve into your consciences, ask yourselves if these are not the 'true' feelings which you too experience. Moral censure raises its hands in a disapproving gesture. And men respond to the question of conscience in the ways shown above; Kienholz has already won them for his cause, and never again will they be able to enjoy an 'unambiguous' game of pinball.

Kienholz may perhaps win women over to his side with this kind of moralism – for does he not highlight the 'despicable' way in which men treat women? And is he not a critic and an opponent of the 'reality' which he portrays? Yet 'opposition' of this kind is in our view both inadequate in itself and at the same time ineffective as a strategy for liberation. After the first fleeting moment of enlightenment, Kienholz's critique of the 'sexual' oppression of women reaches a dead end. It marks prohibition as the only possible means of progress. But what form would this prohibition assume? Thou shalt not play pinball? Since he has reduced all the activities involved in pinball to *one single* pleasure relation, which allows no room for any other form of pleasure, the only solution is to prohibit the activity altogether.

Kienholz has admonished women to be on their guard; the sexual degradation of women is everywhere. In practice, he suggests, we too should begin to seek the 'one thing' which pervades all contexts and situations. Our search, as Kienholz has demonstrated, will be assured of success; for an element of the sexual, to which all other elements may be subordinated, can be found in any context. Within the ordering of the sexual, everything else is defined as the 'symptom' of an essential sex.

In an attempt to escape from our own imprisonment within the particular way of seeing dictated by the ordering of sexuality, we looked for ways of approaching that ordering as outsiders. These we found in the erotic stories of the ancients.[37] There is an element of 'seduction' in these old stories, insofar as they do not focus on dominant men versus subjugated women. There is no such hierarchy in the relationships they portray. Love is taken as read: there is no question that it might be unattainable. The only question is *how* this love can be lived, how any obstacles to it might be removed. To us, this smacked of Utopia, despite the presence in these stories of other structures of oppression which are less familiar to us today – the presence of slaves, serfs and so on – and which we had overlooked.

In an attempt systematically to question the concept of sexuality we take for granted today, we rewrote, transcribed, these old erotic tales as modern love stories, asking ourselves how we might describe the same situation today. What connections should we be making, and how should we assess them? We turned aside from the dominant discourse in search of a different standpoint from which we could join up with it again. Our escape allowed us to adopt the wondering gaze of a stranger from far-off lands, for whom our social relations are anything but self-evident. We were then confronted with a problem. In our attempts to 're-tell' the stories, to 'speak anew' the texts we had read, we were shackled by our own language. Sentences intermeshed of their own accord to form pornographic texts; descriptions became ever more explicit and detailed, as if the problem of the old story lay in its 'concealment' of what had 'really' taken place. To speak in this way is to reproduce the existing sexual order, and yet we had intended simply to make people aware of it.

Sexual Socialization

Let us turn once again to the question of the socializing function of sexuality. It if is indeed the case that 'sex is the foundation of each and every pleasure, and that the nature of sex demands that we celebrate and restrict ourselves to procreation',[38] then surely this discourse requires certain forms through which individuals can become versed in it? If sex and pleasure are regarded as synonymous, and if all human strivings can be formulated in terms of the 'desire for sex – the desire to have it, to have access to it, to discover it, to liberate it, to articulate it in discourse, to formulate the truth of it,'[39] this indicates that there is some 'centre' of which we should know certain things: how it is first installed, how we maintain it. Social necessity seems to demand that the 'reproduction of the species' be the socially established base around which discourses organize themselves independently. Sexuality is represented through a whole set of rules which do not just relate directly to the genitalia but govern the body as a whole, the way it is treated or clothed, bodily hygiene, and so on. Foucault's phrase for the establishment of links between these rules and for how certain concepts are united with others is 'the discursive formation': this, for him, is what determines practice. Let us assume that the dominant discursive formation arranges itself around the monogamous, heterosexual (marital) couple, which constitutes both the envisaged goal and the framework within which we already move. How is this formation constructed; what parts are played by what institutions; what significance should we accord to language as *one* agency of socialization?

The first relevant institution is the judiciary, which lays down guidelines on eligibility for marriage, allocates duties within marriage, and thus opens up the possibility of legal action (so that infertility or sterility, for example, can become grounds for divorce). The law lends the authority of the State to the association between two partners, and addresses itself to questions of property rights. Equally, it delineates the subtle distinction between the serious and the not-so-serious in the sexual domain. In a court of law, there is a world of difference between full sexual intercourse and mere sexual misconduct. Interrogations demanding details of who has touched and/or seduced whom, how and where, produce an 'order of relevance' for parts of the body. The seriousness of any crime is determined according to proximity to or distance from parts of the body which are deemed to be patently sexual.

Equally important are *psychology* and *psychiatry*, whose essential concern is with the drawing of dividing-lines and with efforts at reintegration. These institutions separate the normal from the abnormal through processes of classification and hierarchization. Homosexuality, for example, exists as the antithesis of heterosexuality; thus it becomes a buttress to 'normality', constituting the normal in the process of deviating from it (the reverse also applies here). Then there is medicine, which, through its direct concern with the adequacies and inadequacies of the body, has used the analysis of heredity to place sex in the context of a 'biological responsibility for the human race'. The distinctions between medicine and psychology are blurred; the biological is said to be psychically determined, the psychic to have biological preconditions and consequences. Across and within all these different definitions, limits and exclusions, we find the moral doctrine of Catholicism. Through tne institution of the Church, this doctrine operates within and alongside these other discourses to separate flesh from soul (although the present Pope is something of an exception).[40]

We have found it possible to identify the structural mode of a discourse by transcribing it from the standpoint of one of the above institutions. An 'old familiar story', may, for example, be read from the standpoint of the popular press, of a psychiatrist, a judge, a mother; it may then be reconstructed with the particular meaning created by those institutions and persons. Those meanings are both alien and familiar to us. We are readily able to set up an association between sex and violence; to produce credible evidence that a young boy's leanings towards homosexuality are rooted in his disturbed relationship to his father; to demonstrate that an individual's immoral lifestyle will always lead to social depravation. Today we have at our fingertips a whole range of interpretative approaches which allow us to declare sexual repression, fulfilment or non-fulfilment to be the root causes of happiness or misery. We treat such interpretations as common knowledge that has the effect of a natural law. In reality, however, they derive from psychoanalytic constructions, applied and lived out in everyday life. The advance of psychoanalysis into all the social sciences and into everyday life is most evident in our acceptance of its bid to make us qualified to ask the 'leading' question – are you a nymphomaniac or an exhibitionist; are you homosexual or frigid? Enlightened as we are – we claim that nothing can shock us any longer – we know the 'right' question to ask in any situation, we know the 'proper paths' onto which others are to be directed, and we find potential deviance 'not all that disturbing', at worst. This 'enlightened' attitude, which dismisses all further questions, can be given a jolt through the work of transcription. Since our stories do not present these simple answers as axiomatic, we are able to observe how we come by them.

Ovid's Hermaphroditus

Once a son was born to Hermes and the goddess Aphrodite, and he was brought up by the maids in Ida's caves. In his features, it was easy to trace a resemblance to his father and mother. He was called after them, too, for his name was Hermaphroditus. As soon as he was fifteen, he left his native hills, and Mount Ida where he had been brought up, and for the sheer joy of travelling visited remote places, and saw strange rivers. His enthusiasm made him count the hardships as nothing. He even went as far as the cities of Lycia, and on to the Carians, who dwelt nearby. In this region he spied a pool of water, so clear that he could see right to the bottom. There were no marshy reeds around it, no barren sedge or sharp-spiked rushes. The water was like crystal, and the edges of the pool were ringed with fresh turf, and grass that was always green. A nymph dwelt there; not one skilled in hunting or practised in the art of drawing her bow, nor yet a swift runner. She was the only naiad unknown to the fleet-footed Diana. Often, so runs the story, her sisters would say to her: 'Salmacis, get yourself a javelin, or a gaily painted quiver, and join in the chase. It is good exercise, in contrast to hours of leisure.' But she did not get herself a javelin, nor any gaily painted quiver, nor did she take part in the chase, as good exercise to vary her hours of leisure: all she would do was bathe her lovely limbs in her own pool, frequently combing out her hair with a boxwood comb, and looking into the water, to see from her reflection what hairstyle was becoming to her. Then she would drape herself in her transparent robes, and lie down among the soft leaves, or on the grass.

Often she would gather flowers, and it so happened that she was engaged in this pastime when she caught sight of the boy, Hermaphroditus. As soon as she had seen him, she longed to possess him. But, eager as she was to approach him, she did not do so until she had composed herself, taken pains with her attire, assumed a charming expression, and seen to it that she was at her loveliest. Then she addressed him: 'Fair boy, you surely deserve to be thought a god. If you are, perhaps you may be Cupid? Or if you are mortal, blessed are your parents, happy your brother, most fortunate your sister, if you have a sister, and happy too the nurse who reared you. But far and away more blessed than any of these is the maiden, if such there be, who is engaged to you, whom you will deign to make your wife. If there is such a girl, let my rapture remain a secret: but if there is not, then I pray that I may be your bride, and that we may enter upon marriage together.' The naiad said no more, but a blush stained the boy's cheeks, for he did not know what love was. Even blushing became him: his cheeks were the colour of ripe apples, hanging in a sunny orchard, like painted ivory or like the moon when, in eclipse, she shows a reddish hue beneath her brightness, and bronze instruments clash vainly in attempts to aid her. Incessantly the nymph demanded at least sisterly kisses, and tried to put her arms around his ivory neck. 'Will you stop!', he cried, 'or I shall run away and leave this place and you! Salmacis was afraid. 'I yield the spot to you, stranger, I shall not intrude,' she said; and turning from him, pretended to go away. Even then she kept glancing back till, slipping into a thick clump of bushes, she hid there, kneeling on the ground. The boy, meanwhile, thinking himself unobserved and alone, strolled this way and that on the grassy sward, and dipped his toes in the lapping water – then his feet, up to the ankles. Then, tempted by the enticing coolness of the waters, he quickly stripped his young body of its soft garments. At the sight, Salmacis was spellbound. She was on fire with passion to possess his naked beauty, and her very eyes flamed with a brilliance like that of the dazzling sun, when Phoebus' bright disc is reflected in a mirror. She could scarcely bear to wait, or to defer the joys which she anticipated. She longed to embrace him then, and with difficulty restrained her frenzy. Hermaphroditus, clapping his hollow palms against his body, dived quickly into the stream. As he raised first one arm and then the other, his body gleamed in the clear water, as if someone had encased an ivory statue or white lilies in transparent glass. 'I have won! He is mine!' cried the nymph, and flinging aside her garments, plunged into the heart of the pool. The boy fought against her, but she held him, and snatched kisses as he struggled, placing her hands beneath him, stroking his unwilling breast, and clinging to him, now on this side and now on that.

Finally, in spite of all his efforts to slip from her grasp, she twined around him, like a serpent when it is being carried off into the air by the king of birds: for, as it hangs from the eagle's beak, the snake coils round its head and talons and with its tail hampers its beating wings. She was like the ivy encircling tall tree-trunks, or the squid which holds fast the prey it has caught in the depths of the sea, wrapping its tentacles round on every side. Atlas' descendant resisted stubbornly, and refused the nymph the rapture she hoped for; but she persisted, clinging to him, her whole body pressed against his. 'You may fight, you rogue, but you will not escape. May the gods grant me this, may nothing ever separate him from me, or me from him!' Her prayers found favour with the gods: for, as they lay together, their bodies were united and from being two persons they became one. As when a gardener grafts a branch on to a tree, and sees the two unite as they grow, and come to maturity together, so when their limbs met in that clinging embrace the nymph and the boy were no longer two, but a single form, possessed of a dual nature, which could not be called male or female, but seemed to be at once both and neither.

When he saw that the clear water into which he had descended as a man had made him but half a man, and that his limbs had been enfeebled by its touch, Hermaphroditus stretched out his hands and prayed – even his voice was no longer masculine – 'O my father, and my mother, grant this prayer to your son, who owes his name to you both: if any man enter this pool, may he depart hence no more than half a man, may he suddenly grow weak and effeminate at the touch of these waters.' Both his parents were moved with compassion, and granted this request of their child, who was now but half male, and half female. They infected the pool with this horrible magic power.[41]

The following transcription of Ovid's story is written from the standpoint of a popular newspaper. This presents difficulties, insofar as that standpoint is both alien to us – who would care to read the *Sun* every day? – yet at the same time familiar, since we tacitly assume its contents to be in some sense true. Newspaper reports of this kind are written in such a way as to suggest meanings and associations which are never made explicit; the reader is left to 'think the story through' to its conclusion.

WOMAN PIANO TEACHER SEDUCES FIFTEEN YEAR-OLD SCHOOLBOY

Yesterday afternoon, a fifteen year-old schoolboy, Peter H., was sexually assaulted by his piano teacher Maria S., in her home. The boy's parents are pressing charges for indecent assault of a minor.

Peter H. is a slightly over-serious lad. He looks like a child – but Peter is fifteen years old. We were told how he sits out the rough-and-tumble games of friends of the same age. His teachers at the Frederick Field grammar school know him as an attentive boy. One teacher said, 'He is pleasant, helpful and ready to help weaker members of the class when necessary.' 'He's a bit on the quiet side, but he works hard, and he's obviously got artistic talent,' his music teacher told us. Peter lives with his parents at their home on a new housing estate just outside S. His love of music has always been encouraged by his parents. They arranged for him to have piano lessons at an early age. 'He always dreamed of having his own piano. We made his wish come true on his sixth birthday', said his mother, Hetty H. Hetty and her husband Herbert have no other children.

Sitting facing Peter the first time we saw him, we were struck at once by his serious dark brown eyes. It was obviously an effort for him to pull himself together for us. Peter has the kind of delicate hands you'd expect to be at home on a piano keyboard. But he had them clenched around his knees. He looked tired and sad. He told us his version of the events of yesterday afternoon. As usual on a Tuesday, he had gone to the house of his piano teacher, Maria S. He was in an especially good mood – in two weeks time he was going to play in a Steinway competition. He had a good chance of winning. He was putting in four hours' practice a day. He felt especially sure of himself on this particular afternoon. Punctual as always, he rang Maria S.'s doorbell at 3.30 p.m. She took a long time to come down and open up. As far as Peter can remember, she was dressed in something long, light and low-cut. It reminded him of old oil-paintings. But then her clothes had always been different – not like his mother's. Peter had thought the difference had something to do with his teacher's piano playing – her musical bent. *But this afternoon everything was different. Maria S. seemed in no hurry to open the piano. Instead she asked him about strange books he'd never heard of, and about his girlfriend. He remembers her menacing laugh when he said he didn't have one. Then everything happened very quickly. The boy stood rigid with fear. She whispered things in his ear, words he'd never heard before. She groped inside his clothes, he said. The* **Sun** *asks: What will be the effect of all this on a boy as young as Peter?*

Who is Maria S.? A single woman – she's lived alone since her mother died. We visited her sister. She told us she didn't think Maria had ever been out of the ordinary. 'She might not have been averse to party-going or having a good time – but she never went in for sexual adventures.' Teacher Maria was dedicated to her job right from the start, she said. Even as a schoolgirl, her greatest joy was helping less able children to catch up with class work. When she told us the story of Maria's childhood, her sister realized that the children she'd shown an interest in had always been much younger. Maria had never had boyfriends or girlfriends of the same age. She added heatedly, 'But that's not the point. Maria just enjoyed teaching things to little children.'

All this might be perfectly harmless – but didn't teacher Maria take her enthusiasm a bit far in Peter's case? What was it she was trying to 'teach' him? A first lesson in love? Isn't there good reason to suppose that Ms S. (she still looks attractive, but she's no longer a young girl) was unhappy because she had no boyfriend? We must leave it to the psychologists to establish the real reasons for what she did. According to official police statements, Ms S. is now suffering from shock. On the advice of her GP, she's been taken into mental hospital for observation. Peter's parents may be suffering themselves, but they still feel sorry for her. 'We just feel so helpless,' they told us. 'We can't see how children can possibly be protected from this kind of danger.' As far as they're concerned, they did everything that was humanly possible – and still the unthinkable happened. 'Maria S. must be a very sick woman' – these were Hetty H.'s last words to us as we left her house.

Can it be that this story has started to go 'over the top'? Before writing it, we asked ourselves where the seduction of a young boy by a woman who is a good deal older might actually take place today. It seemed to us that the seduction had to involve a relationship of dependence in a place where such relationships are taken for granted; this was how we arrived at the realm of teacher-pupil relations. We then attempted systematically to establish what questions were more likely to be seen to require explanation in such a case. For example, the fact that a sexually mature young boy has 'as yet' had no sexual experience is just as likely to provoke questions as the possibility of his 'already' having sexual experience. In the latter case, interest might perhaps focus on 'how far he has gone' in the past. Nothing is assumed as a 'matter of fact'; the seduction of a young boy, like any other event, will always be linked to social meanings which refer to events and actions in the past and/or the future. Rewriting the above story from the standpoint of a newspaper's legal correspondent thus produces a whole new range of associations:

Report by a Legal Correspondent

The verdict in the case of Maria S. has always been a foregone conclusion: the law leaves little room for doubt. The accused was charged with 'indecent assault on a minor'; all that had now to be decided was how severe her punishment should be. But there seemed to be a problem in court yesterday. The judge spent a long time discussing the case with the jury. Was it really the boy's welfare which was at stake, and not Maria's, he asked. In the final court hearing, the main issue had been the defence of the boy. For both him and the woman, a neutral psychiatric expert had been called in. At the start of yesterday's proceedings, both parties were cross-examined (for the umpteenth time) on the details of the case. White-faced Peter looked withdrawn and defiant. The slim lad sat with his head slightly bowed – a picture of loneliness. No trace here of the friendly, understanding and helpful fifteen-year-old he once was.

What exactly is it that his teacher found irresistible about him? Could Peter be called attractive? Perhaps it was his body, or his shy good looks. The situation, or her desire. In court, she stayed stubbornly silent. She seemed unwilling – or unable – to say much about the incident. Time and again, we saw Peter casting brief glances in her direction – had he perhaps fallen in love with the woman who raped him? Or will he develop a lifelong hatred of women?

It was then the turn of the counsel for the defence – a woman – to take the floor. She went back over the facts of the case. She said the boy had come to the woman's house for a neutral reason – a piano lesson. She asked, 'Was there any difference between this day and any other?' Apparently not. The court, she said, was dealing with a fifteen-year-old who was completely without sexual experience. The consequences of this psychic trauma for him were as yet unforeseeable. Previous statements in court had clearly established that sex had taken place. Though the boy's body had shown no traces of violence, he had certainly attempted to resist.

It was now the psychiatrist's turn to give a detailed account of the boy's childhood. 'Peter comes from a stable family background,' he said. Until a few years ago, his relationship with his mother was especially close. They often joined forces against his father, who was strict with him. The psychiatrist said there had been no marked peculiarities in Peter's sexual development to date, with the possible exception of his obvious tendency to 'sublimate his drives' in art. So says the psychologist – but what exactly does he mean? We think it unlikely that he could possibly know the problems and emotions of a young boy. Will the report be of any practical use to Peter?

The case continued. The accused, Maria S., had come to court formally dressed. She looked somewhat severe, calm and composed, and showed hardly a trace of emotion. She refused to appear in the witness box. The circumstances of the case were outlined by the defence counsel, who claimed Maria's actions hadn't been deliberate. She said the incident with the young boy had happened spontaneously. Maria had lost her self-control. 'My client's state of shock is an indication of how heavily the burden of guilt weighs on her.' The defence pleaded for acquittal. Once again, the life history was enlightening. Ms S. was the middle daughter in a family of three sisters. Her father died when she was twelve. Her mother was often out of the house. For the children, their relationship with their grandmother was particularly important. At school, Maria's performance was more or less average. She often found herself in conflict with other girls. Her teachers didn't notice her artistic talent until relatively late. Maria then began to work long and hard at the piano. She began studying music and sport. As far as her sexual development is concerned, it's clear she had no close contact with the opposite sex until quite late on. Her love affairs have always been short-lived. None of them has led to marriage.

The defence counsel concluded by saying that the whole of Ms S's adult behaviour had been determined by the isolation forced upon her by the loss of her father, and by her female-dominated childhood, which taught her an attitude of defiance and defensiveness. But psychologists cannot perceive any diminished responsibility in Maria.

Both sides of the case have now been heard. Sentence has been passed. The defendant has been found guilty, and the penalty is a fine. But what, we want to know, are the long-term consequences of this kind of case? Does anyone care what now happens to these two victims of such unhappy circumstances – anyone, that is, except Ms S. and her pupil Peter?

Lessons from the History of Eroticism

This reworking of traditional narratives – if done collectively – is not only illuminating; it is also fun. It becomes particularly productive in discussions of the changes which occur in the shift from a past discourse to one located in the present. Since it is impossible to establish the nature of that shift by examining its product (the new story) alone, we find ourselves directed towards new avenues of research. For example, one thing which the work of transcription made clear to us was the solidity of the connection between sexuality and other human relations, the difficulty of considering sexuality in isolation.

In the first instance, the collective was necessary as a corrective; it was only with the help of the group as a whole that we were able to find ways of questioning our own day-to-day assumptions. Secondly, no one could ever envisage all the possible conceptions of 'reality' by sitting at a writing-desk. In our discussions of Hermaphroditus, for example, one woman delivered a vehement defence of the argument that 'all older women desire very young boys' – by which she meant not all, but ninety percent of women (a group from which she excluded herself). What became apparent in group discussion was that our way of reading the Ovid story was to extract what we considered its 'essentials' on a first hearing. We became involved with the narrative via empathy – in this case with Salmacis. She felt desire for a fifteen-year-old boy; could we experience desires that were similar? In the end, our enlightened *laissez-faire* attitude led us to assess the narrative purely in terms of how 'true-to-life' we had found it; the fact that the problem posed by Ovid was a different one, relatively remote from our own concerns, was left undiscussed.

The Relocation of the Problem.

The narrative complication in Ovid's story is the arousal of desire by the beauty of a young boy – a desire which seeks satisfaction. Ovid is then confronted with the question of the obstacles that arise, and the possible means of overcoming them. The relation between desire and beauty is assumed as a matter of course. In very broad terms, the complications which initiate this and similar traditional narratives are external ones; in other words, what determines whether or not the goals are attained is the configuration of relationships and not, as in contemporary discourse, the 'inner state' of the characters. When a character in love asks how he or she may win the affection of another, it is assumed from the outset that love is a possibility. In the contemporary context, the story becomes quite different: she (an older woman) desires a young boy (age, it is assumed, must be stated as a means of evaluating the appropriateness – or otherwise – of that desire). The first question is, 'Why does she love him?' Might we perhaps be dealing with a woman of 'perverse tendencies'? How is it that the action was uncontrollable? Who was behaving recklessly? Further problems are posed by the fact that it is 'sexual pleasure' which is being sought. In the older story, sexual pleasure is assumed to bring happiness as a matter of course; thus it is taken for granted that the naiad should strive to experience that pleasure. In the transcription, pleasure has been relocated within the individual. Pleasure is not assumed to be 'normal', for human relationships have changed.

Changes in Human Relationships

For any individual today, 'pleasure' can only be pursued within the framework of hunter and victim. Our discourse is pervaded by references to the duo of the seducer and the seduced: to men (less often women) who seduce and violate innocence, who exploit opportunities and force someone to comply with their wishes. Our attention is focused on individuals seen in isolation from the conditions in which they live. Those conditions take concrete form only through human beings, with their poverty-stricken or wealthy childhoods, their mother-father relationships, the present jobs they have – or don't have. What is demanded of the individual is an inner triumph over the surrounding conditions. Individuals are left to come to terms on their own with those conditions. It is not social conditions which are held responsible for individual failure or success, competence or incompetence; what is seen as decisive is the way the individual can adjust his or her response to them.

When any new relationship is embarked on, the question always posed is that of its future goal. The experience of pleasure is not seen to represent an appropriate goal – or rather, if it is presented as such, then it is negatively sanctioned. If, as in our story above, it is 'impossible' from the start that the two characters will ever become a 'couple', or indeed where such a union is never striven for in the first place, the bond between them is considered shameful. If, however, the question of whether they intend to *become* a couple can be answered in the affirmative, then further points present themselves for clarification. Are they capable of the union? Can he provide for her? Can they offer security to prospective children? In each case, all forms and practices which cannot be organised within the available discourse are set apart and distinguished from, reflected upon and annexed by the monogamous, heterosexual couple or marriage.

In the narratives of the ancients, sexual pleasure is taken for granted; in a contemporary context, it appears in the form of 'knowledge' and 'technique'. Pleasure has become something exceptional and depends on a 'skill'.[42] The young boy in our story is said to be still 'ignorant' of sex; as a result, he struggles neither to attain pleasure nor to suppress it. Innocence and pleasure are placed in opposing camps; they know nothing of each other. Within our sexual ordering, there is a value judgement involved in detailing the ages of characters in a love story: they are said to be young, or too young, no longer young, too old, not as young as they were (but still attractive), and so on. It is assumed that the role played by 'sexuality' is, and should be, confined to certain clearly defined life stages. Thus the fact that puberty now begins increasingly early is taken as the reason for the increase in 'juvenile sex'. Biological sexual maturity is the point at which 'sexuality' begins; in women, the menopause marks its end. (Even the special issue of the feminist magazine *Courage* on menstruation works entirely within the terms of this ordering.) Female rebellion against the prevailing sexual ordering has often been couched in terms of claims that sexuality can be proven to operate after the point at which it is said to have died. Yet in making such claims, women are accepting an ordering in which sex and age stand in a fixed relation (a negative one, in our story). In so doing they preserve the old association whereby sex is made the fulcrum, the standard against which the whole of their lives is measured.

Agencies of Welfare and Control

Within our sexual ordering, relationships never 'simply' consist in two people being together; what is involved instead is a whole tangle of relationships which in explicit, implicit or unspoken ways, fulfil various functions of mutual aid, protection and control. In order to *explain* the innocence of the young boy in our story, and the potential perversity of his teacher, it was necessary to bring into play a number of different agencies and individuals: the school, parents, friends (for whom it would have been possible to substitute 'neighbours'), relatives, the police, the family doctor, the institution of psychiatry. There were detailed questions to consider: what were the living conditions of the individuals under discussion? Where were the welfare agencies and agencies of social control at the time of the assault? Could they have been neglecting their duty? Was there any evidence of their part in the affair? There seemed to be cracks across the surface of control; between those cracks, sex was taking place – or at least, the potential for sex was given. And the most difficult question of all: who was to bear the consequences, who could be made responsible – and what unforeseen consequences might arise in future? Would the boy perhaps become homosexual? Or incapable of love?

We exist today in a patriarchal ordering of the sexual, within which women appear overwhelmingly as 'victims' (the objects of seduction) or as objects over which a man, though he may not have the legal *right* to do so, assumes control (for example in rape). In the Ovid poem quoted above, the question of gender never arises in relation to desire. Love and desire are seen as connected to beauty, a quality which may be attributed to either sex. Today, on the other hand, beauty is articulated essentially in association with women; a male youth may be known to be a 'pretty boy', yet the very term arouses suspicions that he may be homosexual. (We have therefore to investigate all the articulations of gender which participate in the organization of women's lives as a single, biological supra-historical and unquestionable 'truth'.)

Up to this point, relations of class have been wholly absent from our considerations; yet these too are built into the ordering of the sexual, playing a part in the operation and reproduction of discourses. The specificities of class are woven into the fabric of patriarchal discourse through the operation of State agencies which, as in our case study above, are brought to bear on the experiences of individuals. Transcription, we believe, has potential as a cultural practice in which utility and enjoyment might coincide. Let us begin with a list of constructive questions and results intended to encourage other groups or individuals to venture on similar work, despite its difficulties.

1) What is the complication in the traditional narrative?
2) What is the nature of the human relationships within it? What events does it relate?
3) Where might it take place today (place or institution)?
4) Who might the contemporary characters be? (Details of name, age and profession.)
5) What position might those individuals occupy within family relations and what is the significance of those relations?
6) What sort of behaviour is expected of them? (This is how to establish 'deviance'.)
7) What is the nature of their connection? (Who is the seducer, who the object of seduction?)
8) What institutions are brought into play (offering warnings, protection, control etc.)?

Programmatic summary of our results:

1) The complication is relocated.
2) Everyday life loses its self-evident aspect.
3) The contrived nature of our everyday perceptions becomes open to scrutiny; insights are gained into processes of control.
4) The prurient and suggestive nature of our language is revealed. . . . . . .
5) . . . . . . as is the alacrity with which we make associations.

QUEEN OUTWITS INTRUDER

It was not without vigorous disagreement that the reworking of Ovid represented by our transcription of his text into a tabloid tragedy, played out between piano teacher and pupil, could be produced. One subject of extreme controversy in the group was whether the construction of contemporary newspaper discourse does in fact demand that age should always be stated, that connections be made between incident and social background, or indeed that parents, relatives and so on should figure in newspaper reports on adult crimes. The day after this disagreement two women read out a new transcription to us. It was the story of a break-in to the Queen's bedchamber. The group felt it to be in some ways relatively successful, but in the end still too exaggerated. The tabloid press, we felt, was not as bad as this. Many a guess was ventured as to the original – was it Ovid? Boccaccio? Balzac? To our immense astonishment, the piece was the original text. We would have been hard pressed to obtain better assistance, or a more explicit vindication of our earlier work of transcription. For the reader's benefit, we have therefore reprinted one episode of an extended series on the Queen's intruder here. The story was handled in a similar way by a number of newspapers, and we can reconstruct in minute detail the elements which are linked together to constitute the ordering of sexual control – age, personal history, marital status, parental details and so on; we can also perceive the unspoken inferences that leave us to make our own associations. Having once constructed our own transcriptions, we were able to view these newspaper articles through the eyes of a quite distant yet knowing observer. Hence there is one further reason for women to try their hand at transposing traditional narratives into a contemporary context. For in so doing we learn, once and for all, not only the simple *fact* that articles in the daily papers are 'made', but also *how* they become constructions of an order which at every turn demands controls and standardization, voyeurism, and the conversion of social problems into the building blocks from which 'sexuality' is made.

Translation of text from *Bild*, 13.7.82

BLOODSTAINED HANDS OF MAN AT QUEEN'S BEDSIDE

'I was in love with the Queen. . . .'

Horrifying new facts have come to light in the case of the man found sitting at the Queen's bedside at 4.30 a.m. only a few mornings ago. His hands were drenched in blood – he had tried to slash his wrists.

Queen:
Mann am Bett
hatte blutige Hände

Er liebt die Königin

Neue ungeheuerliche Einzelheiten über den Mann, der morgens um halb fünf am Bett der Queen saß: Seine Hände waren voller Blut – er hatte versucht, sich die Pulsadern aufzuschneiden. Wollte Michael Fagan (Foto oben) aus Liebe neben der Queen sterben? Jetzt wurde enthüllt: Der Mann war eine halbe Stunde bei der Queen. Lesen Sie weiter auf Seite 8.

From *Bild*, 13.7.82

Einbrecher 12mal bei Freundin Elizabeth"

FORTSETZUNG VON SEITE 1

Es muß ein Schock für die 56jährige Königin gewesen sein, als sie aufwachte: Blut rann von den Händen des Einbrechers Michael Fagan, breitete sich auf ihrem weißen Bettbezug aus. Und dann hielt er auch noch den zerbrochenen Aschenbecher in den blutigen Händen.

Die Queen sah ein blasses Gesicht. Mit zitternder Stimme sagte sie: „Ein Whisky wird Ihnen guttun", drückte auf einen Alarmknopf, aber der klingelte nicht. Peinlich! Die Queen ging in den Salon neben ihrem Schlafzimmer, nahm aus einem viktorianischen Schrank eine Kristallkaraffe und goß Whisky in ein geschliffenes Glas. Fast eine halbe Stunde redete sie mit dem Mann. Dann kam ein Diener auf den Gang, nahm den Einbrecher fest. Da war das Blut seiner Hände schon getrocknet.

Wie BILD berichtete, war der arbeitslose Fagan an einer Regenrinne in den ersten Stock des Buckingham-Palastes geklettert.

Könnte ein Einbrecher auch zu Loki kommen?

Könnte nachts auch ein Einbrecher auf dem Bett von Loki Schmidt oder Veronica Carstens sitzen – wie bei der Queen? Ein Sicherheitsbeamter: „Das ist kaum denkbar."

Das Kanzleramt ist von einem 3 Meter hohen Stahlgitterzaun umgeben, auf dem elektrische Warnanlagen installiert sind. Er wird mit Fernsehkameras überwacht. Tag und Nacht patrouillieren Grenzschutzbeamte mit Maschinenpistolen und abgerichteten Schäferhunden.

Auch das private Reihenhaus der Schmidts in Hamburg-Langenhorn ist gut gesichert: Schußsichere Scheiben, meterhohe Stahlzäune, Grenzschutzbeamte rund um die Uhr, ständig Leibwächter im Haus.

Genauso werden Bundespräsident Carstens und seine Frau Veronica bewacht.

„Er hat die Königin geliebt", erklären Fagans Vater Michael (51) und seine Mutter Ivy (50).

„Er ist öfter über Nacht weggeblieben und hat uns erklärt: Ich war bei meiner Freundin Elizabeth. Sie ist ein bißchen älter als ich und hat vier Kinder, genau wie ich. Sie wohnt in einer feinen Gegend, in S.W. 1." Das ist die Postadresse des Palastes. Zwölfmal soll Fagan im Palast gewesen sein.

Erst vor einem Monat war er wieder mit seiner Frau Christine (38) zusammengezogen (von der er sich ein Jahr vorher getrennt hatte). Sie lebten in einem Armen-Wohnheim, in zwei Zimmern mit Toilette auf dem Gang. Für die Kinder zwischen drei und 16 Jahren teilten sie das eine Zimmer ab. Ein Nachbar: „Er war verzweifelt über das bißchen Arbeitslosengeld, 250 Mark die Woche für acht Personen. Er hat gesagt: Darüber muß ich mit meiner Königin reden. Die kann helfen."

Auf dem Weg zu ihrem Ehemann Michael Fagan im Londoner Brixton-Gefängnis: Christine Fagan (38)

From *Bild*, 13.7.82

Did Michael Fagan (photo above) hope to die at the bedside of his beloved Queen? The latest revelation: he spent a whole half-hour with the Queen. Full story on page 8.

Twelfth visit by palace intruder to 'my girlfriend Elizabeth'

It must have been quite a shock for the 56-year-old Queen to wake up and see blood from the hands of Michael Fagan, her nighttime intruder, spreading across her white bedclothes. When she saw him, he was still holding the broken ashtray in his bloodstained hands.

The Queen could see a pale face in front of her. 'A whisky would make you feel better', she said, trembling with fear. She pressed the alarm bell – but nothing happened! How very awkward! The Queen went into the salon next to her bedroom, took a crystal decanter from the Victorian sideboard and poured out a whisky into a cut-glass tumbler. She carried on talking to Fagan for almost half an hour. . .until he was finally caught by a servant coming down the corridor. By this time, the blood on his hands was dry.

Bild readers already know how the unemployed Fagan climbed up the drainpipe to reach the first floor of Buckingham Palace.

He really loved the Queen, say Fagan's father Michael (51) and his mother Ivy (50).

'He's often stayed out the night and told us he was with his girlfriend Elizabeth. He used to say, "She's a bit older than me, with four children, just like me. She lives on the posh side of town, S.W.1".'

As recently as a month ago, Fagan moved back in with his 38-year-old wife Christine. They'd been separated for a year. They occupied two rooms with a toilet outside in the corridor. The youngest child was three, the eldest 16. A neighbour told us: 'Having to keep eight people on the miserable amount he got from the dole made him desperate. He said he had to talk about it to the Queen – she'd be able to help.'

(Inset): LOKI IN DANGER FROM INTRUDERS?

Are our own Loki Schmidt or Veronika Carstens in danger of

waking up to find an intruder sitting on the bed? It happened to the Queen of England! A security officer states, 'It's almost inconceivable'.

The chancellery is surrounded by a 10-foot steel wire fence with a built-in electric warning system. It's guarded with TV cameras. Police patrol the fence day and night with machine guns and specially trained alsatians.

There is tight security at the Schmidt's private mews residence in the Hamburg suburb of Langenhorn: bullet-proofed windows, high steel wire fences, twenty-four-hour police patrols, round-the-clock bodyguards inside the house.

FEDERAL PRESIDENT CARSTENS AND HIS WIFE VERONIKA ARE JUST AS CLOSELY GUARDED.

The Church and Sexuality

Long before Karel Wojtyla became Pope, his lectures from the years 1958 and 1959 were widely known to an international audience. They appeared in book form in Poland in 1960 and 1962, in London and Paris in 1965, in Madrid and Turin in 1969, and in Germany as late as 1979 and 1980. In one sense, the ethical doctrine of love he expounded in them merely confirmed a number of long-standing ideas about the Church. At the same time, however, Wojtyla's procedure was remarkably modern, revealing him as capable of a quite conscious and sophisticated implementation of a policy of alliances. In the course of the lectures, the hopes and experiences of human beings are woven into a tightly-knit ideological 'network', which makes a totalizing claim on the social being and on his or her actions and behaviour. In our discussion of the lectures we hope to reveal both the workings of their ideological practice and a whole system of relations and interconnections against whose background the partial nature of Wojtyla's occasional manifestations of liberal sexual enlightenment can be better appreciated.

It would be singularly misguided to judge the book only by its more notorious aspects: the explicit commandments and prohibitions it makes. To do so would simply blind us to its ideological effectivity. We should, however, mention briefly the book's 'conclusions' at this point, so that their full severity is not lost in our discussion of Wojtyla's ingenious work of articulation. As a matter of principle, Wojtyla states that sexual love is only to take place within marriage; marriage is for life; abortion is of course forbidden and contraception too is regarded as immoral, or rather, immorality is seen to reside in any sexual intercourse where there is no wish for a child; here, continence is the order of the day.

How can a work which presents such conclusions be considered 'modern'? The answer lies in Wojtyla's approach. It seems to us that his main achievement is to have bound up

231

physical, sexual enjoyment with love – instead of denying 'the flesh' – at the cost of applying ethical categories to sexuality and love. By tracing the way he makes his connections, we hope to identify both the supports on which they are founded and points of resistance to them.

Wojtyla's method, which we have described in terms of a policy of alliances, can be perceived in its most characteristic form in the following quotation from his book. 'Aristotle and St. Thomas Aquinas. . . both emphasize that in relation to the sensual and emotional sphere of one's inner life, one must employ appropriate tactics and even a certain diplomacy. Commands are of little avail here and may even produce the very opposite of what was intended. This view attests to practical experience. Everyone must effectively deploy the energies latent in his sensual and emotional life, so that they become allies in his striving for authentic love, for they may also be its foes. This ability to make allies of potential foes is perhaps an even more decisive characteristic of self-mastery and the virtue of chastity than is pure continence.'[1]

The key category around which Wojtyla's book is organized is that of the *person*. The term functions wherever necessary as a point of interconnection; or it takes effect as an agency of hierarchization wherever value-judgements are being made. In the end, it is through his skilful use of this category that Wojtyla is able to 'make allies of foes'. In fact, it becomes clear in the end that the whole of Wojtyla's sexual ethics is constructed on the basis of this category. The key to Wojtyla's works is a knowledge of what he understands by the term 'person'.

The Person

If we are to understand the notion of the 'person', says Wojtyla, we must understand the categories of subject and object. It is objects (or entities) which make up the world. It is important to take objects as a point of departure, even though the concept object presupposes that of subject and implies a relation between the two. In Wojtyla's view, if we begin with the subject, we run the risk of considering the world of objects 'in a purely subjective way', of judging it, in other words, only from lived experience as it enters the consciousness, instead of perceiving that something 'is objective'. His term for the acceptance of an objective world is 'realism'.

In the realm of objective entities, Wojtyla distinguishes between 'somebody' and 'something' (between persons and things). This first distinction between objects and subjects provides the basis for a subsequent limiting and devaluation of the merely subjective in favour of the objective. Drawing a second distinction between objective things and persons, Wojtyla concludes that a thing has no reason, no life. An animal or a plant is certainly not a thing, but it is also not a person. Who, after all, would speak of an animal as a person? One might distinguish animals as individuals, 'but it is not enough to define a man as an individual of the species Homo. The term "person" has been coined to signify that a man cannot wholly be contained within the concept "individual member of a species", and that there is something more to him, a particular richness and perfection which can only be brought out by the use of the word "person".'[2]

What establishes a person as such is the faculty of reason; conceptual thinking marks out the person as distinct in the world of objective entities. As a subject, the person is distinguished by his inner self. Since cognition and desire are spiritual in nature, they form a genuine interior life: 'Inner life means spiritual life. It revolves around truth and goodness.'[3]

Wojtyla recognizes two human 'functions' or natural tendencies: cognition and aspiration (or desire). These are demonstrably present in what we would call the relationship between human beings and the world. Wojtyla writes: 'A person is an objective entity that as a definite subject has the closest contacts with the whole external world and has fundamental roots in that world because of its inwardness, its interior life.'[4] God is mentioned more or less in passing. The author merely adds that a human being is also in contact with God. The fact that human beings have bodies allows them, like animals, to establish sensual contact with the world. Yet since it is through the inner self that human relationships with the world are entered into, we may conclude, says Wojtyla, that sensual contact is not the 'characteristic way' for human beings to communicate with the world. The human species attains its specificity only in the sphere of inner life. It follows that in their whole relationship with the world and with reality, human beings will attempt to assert themselves, their 'I', to realize the nature of their being. Wojtyla therefore considers it important to specify the whole range of elements which make up human nature. Foremost among these are *self-determination* and *free will*. In the exercise of free will, a person – the human being as a person – becomes his or her own master (a term which in our linguistic usage, as in Wojtyla's, implies that he or she cannot be made into an object). It is upon self-determination and free will that 'all human co-existence rests. Education and culture originate in this principle.'[5]

Since within sexuality other persons continually become the objects of actions, it is important to know who is acting and what rules they are obeying. That knowledge, says Wojtyla, is the starting point for the development of a sexual morality. In what follows, we shall be able to observe how Wojtyla's adoption of this particular starting-point allows him to formulate a complete social order in such a way that sexual practices become integral to it, rather than being encoded in the sort of bizarre hieroglyphics we encounter in books on 'liberated sexuality'. It will also become evident that the 'person' he takes as a starting-point is the private individual in a society based on free enterprise. Along the route chosen by Wojtyla, there are only two possible points of entry into society: either through contractual relations or via morality. Since the subsequent links in Wojtyla's chain of reasoning can be deduced with ease, we shall summarize them only very briefly.

The Subject-Object Problem

In actions, activities or modes of behaviour that are directed towards others, human beings are liable, writes Wojtyla, to treat these others as means to an end (this is his interpretation of the word *uti*). Since viewing a person as the means to an end does violence to their very nature, it poses an ethical problem – a problem that concerns relationships between men and women, commanding officers and ordinary soldiers, employers and employees, and parents and children. To treat someone as a means to an end runs counter to 'the natural moral order'.[6] The remedy to the problem is love, which Wojtyla defines as a conscious joining together with others in pursuit of good: 'If we go on to seek a positive solution to this problem, we begin to discern or at least to glimpse love as the only alternative to using a person as the means to an end, or the instrument of one's actions. Obviously, I may want another person to desire the same good as I do. Obviously the other must know this end of mine, acknowledge it to be good and adopt it. If this happens, a special bond is established between me and this other person: the bond of a common aim and hence a *common good*. This special bond does not merely mean that we seek a common good together, it also unites the persons involved internally, and so constitutes the core of all love.'[7]

There are formulations in Critical Psychology which are almost identical to the above. Here, however, the formulation begins with the person, love being then added as a source of energy, whereas Critical Psychology begins with the social third term which determines the person. Having taken the person as his starting-point, Wojtyla can present the aforementioned entrepreneur as transcending exploitation through love, without abandoning production (or its concomitant, surplus value). 'Inherent in the employer-employee relation is the danger that the employee may be treated as a mere instrument: various defective labour relations are evidence of this. If, however, the employer and the employee so arrange their association that the common good which both serve becomes clearly visible, then *the danger of treating a person as something less than he really is* will be reduced and gradually disappear.'[8]

In marital relations, says Wojtyla, the common good is 'the child, the family.'[9]

Love and Pleasure

What Wojtyla hits upon in his quest for the power of love are the 'emotional-affective elements'[10] of human activity. The forms which the emotions may take in his scheme range from physical satisfaction or a feeling of contentment to a great and profound joy. The battlefield is determined by this tripartite division. Since the distinction between these three forms is a mental one, we can assume that thought will also regulate and determine our choice between the three. Our emotions are chosen of our own free will; they are self-determined. Neither good or bad in themselves, the emotions are seen as raw material, as energies which potentially underlie total joy, or physical satisfaction or a feeling of contentment.

Wojtyla identifies these three forms of emotions as forms of pleasure. Since human beings are persons and are conscious of being so, they always perceive others as persons; thus pleasure must be see as a moral problem. In Wojtyla's view, the question of pleasure raises a problem which always arises in relation to human sensual and emotional impulses, namely that of how to regulate it. His reasoning is quite straightforward: to use another person for one's own enjoyment or lust is to make that person into an object. It is therefore necessary to subordinate pleasure to love.

The same hypothesis runs through Wojtyla's subsequent critique of utilitarianism, a philosophy which he sees as reducing the human being to a being that strives exclusively after enjoyment. Against this, he maintains (knowing himself to be at one with Kant here) not only that enjoyment is incidental to the human being, but that taking it as an end in itself runs counter to human nature.[11] To avoid souring the experience of love for his readers, Wojtyla is forced to bring into play a number of links and connotations to bolster his simple line of theoretical reasoning. He places the pursuit of pleasure in the same camp as the instrumental use of persons and connects it with notions of selfishness, with the necessity of a compromise or contract whose harmony is a contrived one. In the opposing camp stands love, which he sees as genuine and transsubjective; it is nurtured by altruism. For Wojtyla, true love aspires to the happiness of many.

On this basis, Wojtyla concludes that pleasure is only subjectively good, whereas the common good is objectively good, and it is the foundation of love. 'It is clear that if utilitarian principles are followed, a subjective understanding of the good (equating the good with the pleasurable) leads directly to egoism, though there may be no conscious intention of this. The only escape from this otherwise inevitable egoism is by recognizing beyond any purely subjective good, i.e. beyond pleasure, an *objective good*, which can also unite persons – and thereby acquire the characteristics of a common good. This is the authentic foundation of love, and individual persons, who jointly choose a common good, are also subordinating themselves to it. They thus become united through a true, objective bond of love, which enables them to liberate themselves from subjectivism and from the egoism which it inevitably conceals. *Love is the unification of persons.*'[12]

For Wojtyla, the logical conclusion of utilitarianism and egoism is that by treating others only as means and instruments for one's own pleasure, the individual comes to regard himself in the same light. In opposition to utilitarianism, love is presented as a commandment that can be derived from the fact of personhood, and hence from a personalistic norm. 'This norm, in its negative aspect, states that the person is a good which does not admit of use and cannot be treated as an object of pleasure and as the means to an end. In its positive form the personalistic norm states that *the person is so exalted a good that love is the only proper and valid attitude towards it.* This is what the commandment to love teaches.'[13]

As we have indicated, Wojtyla's ethical system does not proceed by issuing commandments and prohibitions, but through rearticulations and reorderings of existing systems. This is the source of its effectiveness, for what is demanded is not that the pleasures or desires of the flesh be renounced, but that they be built into and successfully asserted within the ethical contexts he outlines. Thus it is not on grounds of falsity that he rejects the principles of utilitarianism; instead, he contends, 'Morality goes beyond utility (which is all that the utilitarian principle recognizes) – although it does not deny but only subordinates utility: in dealings with another person, everything that is useful and convenient is contained in the commandment to love.'[14] One of the elements which should be related to love, both mentally and emotionally, is *justice*. What is just is what is proper. And in the context of persons, the only proper stance towards others is love. 'Love is a requirement of justice, just as using a person as a means to an end would conflict with justice. In fact, the order of justice is in a way more fundamental than the order of love – and the first embraces the second inasmuch as love can be a requirement of justice.'[15]

For Wojtyla, justice concerns itself primarily with things as they relate to persons. Thus justice and love – and their bond via the person – lay the foundations for sexual morality. From this starting-point, it is simple to define deviance; between a man and a woman, it lies in seeking after pleasure for its own sake. But for Wojtyla to be able to proceed from his notion of personal love to sexual continence or lifelong marriage with children, a further rearticulation is necessary: a rearticulation of the sexual urge which integrates it within his new discursive order.

The Sexual Urge and Love

In discussing the sexual urge, Wojtyla first refutes notions of the human being as a slave to the sexual drive and therefore incapable of self-determination (a line of thinking which, he claims, can be clearly identified in any number of textbooks on sex, though his own references are largely to Freud). The second target of his attack is the notion (which he identifies as puritanical) that the sexual drive is evil and hence to be combated.

Once again, his aim is to *integrate* sexuality and make positive use of it as a buttress to his ethics. In his view, the sexual drive is a source of energy. Unlike the egoistic instinct of self-preservation, it transcends individual subjects; it is directed towards others as a source of energy for love. 'The sexual urge in this context is *a natural, innate form of human endeavour* whereby man develops and perfects himself.'[16] Since the sexual urge concerns the whole man, it converges with freedom and free will at the point where human beings take responsibility for their actions.[17] Wojtyla does not consider desire to be morally wrong in itself; what would be wrong would be the subordination of the will to desire.

In Wojtyla's scheme of things, any human being who is neither sick nor deviant has a natural predilection for the opposite sex, since man and woman are complementary. He now turns to consider the values attributed to gender (the view of masculinity as powerful and femininity as gentle) and explains the functioning of these values as an effect of the existence of the sexual drive. Because sex, he says, does not exist in the abstract, but only in the whole person, it is towards a person that the sexual urge is directed 'in the natural course of events.'[18] In this way the drive can become a basis for love: 'Always, then, the sexual urge in a human being is naturally directed towards another human being – this is the normal form which it takes. If it is merely directed towards the sexual attributes this must be recognized as an impoverishment or mishandling of the urge. If it is directed towards the sexual attributes of a person of the same sex, we speak of a homosexual deviation. It is even more of an anomaly if the urge is directed not towards the sexual attributes of a human being but towards those of an animal. The natural direction of the sexual urge is towards a human being of the other sex and not merely towards "the other sex". Since it is directed towards a human being, the sexual urge can provide the basis on which the possibility of love arises.'[19]

Here the sexual drive is connected with a love that is antithetical to mere pleasure and also connected with marriage, or at least with the relationship between man and woman. Love secures the connection between the drive, freedom and responsibility: 'The sexual urge can transcend the determinism of the biological order by an act of love. For this very reason, manifestations of the sexual urge in man must be evaluated on the plane of love, and any act which originates from it is an object of responsibility, especially the responsibility for love.'[20]

The Sexual Urge and Society

'Since the urge is a universal human attribute, one must constantly reckon with it in the relations and co-existence of the sexes. They coexist within the framework of social life. Man is at once a social being and a sexual being. It follows that the rules governing the co-existence and association of persons of opposite sex are part of the general code regulating the life of human beings in society. The social aspects of sexual ethics must be given no less weight than the individual aspect. Living in a society we are continually concerned with the various forms of existence of the two sexes and for this reason ethics must put these relationships on a level consonant both with the dignity of human persons and with the common good of society. Human life is in fact "co-educational" in many sectors.'[21]

The above is the only passage in Wojtyla's book to offer a comprehensive account of society as a whole. This general overview allows him to attach notions of the dignity of persons, and of the common good, to the links he has already made between love, the person, responsibility, self-determination, freedom and inner life. These definitions also allow him to refer back from society and the sphere of the common good to a sexuality which he carefully treats as a question of ethics, since 'one must constantly reckon with it.' After all, he claims, the sexual urge is the force behind both what is good and what is deviant. Hence, by logical extension, he calls the subsequent chapter, 'The Sexual Urge and Existence'. Here he argues that, since the sex-drive produces certain natural results, it necessarily determines man's species-existence. Yet up to this point, he has viewed love between persons as a matter of free will, not necessity. Love as the purpose of the sexual urge cannot be the factor which defines and determines that urge. Hence he proposes that the sexual urge, which transcends individuals, be seen as safeguarding existence. The particular context which Wojtyla thus constructs leads him to describe existence as 'the first and basic good for every creature.'[22] Thus, the sex-drive takes on existential significance! In a concluding philosophical overview, he delivers the following pronouncements on the sexual urge and sexual ethics. 'If the sexual urge has a merely biological significance, it can be regarded as something to be used. We can agree that it is an object for man to enjoy just like any other object of nature, animate or inanimate. But if the sexual urge has an existential character, if it is bound up with the very existence of the human person – that first and most basic good – then it must be subject to the principles which are binding in respect of the person. Hence, although the sexual urge is there for man to use, it must never be used in the absence of, or, worse still, in a way which contradicts, love for the person. On no account can one assert that the sexual urge, which has its own predetermined purpose in man independent of his will and self-determination, is inferior to the person and inferior to love.'[23]

It is not, therefore, on a sexual drive relegated to lower spheres that Wojtyla seeks to base his moral system, but, on the contrary, on a drive elevated as a fundamental force to the level of existential significance. Its integration into morality is achieved through the ascription of the property of personhood to the human being – a property which, as we have seen, entails self-determination, free will, an inner life and, by extension, a potential responsiveness in the individual to demands not to offend against his or her nature.

Sexuality and Children

Having begun from a starting-point which accords existential significance to the sexual urge, Wojtyla has no difficulty in arriving at a conclusion which involves married love and children. 'This is altogether the (species-specific, KH, FH) character of conjugal love between two persons, a man and a woman, who have consciously taken the decision to participate in the whole natural order of existence, to further the existence of the species *homo*. Looked at more closely and concretely, these two persons, the man and the woman, facilitate the existence of another person, their own child, blood of their blood, and flesh of their flesh. This person is at once an affirmation and a continuation of their love. The natural order of human existence is not in conflict with love between persons, but in strict harmony with it.'[24]

Here as in previous sections, Wojtyla adopts a hierarchic scheme. Rather than presenting God as the sole creator and human beings merely as his vessels, he represents parents as participants in Creation. To the flesh – the body of the person – which parents bring into the world, God adds the spirit. 'They can therefore look upon themselves as rational co-creators of a new human being. That new human being is a person. The parents take part in the genesis of a person. A person, is, of course, not merely an organism. A human body is the body of a person because it is united in substance with the human spirit.'[25]

The human ability both to participate in creation and to receive further powers leads Wojtyla to accord to parents the main task of educating and perfecting the person-as-child. 'It is here that the full productive power of love between parents is concentrated, in the work of rearing new persons. This is its proper end, its natural orientation . . . all that exists by nature in the human being to be educated is material for the educators, material which their love must find and mould.'[26]

Here once again Wojtyla uses the concepts 'material' and 'moulding' in conjunction with the concept of the 'person'. Both the guiding principles of the moulding process and the ultimate forms achieved are, he says, to be developed from the notion of the person. Together they constitute the tools of a new ethics which derives its efficacy, not from the exclusion of one or more of the forces in play, but from their mutual integration.

In the process, these forces are transformed. Let us look again at Wojtyla's three orders. There is the natural order (in this case the essence of human beings), the biological order with its goal of procreation (this is distinct from, but frequently confused with the natural order, since it is here that natural phenomena take empirically verifiable form) and the divine order. For Wojtyla the divine order is at once a natural and an existential order. The biological order is also a natural order, but it lacks any connection with the Creator (the connection between God and the person). Wojtyla argues that to see the sexual urge only in biological terms is to fail to recognize its connection to God. Here he rounds on the puritans within his own ranks. 'The sexual urge owes its great objective importance to its connection with the divine work of creation.'[27] This readily leads to his opposition to test-tube babies and contraception.

A Desire that has no Object

'A man therefore does well when he uses a woman as the indispensable means of obtaining posterity. The use of a person for the objective end of procreation is the very essence of marriage. Such a use is intrinsically good. Mere enjoyment, on the other hand – seeking voluptuous pleasure in intercourse – is wrong. Although an essential part of use in the first sense, it is an intrinsically impure element, a necessary evil in its own way.

That evil must, however, be tolerated, since there is no means of eliminating it.'[28]

Against what he calls this 'necessary evil', Wojtyla posits a sexual ethics based on a pleasure that has no object of desire. 'The problem for ethics is how to enjoy sexual pleasure without treating the person as an object of pleasure.'[29] To portray persons as merely seeking after pleasure – as Freud did – is, for Wojtyla, to argue from the subjectivist viewpoint of an experience conceived in terms of stimulus and response. From this perspective, he says, man appears as egocentric rather than alterocentric. In Wojtyla's discursive ordering, by contrast, responsibility is posited as an essential category; the human being is held liable for the use s/he makes of her/his sexual drive. In a concluding proposition, he demands of human beings that they *behave objectively*,[30] by which he means that neither can they regard the three goals of marriage – procreation, mutual support and the appeasement of desire – in isolation from one another, nor can any one of these goals become a guiding principle for their behaviour. All three are transformed by love.

A Metaphysical Analysis of Love

Love is seen by Wojtyla as a relationship which aligns itself with the good. It has as its main elements attraction, goodwill and virtue. Let us observe how Wojtyla expounds true love through those elements; his method once again proceeds through the mutual integration of elements to produce acquiescence.

Turning first to attraction, Wojtyla argues that a perception of something as pleasing implies that it is apprehended as a good. As a sense impression, attraction is seen to derive from the sexual urge and, at the same time, to be closely related to intellectual knowledge and to extra-cognitive factors. A commitment to a person can be 'effected only by the will.'[31] Wojtyla makes a connection between one's striving after perfection and what one finds pleasing about other human beings. Thus for him, attraction is directed to a particular *value of the person*; it is here, he suggests, that love begins. But if the value of the person is to play any role at all, it is necessary to perceive persons *as they truly are*. 'Hence in the mutual attraction between man and woman the truth about the value of the person to whom one is attracted is a basic and decisive factor.'[32] This is how Wojtyla explains the deceptiveness or unreliability of *emotional* attraction – attraction based on subjective experience, on feelings, rather than on the objective truth of the person. By expounding attraction in this way, he allows it to represent the core of love and at the same time presents our subjective desirings as sanctioned positively. There now remains the problem of why precisely those subjective desirings should become suspect in our eyes.

Wojtyla's answer is that 'attraction goes very closely together with an awareness of values.'[33] Although we may apprehend a number of different values in another person, only the value which elicits the strongest response is decisive. For an attraction to be proven to be true, it must be ascertained whether it is the person as such who is loved, or mere 'partial values'. It is, says Wojtyla, the value-character of personhood which allows its most unfathomable qualities to be identified as elements within ordered systems, which then function as signposts, pointing the emotions along a responsible path. Wojtyla's ultimate goal is an integral or *integrated* love, which incorporates all human impulses. Or rather, human beings can achieve this act of integration. Of the beauty of the person, for example, Wojtyla says: 'The attraction on which this love is based must originate not just in visible and physical beauty, but also in a full and deep appreciation of the beauty of the person.'[34] A further example is a relationship that constitutes one facet of love, namely the relationship between love and desire. The existence of the two is evidence that persons are not sufficient unto themselves, and that their sexual nature defines them as incomplete; they are limited, but strive to transcend their limitations. The decisive distinction is between 'desire-as-such' and 'love-as-desire'. 'A man may, for instance, desire a woman as an apparent means for the satisfaction of desire, just as food serves to satisfy hunger.'[35] 'Love-as-desire' is defined by contrast as 'a genuine love . . . in which the true essence of love is realized – a love which is directed to a genuine (not merely an apparent) good in the true way, the way appropriate to the nature of that good.'[36]

Finally, Wojtyla talks of a reciprocal and altruistic 'love-as-goodwill' which has moral significance. 'In any case, it is clear that love is by its very nature not unilateral but bilateral, something 'between' persons, something social. Fully realized, it is essentially an interpersonal, not an individual matter. It is a force which joins and unites; its nature rejects division and isolation. For love to be complete, the route from man to woman and the route from woman to man must converge. Mutual love creates the immediate basis on which a single being can arise from two 'I's.'[37]

Sympathy and Friendship

Wojtyla is not content simply to expound love within marriage. All the other possible human associations are worked into his discursive ordering, or rather assigned a particular status and coherence within it. He begins by breaking down the word sympathy and reassembling it to produce a notion of 'feeling together'. The term 'feeling' implies a connection with the emotional life and with experience; yet we already know that experience is not determined by the will. Indeed, the will may be unconsciously captured by the pull of emotions and sensations. From this Wojtyla deduces that 'sympathy is love at a purely emotional stage, at which no decision of the will, no act of choice, as yet plays its part. At most the will merely consents to sympathy and the direction it takes.'[38]

For Wojtyla, the weakness of sympathy lies in its lack of objectivity. Sympathy, he contends, is subjectively intense, a subjective expression of love. 'Mere intellectual recognition of another person's worth, however whole-hearted, is not love (any more than it is attraction, as we said at the beginning of this chapter). Only sympathy has the power to bring people palpably close to each other. Love is an experience, not just the result of reflection. Sympathy brings people close together, into each other's sphere, so that each is aware of the other's whole personality, while also discovering that person in his own sphere. For this reason, sympathy is that very important thing in relations between men and women, an empirical and provable token of love.'[39]

By association, Wojtyla links the deceptive side of subjective experience, its lack of objectivity, to the fallacies of love. 'As soon as sympathy breaks down, it is usually assumed that love has also come to an end. Yet sympathy is not by any means the whole of love, any more than moods and emotions are the whole of a human being's inner life.'[40] There is also the will, which moulds human beings. As far as the relationship between love and sympathy is concerned, Wojtyla argues that 'a deeper, far more important element is the will, in which the power to mould love in a human being and between people is vested.'[41]

At this point, he introduces the concept of comradeship. Unlike sympathy, comradeship does not rest on subjective foundations but on working together, sharing common goals and interests. Though the goodwill which characterizes friendship is not yet present within comradeship, it does provide a sound basis for marriage, since it represents an objective common interest. 'This is why comradeship may be very important for the development of love between a man and a woman, if their love is to ripen into marriage and become the cornerstone of a new family. People capable of creating and living in a milieu of their own are undoubtedly well-equipped to impart the character of a closely-knit group to the family, and to create a good atmosphere for family life.'[42]

Lastly, Wojtyla turns to the paradox of betrothed love. It derives from the nature of betrothed love as both a giving of devotion to another, and the giving away of oneself. 'Betrothed love can never be a fortuitous or minor event in the inner life of the person. It always constitutes a special crystallization of the whole human "I", determined because of its love to dispose of itself in this particular way. In giving ourselves we have compelling proof that we possess ourselves.'[43] Betrothed love concerns both partners and this creates a basis for the impossibility of adultery. 'When a woman gives herself to a man, as she does in matrimony, this – morally speaking – precludes a simultaneous gift of herself to others in the same way.'[44]

Conclusion

Here we shall break off our analysis of Wojtyla's work and summarize the specific methods by which he articulates processes and events to produce acquiescence and subjugation. Wojtyla deals in concepts of supremacy. 'It is the knowledge of this truth that awakens the need for the integration of sexual love, and demands that the *sensual and emotional reaction* to a human being of the other sex *be raised to the level of the person.*'[45] All qualities of experience are admissible; in their non-integrated form, however, they reveal themselves to be truncated and merely subjective, bypassing what objectively defines the specificity of the species – the person. It is to the category of 'person' that Wojtyla accords the task of achieving integration.

Wojtyla conceives the domain of love and sexuality as a battle-field. It is so in a dual sense: firstly as a field upon which individuals do battle and, secondly, as a field on which he himself fights as he imposes an ethical order upon it. His weapons are rearticulation, repositioning, structural analyses, the definition of certain elements as raw materials and others as moulding those materials, and so on. His work of ordering is total, and his own choice of words and concepts reveals that he is making associations and connections. Thus he says, 'sexual values, which in various forms constitute the catalyst of sensual and emotional eroticism, must be connected in the individual consciousness and will with the attitude adopted to the value of the person who provides the content, as it were, of those erotic experiences.'[46]

Such familiar values as abstinence, chastity and virtue are not advocated by Wojtyla as absolute, unargued values; they arise out of his analysis of values and of human attitudes to them. He presents his system as the conclusion of an argument, not as an hypothesis. And the conclusion which his analysis of values produces is the necessity of their objectification. His argument has come full circle; with the objectification of the value of the person, the value takes precedence over all other values.

The Anti-Ideological Struggle: A Contribution to Liberation

What is the point of analyses of the kind presented here? What purpose do they or could they serve? We began by asking ourselves at what point Wojtyla intervenes in concrete life and figures as one of the organizing ideologues in whose nets our actions are entangled.

Throughout this volume, we have been dealing with systems with which we are familiarizing ourselves because of their emergence as social structures and material practices. Catholic social morality pervades our thoughts and our actions; it is present throughout everyday life. Wojtyla's work represents a theological doctrine that has learnt from Marxism, that has digested the experiences of a socialist country. Locating its reality and the mode of its construction seems to us to offer a useful means of working against it, a contribution to the struggle against ideology, and a first step on the road towards greater self-determination. Our perception and grasp of any discursive ordering allows us to live our lives more consciously, or rather – extending an earlier metaphor – to escape the entanglements of ideologies which we might otherwise have taken to be the world in its entirety, and to examine that net as a set of discursive links. Hence, we can recognize a potential for new and different connections, to be made by our own activity and 'from below'. We may then re-make our connections, working them into an ordering in which self-determination is possible.

Women and Bodies

A critical review of some texts from the women's movement.

Preliminary Remarks

The central focus of the following review will be the book 'Unser Koïper–Unser Leben' (*Our Bodies–Ourselves*). 75,000 copies of the work have been printed in the German-speaking world since April 1980. According to the American feminist philosopher Londa Schiebinger, the book's publication sparked off a wide-ranging new movement amongst women. They demanded information from doctors, formed self-examination groups and got together to talk about health problems, abortion and childbirth. The book has helped many women overcome their ignorance and anxiety about bodily processes. Its authors even came into conflict with the State. Some of them had set up self-examination groups, and were prosecuted for having 'practised as non-qualified doctors without a licence.'[1]

The first question we asked ourselves in group discussions of our unease in relation both to this book, and to the others we shall be looking at, was what advice we might substitute for the advice they offered. Since all these books clearly were and are useful to women, it seemed to us that we were being hyper-critical. But the conclusion we reached in many of our discussions was that it was nøt the individual propositions that caused us disquiet, but the way the material was 'ordered'. The notion of 'ordering' allowed us to see the individual propositions put forward as more than answers to isolated individual problems. The various recommendations are connected by a notion of the very much more general goals towards which they are directed. Thus Reitz, for example, links together a number of her proposals under the heading of 'self-determination'.[2] What came to interest us was the set of connections through which different proposals were formed into a whole life-view, grounded in and at the same time productive of a particular world-picture.

At this point we began to ask ourselves what kind of life a woman would lead, were she to follow the advice provided.

What sort of self-determination would she be wrestling to achieve? What insights would she gain into her place in society, her oppression and the possibilities of liberation? What we had to bear in mind was that the ordering is more than the sum of its elements. It is quite possible for the same or similar proposals to appear in different contexts, to be associated with different goals, or to be given a weighting which communicates a different conception of life, a different world-view.

A Body Gained

'By learning to understand, accept and be responsible for our physical selves, we rid ourselves of many fears and obstacles and can start to make better use of our untapped energies.'[3]

'At last we see ourselves as we are and can thereby become better lovers, better *people*, more self-confident, more autonomous, stronger.'[4]

'It has given us fresh room for manoeuvre in our lives. This includes the freedom to make one's own decisions.'[5]

'My hope for this book is that it will help us to rid ourselves of our negative streaks, so that we can enjoy the change of life, instead of fearing it.'[6]

In our study of the texts cited above, the first thing that became clear was that they use the body as a starting-point for much more ambitious goals of liberation. They are concerned with *freedom* and *self-determination*, with *self-confidence* and *autonomy*, with *enjoyment* and with becoming *better people, better lovers*.

This discursive linking of the body with such general goals as freedom and self-determination makes unfreedom and heteronomy appear the causes of a false relation to the body. The body is seen as the focus of oppression – and thus as also a potential focus of liberation. In our project on the body, we attempted to work out how, in developing a relationship to our bodies, we work our way into and shore up the social order. These women authors propose that we struggle against oppression; what forms is that oppression seen to take?

Women's Suffering

The authors describe a number of fears that women share: fear of menstruation or the change of life, or a sense that lack of knowledge places women at the mercy of doctors. 'As we discussed our experiences with one another, we realized just how much we had to learn about our bodies.'[7] The authors see women's suffering as stemming from social conceptions of femininity, and from the determination of women's value by others. 'We discovered notions of femininity which we had in some sense shared: woman as inferior, woman as passive, woman as beautiful object, woman as wife and mother.'[8] 'We expect everyone else to be the final judge of how well we have displayed our "pluses" and minimized our "minuses".'[9]

Viewing oppression in this way produces its own particular way of viewing liberation: knowledge is seen as the antidote to ignorance, new 'values' as the remedy for false conceptions of femininity. No longer are our 'pluses' and 'minuses' to be determined by others: we are to determine our own value 'by ourselves', to decide our lives 'for ourselves'.

Liberation, then, means reversal. Certainly this idea contains an insight into the ways in which we reproduce patterns of domination within existing social forms; yet it presents those forms as the effect of prohibitions. In our section of Foucault, we discussed his notion of power as working not simply through prohibition, but also 'positively' for the creation of new forms. In criticizing social conceptions of femininity, the authors of *Our Bodies – Ourselves* implicitly endorse Foucault's argument for the 'positivity' of power: for what they are resisting is the *production* of particular orientations in our lives. For them, the problem is not one of being *denied access* to femininity, or of femininity being *suppressed*. Yet repeatedly in the books we looked at, it was women's *oppression* that we were exhorted to resist. And in general, that resistance was to consist in doing the opposite of whatever was regarded as prohibited.

My contention about the elements and proposals within these books is that they are ordered according to a *logic of contraries*. The ways in which this ordering is produced will be examined in greater detail below. What I hope the following analysis will also reveal is the *type* of autonomy and self-confidence contained, either implicitly or explicitly, in these writings.

Forms of Liberation

Knowledge

One of the forms of oppression discussed in these books is the withholding from women of knowledge about their own bodies. Thus substantial sections are devoted to the presentation of medical information about the body (relating essentially to the sexual organs and hormones). Although there are occasional accounts of the healing powers of herbs and other natural substances, the majority of the books discussed here reproduce information from orthodox medicine. Female ailments are described at some length, as are the appropriate methods of treatment, various methods of abortion, and what occurs in the body during orgasm. Doctors are certainly criticized for not giving women sufficient information about the causes of their illness and the course it is likely to take; they are reproached, too, for their over-eagerness to operate or to hand out drugs on prescription. But despite the criticism, the conventional wisdom (in other words, the orthodox view of health and sickness) is allowed to stand.

In medicine, the human body is treated as a physio-chemical system with a specific set of reactions that function independently of the individual's social context. The sociologist Boltanski has given an account of the various disciplines that examine the body in an article entitled 'The Social Uses of the Body'. He makes the following criticism of the categories with which each of these disciplines attempts to comprehend the body. 'Since they (the categories – NR) are based on the practical necessity of mastering the body in particular situations, each of the various problem definitions of these special disciplines tends to reduce the body as a whole to a single sector or a single dimension. For the nutritionist, it is a thermic machine, for the ergonomic scientist, a system of levers, and for the doctor and psychiatrist an involuntary transmitter of symptoms and signals.'[10]

The same criticism can be applied to medical science, which reduces the body to a defective stimulus-response system.[11] A wholesale adoption of medical concepts and definitions has definite consequences for the image of humanity – or the image of women – which they convey. Those consequences are particularly evident in the 'Sexuality' chapter of *Our Bodies_ Ourselves*. Here the body is treated from an essentially functionalist point of view as a system that either achieves or does not achieve orgasm. Old age, youth, or the differences between women and men are all considered in terms of the capacity for sexual arousal. The subsequent chapter discusses various forms of living arrangements, including communes, marriage and living alone. The separation of the two chapters and the absence of cross-referencing between them produce an impression of sexuality as something entirely divorced from living arrangements; it is seen as reducible to the manipulation of particular parts of the body.

But what of the woman who achieves orgasm – having been properly 'handled' – and yet remains unhappy, perhaps out of dissatisfaction with her marriage or communal living situation? In their compartmentalizations of women's lives, the authors reiterate the reductive view of the body that is taken by the medical profession, among others. It does not suffice to accumulate information. However useful that information may be, it carries with it the dominant conception of ourselves as the dominated. If liberating forms of thought and action are to be possible, it will be necessary to transform the very concepts through which knowledge becomes accessible.

One of the further misdeeds of orthodox medicine is reproduced by Rosetta Reitz in her calls and recommendations for healthy living. Her claim that 'yoghurt too is especially good for the skin' is delivered with no further attempt at explanation.[12] What difference is there between her statement and one which tells me that medicine X is 'good for me'? In neither case is the assertion substantiated. If we follow our women authors, we are simply exchanging our old faith in doctors for a new faith in an author whom we are supposed to believe because, as a woman, she is on our side. But is it really *faith* that is necessary? How are we to achieve self-determination if we have no way of verifying information? It is not primarily ignorance that shackles us (though it certainly plays a role). Power relations exist within knowledge itself, in its apparently incontrovertible status, the supposed objectivity with which it is presented, the respect which we confer on it and our refusal to allow of any doubts. In all these forms, knowledge is connected with power, and we are subjugated to the latter. If, however, we question our previous knowledge, we can begin to see the mechanisms to which Boltanski referred. We have a potential for new knowledge through which we can recognize the set of connections that will be of importance to our liberation.

Domination through Language

In all these books, we are advised time and again to talk about everything. 'For most of us it is difficult to be open about sexuality. . . .We urge all women to discuss sexual feelings with friends and in small women's groups. Here we can free ourselves of sexual inhibition and misinformation by educating and supporting each other. In the process we will learn to express our sexuality and communicate it to others.'[13]

It is true that there can be no liberation without discussion. In talking, the problems become clearer, or at least it becomes clear that they are unclear, and at what points they become so. But the converse thesis, namely that we can 'free ourselves of sexual inhibition'[14] by talking, is unsatisfactory; it overlooks the treacherousness of language. Some of what this constitutes has been mentioned already in our chapter on memory-work: the occasions when words fail us, when the words to express our emotions and feelings are not readily available. We have seen language functioning as a straitjacket, with cliches that force us into pre-ordained worlds of feeling; we have seen, too, how the abstraction of even everyday language prevents us from grasping the diversity of actions and their consequences. There may be no liberation without discussion; but in talking we also confirm our subjection. It is through language that we are socialized, that we fit in with the social order. The authors we have looked at demand that we talk about 'sexuality'. In so doing, they have already consented to the construction of an object known as sexuality, and thus to the strategies of power which it contains.[15] Discussion belongs to two opposing camps; it stands on the side of subjection as well as liberation. If we are to use speech as an instrument of liberation, then we must understand how we bring about our subjection through particular forms of speech, or how we use particular words to cement our subjugation.

The Interpretation of a Community of Women

In these books for women, one use of language struck me particularly forcefully: the almost universal use of 'we'. After a hundred pages, sentences like the following began to annoy me: 'We began to look at each other differently. We rediscovered a common bond that allowed us to stop judging ourselves and other women by men's standards. We tried to stop competing with one another. We worked to respect our emotions and to support each other's strengths. We learned to take each other seriously.'[16] Or this: 'Of course, some men will not face this involvement and either leave us or withdraw emotionally. This is when we have to turn to a friend or counsellor for all our support.'[17]

Why do I find this irritating? Surely one of the strengths of the women's movement is its use of 'we' as a means to combat the isolation of women? It is a figure of speech in which women learn to recognize their private problems as more general. Indeed the group to which I belong often uses the 'we' form in its books. In an attempt to get to the bottom of my irritation, I set about comparing different styles of writing.

'We all grew up with these assumptions. People outside our families were defined as "outsiders". We expected to be part of a couple and part of our own families when we grew up. We might be single women and do exciting things for a while, but that would be just a breathing space before marriage.'[18] Reading a text of this kind, I am immediately aware of the temptation to agree. It is written as though it were reporting processes that every woman has experienced in the same way. What is presented does not seem to be an interpretation of reality, but reality itself. Yet that reality which the majority of us have supposedly experienced is only an interpretation. The above quotation couches its account of childhood in the concepts of external limitation: it talks of expectations, assumptions, exclusion.[19] Since this interpretation conforms to the experience of most women, they will acquiesce in it spontaneously without recognizing its *specificity*. Through the use of 'we', the authors together with their readers form an interpretation of a community which will be taken for an actual community. This spontaneous acquiescence provides the basis for a false mutuality – false in the sense that the readers who become part of this community have made no conscious decision to join it. Whether she likes it or not, every reader ends up 'belonging', since in the course of the book, almost every possible experience that women may have as women is treated in the same way.

Interpretations of reality are presented unquestioningly, as reality itself; similarly, proposals for change have the semblance of sole and ultimate truths. 'By jointly reliving the experiences of our own adolescence, we can help our children to grow up differently, with healthier feelings about their bodies and their sexuality.'[20] But what makes a feeling healthy? What is sexuality? What does it mean to relive our own experiences? *Why* should this be helpful to our children? And what general significance does family upbringing have in the development of feelings about our bodies and the formation of a domain of sexuality? There is a degree of personal effort involved in asking questions such as these, simply because the passage is written in such a way as to suggest that the answers lie in experiences we all share. And yet the standpoint from which it is written is not – as the use of 'we' leads us to believe – that of a subjective account of sexuality. Instead, what is established is a set of relations which appear to have the objective validity of a universal law. This becomes clear if the sentence is rewritten without the personal-sounding 'we'. 'By jointly reliving the experiences of their own adolescence, adults can help their children to grow up differently, with healthier feelings about their bodies and their sexuality.' Presumably, anyone who distrusts simple causal connections will immediately question a statement of this kind. The same person might, on the other hand, have concurred in the preceding formulation which, since it presented itself as immediate experience, could not be suspected of representing any particular theory or world-view.

I found a similar instance of the use of 'we' in the book immediately preceding this volume, *Frauenformen I*. 'There was a time when we were quick to express irritation with homosexuals. We found the way they acted towards each other more or less absurd; it was not what we expected of men. . . .We are more enlightened these days; we consider ourselves progressive. It is no longer the behaviour of homosexuals that we find irritating, but the people who are still irritated by it.'[21] Here too a 'we'-community is being constructed. It embraces all those who have held or still hold certain opinions. Those opinions are, however, presented as just that; they are not served up as immediate experiences.

In the second example, as in the first, the reader spontaneously assents to the text, since it presents familiar ways of thinking with which she is in agreement. There is, however, the difference that here assent is produced only in order to throw it into crisis. In the remainder of the passage, the thinking *about women* contained in an 'enlightened' attitude to homosexuals is used to undermine the reader's assent. It is argued that in accepting the behaviour of some male homosexuals as part of the everyday run of things, we are overlooking the insights that can be gleaned from the strangeness feminine behaviour assumes when adopted by men. The point is not that 'effeminacy' in men is ridiculous in itself, but that 'what we have become used to accepting as feminine is in fact inhumane.'[22]

To return to the first example: it was not the use of the 'we' in itself which annoyed me, but the fact of being drawn into an interpretation of a community which failed to identify itself as such. More annoyingly still, the 'we' had the effect of cementing me into experiences presented to me in the same old ways, the ways I had always thought about them and suffered from them. Quite unexpectedly, I found myself participating in a community of suffering which told me things I already knew. What I was being offered was precisely the kind of knowledge that had failed to bring about my liberation.

This conflation of experiences and interpretations into a unifying 'we' implies also that our experiences are determined exclusively by gender. It takes no account of our different lives and experiences, originating in different social locations – allegiances of class, for example. It ignores our disputes over different conceptions of our paths and goals. If we present ourselves simply as 'we women', then all these differences – which might teach us a great deal – disappear.

In writing this book, we ourselves have occasionally used a 'we' that demands the reader's assent. (The reader should beware of the points at which we have overlooked and failed to correct this error.) The device is tempting, since recourse to the evidence of experiences we have 'all' supposedly had releases us from the need for careful argument. This is not to say that the technique may not be legitimate. Many women writers begin as we do with experiences, in an attempt to theorize and to learn from them. And indeed, what is there to be said against reminding our readers that they are likely to have had experiences similar to ours? The process whereby we work with experiences, theorize them, and formulate proposals must, however, be brought out into the open. If we are scrupulous in presenting the different levels of our analysis, the 'we'–device can indeed have its uses. In making clear who is speaking, and from what standpoint, it strips the statements we make of the semblance of objectivity which scientific language has traditionally lent them.

Individualization

Responsibility

All the books we looked at reflected contradictory conceptions of the relationship between the individual and society. 'Since we ourselves are stamped by the prevailing conditions, we find it difficult to criticize and to change them, for this means questioning of our previous thinking.'[23] Since our own thought is couched in the categories of the dominant order, it should be clear that a critique of prevailing conditions should question our previous ways of thinking.[24] Yet how can this be possible, if we see ourselves as 'stamped' by these conditions, and thus as passive victims of an alien process? No further consideration is given to this problem in *Our Bodies-Ourselves*; yet elsewhere in the book, it is asserted that 'we' might become different, despite the 'stamp' we bear. 'We can acquire knowledge about our bodies. . .and begin to take responsibility for them.'[25] At first glance, this too appears self-evident. In the past, it has not been women themselves, but fathers, husbands and brothers who have determined women's lives. Now at last women are to rise up and assume responsibility for themselves. But responsibility is a dangerous concept; the call to assume responsibility for one's own life implies that the conditions of one's life are determined by the individual.

We have been hearing more and more of such concepts as the 'personal responsibility *of the individual*' since the CDU-CSU-FDP coalition came to power in West Germany. As ministers, these publicly-elected representatives of the State administer the public purse, control the building and equipping of hospitals, schools and universities; in the last resort, they can use force to ensure that laws and decrees are obeyed. Yet these are the people who are calling on every individual to feel responsibility for her or his own life. It is a call that isolates us. Their power derives in part from our feelings of responsibility. Our scope for action as individuals is limited; they see to it that it stays that way. If we act on the basis that individuals as individuals are autonomous and responsible, we are also accepting the notion of prescribed areas of competence for which various different individuals are solely responsible. Production, for example, will be the proper realm of the entrepreneur, since it is his means of production that are being used. High-quality work, on the other hand, is the responsibility of the worker, since this is what she is paid for.

The women's writings apply the concept of responsibility to health. And the way they present it, this responsibility could be impervious to the social agencies on which health depends. The above paradox might then be explained thus: a woman is responsible for herself, yet she bears the 'stamp' of a society whose structures are outside her field of action. Only after transcending this dualism, by regarding the whole of society as something produced by our own actions (though not with conscious intent), can we ask why we should not set ourselves the production of society as a conscious objective. Does this not mean simply extending our range of responsibilities? This was certainly how Brecht saw the issue. 'What I am not to blame for troubles me very little, but the unhappiness for which I am to blame depresses me. Indeed I consider myself responsible for many more things than are usually laid at someone's door. Illnesses and even wars cause me to reflect on what wrongs I may have committed.'[26]

For individuals to live out responsibility this way would be to carry it, in the sense in which the State agencies and institutions require it, to absurdity. If, for example, individuals were made to feel responsible for war, they would have to involve themselves in the business of the State. To redefine responsibility is to explode existing constraints on action. Thus we are no longer saying that women can assume responsibility for their bodies, but that by so doing, they will be demanding 'responsibility' for the health system.

For Ourselves

In being invoked as a responsible person, the individual is both elevated and constrained. She is entrusted with the task of taking care of herself and at the same time thrown back on her own resources. 'Responsibility' for society as a whole is held from her. These books all devote a good deal of space to advising us to 'think of yourself'. Yet the first thing we encounter 'within ourselves' is a set of interests we have learned to regard as ours in the long process of becoming women.

A special issue of the feminist magazine *Courage*, on ageing, includes a discussion of the body and beauty. One woman defends herself against the charge of having submitted to the conventional norms of beauty. 'When I am at home on my own, I make myself up to look ravishingly beautiful. . .when I pass the mirror in the hall, I grin at myself and take pleasure in how good I look. There's no one else there to see me; I do it for myself.'[27]

The absence of other people gives no clue as to whether the criteria by which this woman defines herself as beautiful correspond to the social norms she things she is escaping. The fact that she is alone in front of the mirror does not necessarily prevent her from seeing herself through the eyes of others, or from imagining another man or woman whom she will please. And yet her 'for myself' does contain an element of revolt against heteronomy, against the slavishness that women are called upon to adopt. On the other hand, it is possible to see everything one does as being 'for oneself'. A woman who obeys all the rules of beauty-care, subjects herself to the most exhausting slimming routines and forces her feet into shoes a size too small will probably say she is doing it for herself; it is fun for her to know she is pleasing to others.

Is it perhaps that women separate the things they do 'for myself' into actions performed for a self-related purpose, and those that involve giving themselves away to a stranger? If so, the future might lie in pursuing the autonomous purpose, the 'for me' rather than the 'for others'. But we would question the idea that actions performed wholly for the self allow women to escape heteronomy altogether, or that heteronomy, on the other hand, is manifested independently. They occur as one within the other; thus the unambiguous claims made above are impossible. We need to discern what bestows meaning within heteronomy in general, and how it might be made to work for self-determination.

The Group

The Failure to Remember

Books on women's health groups demand that women discuss their problems, exchange their experiences and thus find some kind of resolution. In Reitz's book, the groups are based on one particular experience common to all women: the change of life. The term is claimed to designate a biological fact; but what actual biological occurrence is there to justify the term 'change'? The only tangible thing seems to be the fact that women can bear no more children. Even the timing of the menopause is not determined by biological law; in recent decades, its onset has come increasingly later. What women suffer from is not biologically conditioned infertility, but the social meaning it carries. The objective of the groups is therefore to develop their own positive meanings to set against this one. In the attempt, however, the groups themselves become embroiled anew in the dominant value system. The main topics of discussion are slimming treatments, body care, sexuality. Thus the groups become involved in reproducing the conditions under which the social meaning of the menopause, as a time of bodily decline, holds sway.

I was particularly astonished in this respect by the special issue of *Courage* referred to above. Out of forty-eight pages, two-and-a-half deal with the political activities of the editorial group. The remainder consists of discussions of the family (10 pages), sexuality (7), the body (5), housing (4), pensions (3), dying (3), leisure time (2), sickness and health (2), competing for men (2), work (2), and education (1). The sequence clearly represents an order of precedence and reflects the significance these individual domains traditionally have in women's lives. The discussion of the group's activities is prefaced by the comment: 'Reading the transcript of the tapes, we discovered that a substantial statement about ourselves was lacking. Our political past and present were absent. Without this however, only a very incomplete picture of our group can be given.'[28] There follows a brief description of the women's political past, together with one sentence relating to the present: 'We work in trade unions, public campaigns and other progressive movements.'[29] At the end of the issue, there is a one-and-a-half page account of the group's activities between 1979 and 1981.[30] But how, I asked myself, could a group of politically active women calling themselves the 'Age Offensive' have simply 'forgotten' this part of their lives? In the first instance, of course, it can be interpreted as 'typically feminine'. Women are not brought up to invest their emotions in political activities. They direct their love towards their families, to children, to everything that goes to make up a 'woman's life'. Yet the women writing here are already living differently. They must have developed some motivation for doing so; but they say nothing of what this might be. Up to this point, I had always considered changes on the level of action to be significant, and assumed them to have been preceded or at least closely followed by reflection. I was therefore astonished to find that women with such a broad range of experience and political activities still seemed obsessed with the Sisyphean task of cultivating an immaculate body. How intense this tribulation over bodily decay must be if it still occupies the centre of these women's lives.

It seems that even groups are unable to eradicate women's isolation; always thrown back on themselves, women continue to place their concern about the body at the centre of their lives. Perhaps this is one reason why the *Courage* women were unable to bring themselves to live together, even though they no longer had families.

Regimented resistance

Despite what we have said above, much that is new goes on in the groups. In *Our Bodies–Ourselves*, the suggestion that we form ourselves into groups occurs under the heading, 'Talking together about sex.'[31] The phrase reminds me of similar ones from my childhood: 'It's time we had a serious word with each other', 'Come on, cough it up', 'You don't have to hide anything from me'. What was invariably required was a confession of some kind.

The word 'together' indicates a relationship between supposed equals. It also occurs within revolutionary groups: 'Together we are strong'. It is equally at home in the mouth of the priest: 'Let us pray together. . .' The statement may be articulated either 'from above' or 'from below'. If we accept Foucault's analysis of how sexuality arose via the various customs according to which it was discussed, pursued and practised, then this new way of speaking about it may be seen as constituting a new 'sexuality' and new personalities. But what would be the effect if I were to form a group with women in which we talked about sexuality in the manner suggested, going over 'childhood and adolescent memories of sexuality', 'masturbation', 'sexual fantasies', 'our sexual responses', 'virginity', 'relations between women', 'love-making', 'intercourse', 'orgasm', 'feelings about touching and looking at our bodies'? A group in which we kept 'personal journals and read them out to one another; made a collage of sex comics or cuttings from advertisements at the beginning of a meeting, saw a porno film together or visited a sex shop'?[32] In a group of this kind, I believe, we would discover that the things we keep secret are part of every woman's daily life. We would form a new community of women in the know. Each one of us would know the character of the others' sex lives; dislikes and pre-ferences would attach to one's knowledge of each woman's secret fantasies. The fantasies of some would be quite out-landish; others would simply have none. But we could not leave it at that. Fantasies would have to be teased out of these other women, manufactured if necessary. We would indeed be dis-covering the 'truth' about ourselves; a truth that would be pro-duced and mutually confirmed by the group. The group would function through mutual surveillance, to form personalities defined via sexuality: she's the one with fantasy X, favourite position Y and childhood Z.

Since sexuality as a separate domain would be the sole object of the group's study, the new identities that arose would coalesce around sexual behaviour and sexual preferences. If there is already a tendency for us to 'sexualize' things, words and forms of behaviour in our everyday life, in other words to reduce them to a single sexual meaning (every long object becoming a phallic symbol, every opening a symbol for the vagina), the same practice would merely be perfected in a group of this nature. Every childhood memory would be turned into a memory of sexuality. Speaking, writing, even going to the cinema would be primarily subservient to the search for 'sexuality'. Yet a practice which does not ask how what we call sexuality arises, but simply strives to recover its traces all around us, would be joining in the game of 'tracking down sex', the hunt for the 'truth' of sex which we discussed in the chapter on sexuality and power. Although these women may be partially freeing themselves through their practice from the institutions within which sexuality has been hitherto construed (marriage, the medical profession, the church), they have a long way to go before they achieve liberation.

Intimacy with Nature and the Alien Character of Society

The Myth of Original Unity

In the texts we have looked at, the authors link the body – or, more precisely, its naturalness – with freedom, self-determination, self-confidence and autonomy. The yearning for self-determination and self-confidence finds expression as a return to nature and as a critique of society in general – a fact which indicates the extent of the adversity suffered under prevailing forms of alienated socialization.

The orientation towards nature is formulated as a response to the destructive consequences of existing methods of its exploitation. What is lamented is a distancing from nature, the destruction of an original unity: '. . .then sexuality may become again what perhaps it once was, a powerful feeling of *connectedness* with other human beings and with *nature*.'[33] Anna Tune speaks of women never having lost their 'original intimacy with what is fundamentally physical'.[34] Certainly it is true that the men and women of previous centuries were in closer contact with nature. Their work had more immediate effects on nature; there was less 'secondary nature' – nature formed by human beings around them, less intervening machinery. We are now aware of the knowledge of nature that women in particular used to possess, such as their expertise with medicinal herbs. Today, by comparison, most women know little or nothing about the nature on which their lives depend. They buy food pre-packed, some of it in powdered form or deep-frozen.

I doubt, however, if proximity to nature can be adequately described by words like connectedness and intimacy. In the past, both men and women were much more at the mercy of nature; infant mortality was high, storms could destroy great tracts of land at a stroke, and men were worn out more rapidly by work that was closer to nature. There was danger in this relationship of intimacy; to be connected to nature was also to be at its mercy. Before nature can be thought of as pleasurable, one must cease to spend one's whole life in the exhausting exploitation of it. It must be the case that in our part of the globe, nature contains little of the threat it once did. Only yesterday (17.12.1982) an earthquake killed two thousand people in Africa in the space of forty seconds, and left another twenty-five thousand homeless. Paradoxically, then, 'distancing' from nature, a lesser degree of exposure to it, is a precondition of pleasurable intimacy with it. Whatever the extent to which individual nations' knowledge of nature has expanded or decreased, our knowledge is greater in global terms. The ecology movement, for example, bases its fight for the protection of life under natural conditions on a knowledge developed essentially over the last hundred years (the age of ecology as science). While the overall effect on nature of interference in one of its domains had always been known, the precise connections between water, earth and air, the interaction of elements, plants and animals were first *scientifically* investigated only when ecology arose as an independent discipline.

When our authors speak of intimacy and connectedness, however, they are referring to a different aspect of our relationship with nature; and its implications seem to me to be worth considering. They are speaking of an attitude which does not consider nature simply as a source of raw materials to be ruthlessly exploited, but as a part of our lives that we must preserve and protect. But this attitude is not natural in itself: it involves social action. Nature can only be conserved on the basis of a knowledge of nature, and the more differentiated that knowledge is, the greater the *possibility* of protecting and conserving nature. We should therefore guard against seeing the past as a time when all was well, a time of 'original unity'. Yet there are echoes of such a view in both the passages quoted – indeed, in all the women's writings we have looked at. Were we to accept that view, we would gain only a partial insight into our socialization into heteronomy, and into the destructive consequences of specific ways of exploiting nature. Not only would we be equating sociality in general with *one particular type* of sociality; we would also be removing all contradictions from our relationship with nature. Nature is both necessary to life and a threat to it, a source of both pleasure and danger. As far as women are concerned, their intimate relationship with their bodies – their struggle to conform to conventional standards of beauty, for example – has been and still remains self-destructive.[35] Our intimacy with our bodies has at the same time represented a retreat from social struggles: a retreat that goes hand in hand with a demand for this particular 'intimacy regained'.[36]

It is not only romanticized versions of the past that take the contradiction out of life, but also rosy visions of the future. Women's erotic poetry presents a vision of a society – a vision already partially attainable and realized – which has eradicated exploitation and oppression not only in sexual relations but in all spheres of life. The poems reveal also the meaning of feminine eroticism in such a society: women will be 'tender and strong, eager and alive': there will be 'tenderness, gentleness, laughter, play, flowers. . .'[37] To me, a vision of this kind appears both abstract and sickly-sweet. It is abstract, in that it only amounts to a stringing together of positively charged words, with no clear indication of how they might relate to reality, nor of why these particular words have been preferred to any one of a thousand others with similarly positive resonances. And sickly-sweet, in the sense that it presents a Utopia in which there are no struggles, no arguments, no contradictions. Yet struggles are not directed solely against exploitation and oppression. We struggle against our own mistakes as well. And to make no mistakes is to do nothing whatever – to opt out of living. Utopias of the kind outlined above also seem to me disheartening. They make everyday life with all its conflicts and our own inadequacies separating us from that ideal state seem insurmountable barriers. If we do indeed desire that women develop this particular kind of relation to their bodies, we will have to release it from its old shackles.[38] In so doing, we will encounter new contradictions – between the enjoyment of sensual delights and the enjoyment of social activity, for example (since we cannot enjoy both at once). There will be contradictions, too, between the desire for transformation and the massive demands it imposes: demands that we change ourselves, our own priorities in life, our identity.

Nature as an Ideological Value

Where in the women's writings can we locate the ideological aspect of the orientation towards nature? One example occurs in Reitz's association of independence and self-determination with the use of natural products. She wrote her book in 1977. Today, five years later, we find 'pure natural products' in every chemist's shop and drugstore, on every cosmetics counter. New firms entering the market are advertising their products on recycled paper. There are creams with 'naturally pure lemon juice' (organically grown, of course), fragrant oils of rosemary and roses. It will not be long before every cosmetics firm has 'naturally pure' products in its range, and it is already possible to buy organically grown wholemeal bread made with stoneground flour at the supermarket. A victory for the women's movement? For the ecology movement? To the extent that natural products are actually healthier, it is indeed a useful achievement. But on the other hand, what have I gained if I am still hopelessly torn as to what type of lemon-cream to buy? A recognition of the harmfulness of certain intrusions on nature can turn into something quite different: the false perception whereby nature – in whatever form – is seen as good, while everything produced by human beings is seen as evil. And yet uranium is a natural product, and some chemical drugs are life-savers. Viewing nature as the supreme good leads us to act as though all further questions were superfluous. Take the question of why women use beauty products in the first place, and whether they are not restricted to a life centred on the body if they follow all the available advice on natural beauty care as much as if they use chemical products. Taking nature as an ultimate reference point is an instance of 'ideological socialization'. It no longer seems necessary to examine the goal or purpose of particular actions; the mere fact that they are natural, or serve nature, is regarded as sufficient legitimization. Values such as these, which are manifested as unsubstantiated guides to action, can be built into the most diverse political strategies. At the time of writing (December 1980) 'Nature' is being incorporated into the strategies of the West German Christian Democrats. 'Environmental conservation' now figures in their campaign slogans for forthcoming elections.

From *Meisterfotos*, S.120

Marxism and Sexuality

'Surely it is above all Marxists who should be developing and attempting to live out, not only a new culture of sexuality, but also a different morality?'[1]

It is tempting to concur all too quickly with arguments such as these. At the same time, our first hesitant attempts to interpret them – even just in theory – throw us into a turmoil of uncertainty. Too much is presupposed by Menzel to be knowable and unequivocal: the nature of a new culture, of sexuality, of a different morality. Having ourselves completed one attempt at research into sexuality, should we not now be able to provide some more concrete guidelines? Our aim in this book has not been to purvey techniques that would guarantee sexual happiness, since we do not accept that unhappiness is attributable to a lack of skill or information; or rather, we do not see these as the most significant issues. But which issues are the most significant ones? In attempting to locate them, we seemed to be running through a maze of signposts. Over and over again, we were directed to new places, only to find ourselves pointed once again in different directions. A lesson we learned in the process was that our desire to find a complete, all-embracing theory, one which retained its explanatory force in any given context, reflects a very peculiar understanding of reality. It conceives the world as structured through and through by a single logic, according to which everything has an attributable cause and effect, a plan that we simply need to uncover. As an alternative to this way of thinking, we would propose thinking in terms of human-made orderings. Those orderings are not necessarily seamless; their individual elements may be assembled in a variety of ways. Our studies are addressed to the ordering, and proposals for changes should be couched in terms of a reordering of elements.

For that reason we shall not attempt to summarize the various findings scattered through this volume. Instead, we shall retrace our steps across the familiar ordering of the problem of sexuality and power, in an attempt to develop a few proposals for re-ordering and to voice some provisional thoughts.

Sexuality and the State

A preliminary survey of our terrain: if we think of sexuality, we inevitably and immediately think of bodies. Mostly in twos, sometimes individually, always suggestive of the intimate and personal. Bound up with this intimacy is a vague feeling of guilt; something is somehow 'wrong'. Never, however, would thinking about ourselves and our desires in this way lead us to connect sexuality and the State. What happens, then, if we take up the challenge of finding a relation between the two by pursuing a different line of thought – from the State to sexuality? Immediately we uncover a host of relations: in law, marriage, the family, sexual relations, pornography, censorship, prostitution, religion, morality, art, regulations about hygiene and contagious diseases, medicine. . .in any area that is in any way connected with sexuality, we find State regulations. The State is everywhere. What could be more obvious than to develop all this in terms of a hypothesis of repression? We suspect that the State has an interest in repressing sexuality. The nature of that interest is easy to identify: it is power. Thus we may conclude that sexuality is repressed by the State in order to maintain class divisions and to propagate society in its totality.

As has been argued above,[2] this thesis is hard put to explain sexual 'revolutions' and even liberal policies in sexual legislation. Moreover, given that we are attempting to elucidate problems of feminine sexuality, this approach unacceptably ignores both sexual difference and the specific forms taken by sexuality and its repression. In our view, a strategy for sexual liberation must pose the question of sexuality in gender-specific ways. First and foremost, it must confront the sexual or sexually-based subordination of the female sex by the male sex.

On Subjection within Sexual Ideology

Let us tackle the complicated question of how class domination, sexual oppression and the social identities of man and woman are connected. We shall start from the assumption that class domination exists as sanctioned by the State; this we term ideological socialization.[3]

Our question might therefore be formulated as follows: how

does ideological socialization take place through sexuality? We know from our work that man and woman as different sexual beings must be viewed in terms of social identities; in other words, that it is necessary to conceive the process of their socialization as a construction in which individuals subject themselves to a social power relation on the basis of biological features. We have termed this process sexualization. In this context, we found that we could usefully draw on the arguments of Foucault, who analyzes the construction of sexuality as a specific domain, a constitution based on power. According to Foucault's schema, it is the very process of acquiring normal sexuality which confirms and produces power relations. And in our attempts to discern the liberating aims of works of so-called sexual education, we have found partial confirmation of our suspicion that sexuality itself involves a drawing of the boundaries within which domination can be upheld.

The title of one West German best-seller should serve to illustrate the point: it is called *Show Me*.[4] This is a book with large frontage photographs in which 'everything' is shamelessly displayed. The highlighting of each and every bodily detail of father, mother and their infant son and daughter conceals the fact that there are other things which the book fails to show. What remain invisible are the social identities into which we are initiated through sexual play, together with all the problems, crises and disasters that involves. Wishes and desires are plainly channelled into the social identities of father and mother, of the nuclear family and normal heterosexual genitality. The two frames of reference are a notion of normality (and thus the possibility of guilt in deviating from the normal), and our capacity for socio-sexual action. We become woman and slave-girl, and that is what we want. Books on sex education more liberal than *Show Me* attempt to deal with the problem of normalization and the issue of guilt that it raises. Their aim is to counter feelings of inadequacy by affirming normality. Our own questions relating to woman as a socio-sexual identity led us into areas which are far more primary. If we assume that power is latent in the constitution of sexuality, we will seek out the ways in which subjection – which includes the subjection of women to men – takes place through the organization of bodies into a society. The process of our socialization operates on these two levels. Therefore we shall first examine our own relations with our bodies, and in so doing, examine our position within the said society.

The Body and the Senses

We found this shift in focus from the issue of sexuality in general to our relations with our bodies to be immediately fruitful. Released from the shackles which seemed to limit our capacity to remember, to write, feel and think productively, we found ourselves thinking up one story after another. Those shackles had been a crutch as well as a handicap. In particular, the loss of stability, crises and guilt-feelings we now began to experience revealed the ways in which ideological socialization exercises power over our bodies. It became clear that it was not primarily our sexuality, but our bodies as a whole that normality affected as a controlling principle. None of us was normal. In every case, there was something to be criticized or hidden or slimmed down, something that showed us to be inadequate in relation to a body that was truly feminine.

To gain control over the conditions that govern our lives: up to now, this had represented little more than a theoretical goal, something conceived in terms of future plans for the control of social production. Factories and offices – inwardly, we postponed the concrete visualizations of their future communal and social control to some distant date. We had failed to recognize that our own corporeal existence was itself both a form of life and a condition, and that the gaining of control over bodies is an important factor in the propagation of society.

How are we to live with all our senses? How are we to build our bodies into the world? Our attempts to recall the history of the body and the senses in our lives have left us with a strange feeling of sadness, of something lost, past and irrevocable. It is as though we no longer desire something that we possessed and desired in childhood. We mourn our lack of a desire for a different relationship with the world. Or to put it another way: in thinking of the body and the senses, of the convergences we describe in terms of a sexualizing process, we experience a sense of limitation, of constriction and reduction. Growing up in the context described is experienced as a process of alienation and canalization. Sexual socialization is undergone in reality as a kind of centering of the senses. Even in our work on this volume and in the standpoints we occupy today, there are distant echoes of different realms of sensuality.

Sensuality: Three Essays

Nora: the body and pleasures

pleasure can't be written about; you have it or you don't
so say my friends, counter-cultural to a woman

and they have it, truly they do
bioenergetics, the first example:
she lies on the floor, can't sit up,
can't ask for help
and learns
as she has always done in life.
today she learns to make her body looser,
to feel,
to move,
and so to adopt different postures in life,
or so they say.
and why not?

or eurythmics:
release the streams that flow through a body,
break the barriers.
a teeth-gritting smile in the mirror as she practices,
loosening up already.
why not indeed?
relax! it's worth the effort

and what of me?
aching shoulders as I write
completely stiff
they say it's psychological.

but how does this relate to our theme?
ask my friends
thirsty for knowledge.
don't tell us you believe in all that rubbish
or are you just making fun of it
in your writing?

just your style
DOGMATIST
THAT

YOU
ARE
honestly, I don't know.

I have written:
we must build ourselves into the world,
with our bodies
not build the world around them.

Barbara tells me:
the women who have read this
have not understood.

my first thought:
barricades
my first demonstration,
we ran across a bridge and
yes, really, the earth shook beneath our feet,
the singing
walking, running in rhythm.
the slogans – they all made you laugh –
how many we were!
and I thought
this is frightful, this mass hysteria.
this excess of emotion.
my first orgiastic experience –
dogmatists are like that.

and writing now,
this feeling in my stomach
like falling in love –
no, not always
but sometimes.
happiness mixed with anxiety
I find what I write now
pleasing
but will they understand it?

and I read a text by Ute
voraciously.

and then the euphoria of discussion
explaining, offering evidence,

presenting a case
all very calmly
before they pounce
on you.

you join in the writing
while inside you there is chaos.
collecting, ordering
devising strategies
how to be convincing without naivety
how to be stirring but still provoke debate?

you leave in the end
warm with joy and rage
counting two at best who've been won over
or at worst
only you are the wiser
Christ, here we go again
Frigga says,
Nora's frightful politics
hara-kiri style

when I look up
I see desert images
three times I have been there
in a desert that is useless
even harmful
advancing year by year
on to fertile terrain.

on a red rock
the stars shine red
the sky above me
naturally blue
I hear only wind
rushing round my ears.

the desert is useless.
I can cross it,
smell it, feel it, taste it,
sand between my teeth.

a question from Herbert:

you mean to say you've written nothing about us?
But what am I supposed. . .?
the way we were the other day after lunch
– potatoes and cream –
in an ice-cold bedroom,
as usual you'd forgotten to shut the window!
then Peter coming in
about the telegram
then leaving
then the way it got warmer,
then. . .
it doesn't work, the words won't come
after all, it wasn't language we looked at
not in this book.

so that's how I'd imagined
the world
and the body
and building ourselves into it.
but for the life of me
I can't put it down
in writing.

Frigga: Change

Hemmed in by general 'correct' political slogans – the right to
work, peace, emancipation – and my own reflections on divisions
in the working class, on how to forge a unity, on how to incor-
porate women here, their restlessness, their views on winning back
the night, on having children at home, on new debates, new forms
of dress – the radicalization of their hopes, their actions – again
these manipulative pronouncements from on high – but how can
one think it out without attempts at organization? Hemmed in
then, by doubts regarding how best to be political, shocked too by
the feeling of triumph these groups dispense right and left, which
used to seem so pleasant, I am going home to Mintard, Mintarden-
berg. For the third time in a long while. Fearful of what I will find,
I avoid travelling straight to Langen's meadow on the hillside I
know to be no longer populated by grazing cattle, but by the
residences of Düsseldorf suburbia. Nor do I walk to the holly
grove which now borders a motorway. Inconceivable and better
left alone. Difficult enough to return, then easy too to be so small
again, the whole world in this holly grove – too late, already I

begin to feel its scratches, we play hide and seek, it's always dusty, the smell of it, the taste on the tongue, arms scratched sensuously, and Hans Langen creeping up behind me – suddenly older and strange and coming threateningly closer, the boy I sat with yesterday in the plum tree. Recoiling, I shout out loud for his younger sister. He looks at me and creeps away, both of us knowing what we do not know, knowing why it's the sister I call and not the other brother. A dawning awareness that the uncanny is related in some way to the opposite sex and that protection is afforded by our own. All of this forgotten in an instant, we went on playing, but I avoided him from then on and the memory still lingers. No, I have no wish to drive along a stretch of asphalt past the splendours of suburbia. So I leave the car in the schoolyard, still recognizable even though it's now a car park and the teacher's house a bank and the school a block of flats. The village has shrunk, but many old houses still stand as they always did, the old names on the doors: Klages, Kemperdieck, Apeltrath, and the newcomers from Saxony, foreign no longer, but old and familiar. I still doubt the wisdom of travelling the old paths and seeing in the traces, the few that linger after modernization, civilization, only the ways they have changed.

And yet the narrow opening by the schoolyard pulls me up the hill with a force that defies me to pause for reflection. And now the sameness of everything, nothing has changed, the gullies crammed with fallen leaves and the ferns, even the ferns on the same slopes, but no more courting couples to be overheard, and where are the voices of the other children? But most startling, the bodily memory, steps dragging at the same places and quickening at others – the same ghosts still haunt the tree-stump, and I speed up to pass it – a change of pace demanded, not by steepness, but by urgent voices still ringing in my ears, run away from the boys who lie in wait behind the tree-stumps, they have pocket knives to threaten you with. And now the path ends, my body moves through the trees and my feet accurately follow the same unseen traces, which my eyes play no part in identifying. And again later, where the homeward path should start, my body pauses. Only now do my eyes search out and actually find a track, which no one has used since. The beech tree, planted at my birth, now decaying, the willow tree no more than a stump, dead now and hence all the brighter in my memory. The steep slope behind the house is gentle and short, here I often used to run with arms outstretched against the wind, only a step or two and the distant Italian pear-tree stands right by the house, by a wall that is still there. Distances shift now –

everything is close together in the cemetery, with its great grave-stones and all the names: Apeltrath, these were the boys, the epitomes of evil who lay in wait behind the stumps of dead trees. Langen, Langen's meadows and Hans Langen. He got married while I was still at school, that's how I remember; Kemperdieck the baker, we queued up for cakes in front of his counter, and Angela Schmitz who had the little shop and was somehow peculiar. Not that she actually looked peculiar, but that was how she was described by others, rousing our curiosity when we shopped there. We tried to see in her, to descry in her what it was that set her apart. She was a maiden lady.

The shop has gone. A smell of roast pork is coming from the house, good when I pass the first time, burnt the second. Manzius. They had 17 children and if he'd married my mother it would have been 21. And the customs of giving the names of children who died to the newborn – thus there is still a Sebastian. The house is still standing, the same as ever, small, squat, crooked, with tiny windows, the same curtains still hanging. But Mr and Mrs Manzius have a large grave in the cemetery. Strangers come out of the church. Under my intently enquiring gaze they eye me with hostility – but no, it's just my cord trousers and jacket on a Sunday, a woman from a different era, a different time, no one knows me any longer.

The Little Ruhr – I swam over sometimes to the other bank, strange and distant, another country. You can almost spit from one bank to another, but this is the same Ruhr and there are still the same ships pulling in to the same moorings, the same fields and the smell of the grass and the wild roses under the broad vault of the motorway bridge which draws Düsseldorf closer to Essen, and the sound of the water on the stones. The names, Baggerloch where Harald nearly drowned, Dicken am Damm, the tavern where I drank my first fizzy drink with flakes of artificial flavouring, the narrow street, infinitely wide, where I walked innumerable times and led the class on excursions. Proudly taking charge, even when I was ill with a temperature, I knew myself to be indispensable, walking in front of the others, town children who didn't like walking, they had the wrong shoes and had to be led by me and kept in good spirits and organized – in that child, I can already recognize the woman I am today.

The tennis court laid out by my father. We went there sometimes as children, saw the strange red clay, the high fencing and the decay, as sad and natural as my father's death. The tennis court spoke of another kind of life which we did not live – perhaps we

should have – an alien promise. A glimpse of a present which, as
we looked at it, we related like a fairy tale that we loved and that
belonged to us, without our needing to experience it. Now, the
tennis court is a tennis court once more, new nets, paint, no moss.
It has been destroyed, the old one, and the fairy tale vanishes.
People playing tennis, as no one did when we were young.

Back to the cemetery, the Tacks, wife and husband, an inscrip-
tion in loving memory of a son killed in wartime as well. I never
knew they'd had a son, even though they had the next-door house
we had to pass on the way to school and didn't like because they
had a dog called Bubi with a bark so long and vicious as to make
him one of the signs, the symbols of the haunting evil that sur-
rounded our childhood days and pervaded our dreams. Bubi
Tack, a dog with the name of the family which owned him. I don't
remember our calling other dogs after their owners. The Rutsch-
manns too had a son killed in the war? And I was so sure until now
that the war had touched only us, for no one else mentioned it.

Attempt at a General Formulation

I

Abruptly now, all the stirrings of a childhood yearning which
resided in colours, in the forms of the hills, the shimmering of
rivers, the breath of wind on the skin, the first glimpse of mountains, sunlight on the fields, are bundled together, their energy
directed towards one person. Bewitched as we are by that one
love, we strip the rest of nature of a magic we can only revivify –
though never in its previous glory – through the beloved.

Where is the strength that would derive from a twofold love: a
revival of the magic of childhood both through the person we
love, and through the joy we experience with them in nature?

How banal it is to call this magic sexuality, to cultivate it for its
own sake, to restrict it, indeed assiduously to incarcerate it
within a relationship between two people, in a grey world where
feelings are subjected to the fitness test of a life that is only a
response to external stimuli. From this point on, there will be
only one place for feelings. Once their boundaries have been this
tightly delineated, we can be sure not only that they will be
short-lived, but that they will be experienced in isolation from
the world. They are not made any deeper by being invested in
one other person. It is this which causes the individual ultimately

to see herself merely as an object of desires. The supplying of an emotion, the movement which connected her with the world, reverts to the individual.

II

Our diverse emotions lie grieving on the junk stall we call sexuality. The links through which we felt nature as longing are now severed, and a new upheaval still awaits us. Once again the restless waters overflow the channels of the river bed. My gaze rests on the feet of a child who has yet to walk, on its warm living body resting on my stomach. The mingling of its soft skin with mine, the smell of milk. Our feelings can be roused and drawn within a being as tiny as this. Where do they go to?

Relations between the Sexes and the Socio-Sexual Capacity for Action

What, then, are the implications of such childhood memories? Sexualization is at one and the same time a reduction, a concentration and, for women, a subjection of their bodies to a constant requirement to arouse desire, to be 'normal'. Slavegirl and mother: it is within these identities that women acquire the socio-sexual capacity for action. Our efforts to maintain external composure conceal the manifold disturbance and unrest we have attempted to document in our stories. But what becomes of class issues in this context or, more precisely, just what has class to do with sexuality? Two consequences flow, it seems to us, from the ordering of bodies in the ways described: the subjection of women to an actively slavish existence and, at the same time, their subjection to standard social relations. We are defined as social beings by our own social significance, our position in society and our general capacity for action: all three definitions are shot through with the questions of class and gender. In relations between the sexes, the subordination of women ensures the dominance of men, who can thus receive compensation for and validation of the general subordination of either sex.

How might we extricate ourselves from this situation? Or, more simply, how might our relationship to our bodies be transformed? A socialization that proceeds via the body leads inevitably to isolation. Each and every woman confronts the reflection of her failings and abnormalities alone. In this context, simply to develop techniques for a more satisfying sexuality seems absurd. It is not only relations between the sexes, but equally our own relations to our bodies which contradict such simple solutions. We cannot imagine a better relationship to our bodies, an independent way of building them into the world, within relations of sexual subjection as they exist today. In order to revolutionize those relations, it will be necessary to form collectives of women in which we must learn the first steps towards standing alone. Writing the stories of our bodies has seemed to us a first faltering attempt to arrange a new social perception of the multiple connections we inhabit, with a view to developing a different organization.

Love and Production

Attempts to reconcile sexuality and love run up against the barrier of property fairly quickly. The family unit, together with our possession of the loved one, clips the wings of what we dream of as love. The situation changes, however, if the same elements are reorganized. If we begin with our senses, we can arrive both at love and at a transformation of the world. The steps we have taken above should by no means be regarded as true knowledge, but only as an attempt to conceive of a framework.

Let us begin with childhood once more. As we grow up, the range of our experiences increases. We may or may not learn from them: what is certain is that we leave a little of our soul behind in each. From time to time, we feel that loss as a certain fragrant memory that seems acutely painful, a sound or an image to stir the emotions before releasing them again into the quieter regions of the present. We grow stronger in knowledge and in experience. Our world becomes richer, but poorer too. For whenever we move on, we leave a part of ourselves behind. What would it be like if we could hold on to everything? *Sturm und Drang!* (Storm and stress!) This way, too, life would be impossible. As we grow older, the soul disperses and settles in fragments of our lives. Old longings are never realized, old strivings gather dust and are abandoned. Hopes are relinquished. Unhappiness and happiness lie half-forgotten in furrows of the mind. We march onwards, happy or sad, or even restless, but careful not to lose our balance. The powers of our soul in transit will suffice for this life. We live in the here and now.

When we love, however, we regain the power to retrieve the

lost and infinitely ramified, buried and forgotten stirrings of our soul: to live many lives anew, to retrace our steps to childhood, to recapture with one mighty effort all that we have lost. The power that comes to us and yet from within us is almost unendurable, bearable only when directed towards the loved one and simultaneously a source of sorrow. Now our perception of the world can also be different – a difference manifested in the most banal of everyday things. Colours become more vivid, the air softer. The year disperses into different periods of intensity, voices take on many registers, and everything is a little ethereal. The power with which the soul is retrieved and redirected is at once healing and destructive. Calm dissipates before the storm. The reorganization of the forces of the soul engenders new life, new directions, meaning. Orientation instead of dispersal. Can we not consciously take up the joy of love as a form of happiness that enables us to direct our powers anew? Can they not be redirected toward transforming the world at the same time? Is not the power to love made endurable by being thus directed, and are not our efforts at effective transformation realizable in this way?

But what is love? Love and hatred are the names we commonly give to the feelings roused in us by a person's actions, appearance and movements. Love transforms both the self and the loved one, who in turn reinforces the forms of action and behaviour for which s/he is loved. The loved one is thus moulded by another and moulds her/himself at the same time. Lovers perpetually produce each other of their own accord. They recognize themselves in the actions for which each loves the other; thus lovers work constantly at their own feelings, to produce *humanity* in their lives as human beings. In this way the production of love is combined with other forms of production which make the world more human. It is for this reason that we love those persons who create in us an attitude of productivity (probably because of a feeling that we will then have a greater self-respect). Love may be defined as a blessing without which the soul will be dormant. Lovers grow perpetually for one another, they have no fixed characteristics, but so live and act as to become like their partner's image of them.

Taking Off to Touch the Ground

Is it the case that women in lesbian relationships can suddenly shake off all forms of obstruction and subjection? One depressing film from the women's movement [Alexandra von Grote's *Weggehen um Anzukommen,* ('Taking off to touch the ground')] demonstrates how difficult the path still is, if one is to shed the effects of a socio-sexual development which is so firmly established in our society.

The contents of the film can be quickly summarized : two women separate after a tangled love relationship which 'isn't working any more'. Anna, the heroine of the film, has always loved girls and women, while Regina, an older woman who has been married, is the one who is 'new' to all this – to her, it represents new departures, revolutionary change. Anna travels to Provence for several weeks to 'find herself'; flashbacks from Anna's memories reveal the dynamics of love and hate in their life together. Anna's tone in the film is accusatory; she complains that what she lacks is love, intimacy, affection, time, consideration. But in spite of this, or perhaps because of it, this is not a film that accuses: it inveighs against neither relationships nor inhumane conditions. Details of social relations – work relations, for example – are not filled in. Work appears nowhere within the film. The only scene in which production takes place – when Regina is writing an article for a magazine – is interrupted by Anna when she destroys her friend's means of production, the typewriter. Thus work is presented as an obstacle to the relationship. 'Why can't you pay attention to me?'

The women's movement is marked by its emphasis on culture. It has developed alternative cultures of food, music and the body – yet none of this appears in the film. The aspects of culture in which pleasure and meaning might have been found are as little in evidence as production is. And what about sexuality? It makes a single isolated appearance, in one long scene in which we are invited to observe women making love together, at the very beginning.

For the rest of the film, we are called upon to sympathize with states of mind whose origins are never made clear. There are references to intimacy and openness – but what are these qualities and why do we need them? What kind of alternative do such relationships represent, if they only revolve around themselves, never directing any power outwards to a movement against oppression? What is meant by a love that constricts the characters until they can move no longer and are exposed to constant surveillance? Love, said Brecht, is a production which is hard to live out in heterosexual relations; since those relations are not free of domination, production cannot take place in communal ways. Surely any model of lesbian relations must at least face up to the obvious challenge, and at least consider the potential for a culture and a production which are free of domination. Instead Alexandra von Grote treats us to a fashion show. In each successive scene, the heroine wears a different expensive outfit. The impression of the relation between sexuality and class unwittingly conveyed is that it is structured to allow only the leisured class to live as lesbians. This view contains nothing that could be of universal relevance.

The Third Term

For all the one-sideness of this film's attempt to enact love 'in itself', and thus to link it to sexuality, we have met with just as many problems in our attempt to reorganize the connection between love, production, sensuality and power or its absence. The kind of impasse depicted so agonizingly by von Grote tempts us into adopting an ascetic total commitment to production. To conclude, we shall reproduce an account by Sünne Andresen of the experience of producing this book, which makes it clear how far we have still to go to find new ways of living. Let us go on striving for a world in which it is worth living, with all our senses.

The Sex Book

'Me-ti said that the relationship between two people was good when there was a third term present, a point at which their interests coincided. Mi-en-leh added that this was also true of the relation between larger groups of people.'

We would concur with Brecht's notion that relationships are produced through a common third term, whose nature may change the form they take. The third term which united us as women, for example, was our intention to write this book. In our different fields, we have all been working on our liberation as women. In producing this book, we had to confront a number of problems, whose principal cause was the intimate nature of the thematic complex that surrounds sexuality. The fact that our whole lives, every statement we made, every area of living seemed colonized by and linked with sexuality had aroused our interest in investigating it further. The way in which we experienced sexuality was, however, to become a problem in writing and working through our stories. Our problems became evident, for example, in our lack of distance, our inability to look beyond concrete experiences of 'suffering' and to make out the new terrain that lay beyond them. We had to transgress boundaries, to develop an inquisitive attitude towards ourselves and our histories. There were problems, too, regarding our different levels of competence. Some women had had more and better formal education than others. Since we wanted to overcome the division between 'practical women' who 'just' wrote stories and 'women of theory' who performed the entire task of theorization, we had to teach ourselves and each other in the process of writing. Then there was the problem of working in different parts of the country. Since some of us live in Berlin and others in Hamburg, we either had to travel backwards and forwards between the two cities or meet up elsewhere for extended periods of work. We had ample opportunity for bickering and irritation: there were frequent complaints that not enough work had been done, that the meetings had been badly prepared or scarcely coordinated, that some of the women involved weren't shouldering their share of responsibility, and so on. Though we had our project in common, the book still demanded a certain amount of interest, stamina, work and time from each individual. All the texts had to be discussed several times before being rewritten or modified. Each of us had to accept a good deal of criticism of what we had produced, then think through the criticisms and incorporate them into a revised version. And yet none of us left the project or gave up before it was finished. Having come together around a common issue, we found it was that which held us together.

Collective projects such as ours, which present each participant with the opportunity of learning, of becoming more skilful both in thinking and in writing, and of moving closer to some form of liberation, seem to me to constitute an important element of interpersonal relations. No research has yet been done on the effects of working relations of this kind on relationships between people in general. One thing our experience suggests is that work of this kind makes it possible to negate *arbitrary* criteria for hostility – an antipathy based on appearance or behaviour, for example – and thus, perhaps, to negate dislike itself. There is still work to be done in all the following areas:

We aim to develop ways of living collectively, and thus to escape individual isolation.

We demand a body that is not itself the means and also the end of our socialization: a body that is not made over to us as though it were something owed to others.

We aim to unravel the processes whereby sexualization comes to constitute class barriers which are guaranteed by the State.

We aim to practice a politics of the body which enables us to live a life of resistance, to perceive in different ways, to forge new connections, and not to subjugate ourselves.

Our aim is not to take the life out of life, nor to imprison the social sphere in an area constituted specifically for it, and labelled sexuality.

Our aim is to change the world lovingly.

Notes

Translator's Foreword

1. Our notable accent exception is a collection of essays edited by Gisele Ecker, *Feminist Aesthetics*, London 1985.
2. Rosalind Coward, *Female Desire*, London 1984 and Susan Brownmiller, *Femininity*, New York 1984.
3. Angela McRobbie, 'Girls and Subcultures', in *Resistance Through Rituals*, ed. John Clanet et al, London 1976.

Preface to English Edition

1. See the 'body project' later in this volume.
2. See Chapter III, Section 4, 'Marxism and Sexuality'.
3. See the 'Legs' and 'Slavegirl' projects, below.
4. Donna Haraway, *'Lieber Kyborg als Göttin. Für eine sozialistisch-feministische Unterwanderung der Gentechnologie'*, in *Argument Sonderband 105*, Berlin 1984 (no page ref.).

Introduction

1. Our investigations into the social construction of women first began in the volume preceding this one, *Frauenformen. Alltagsgeschichten und Entwurf einer Theorie weiblicher Sozialisation* ('Women's Forms: stories of the everyday, and outline for a theory of female socialization'), Berlin 1981.

Chapter I. Memory-work

1. Karl Marx & Friedrich Engels, *The German Ideology*, transl. C.J.Arthur, London 1970, p.46.

2. D.Peukert, 'Arbeiteralltag – Mode oder Methode?', in Haumann (ed.), *Arbeiteralltag in Stadt und Land. Neue Wege der Geschichtsschreibung*, Berlin 1982, p.24.

3. K.Holzkamp, *Grundlegung der Psychologie*, Frankfurt/M 1983.

4. See our later chapter on 'Sexuality and Power'; also W.F.Haug, 'Der Körper und die Macht im Faschismus. Zur Analyse einer Faszination am Beispiel Brekers', in *Sammlung 4, Jahrbuch für antifaschistische Literatur und Kunst*, Frankfurt/M. 1982, and Projekt Ideologi-Theorie (PIT), *Faschismus und Ideologie 3, AS80*, Berlin 1983.

5. Amongst others Brigitte Wartmann, 'Schreiben als Angriff auf das Patriarchat,' *Literaturmagazin 11*, Hamburg 1979.

6. S.Tretjakov, in W.Thomczyk, 'über das schreiben hinaus. . .erfahrungen mit dem andauernden versuch, über das ziel eines schriftstellers hinauszukommen', in *Literaturmagazin 11*, Hamburg 1979, p.133.

7. See the later section of this chapter on 'Language'.

8. For example Paul Willis, *Learning to Labour: How working-class kids get working-class jobs*, Farnborough, Hants., 1977.

9. W.F.Haug, 'Standpunkt und Perspektive materialistischer Kulturtheorie', in *Materialistische Kulturtheorie und Alltagskultur, AS47*, Berlin/W. 1980.

10. See Chapter III, Section 3 of this volume, on 'Women and Bodies'.

11. See the later section of this chapter entitled, 'The Constraints of Subjectification – the Project'.

12. Cf. the final section of this chapter on 'Tools of remembering'.

13. These questions are examined in greater detail in our discussions with Ute Holzkamp-Osterkamp: U.H.-Osterkamp, 'Unterdrückung oder Selbstunterwerfung? Zu Frigga Haugs "Opfer-Täter'-Konzept", in *Das Argument 136, 11/12*, Berlin/W. 1982.

14. Cf. Frigga Haug, 'Einfühlung als Methode' ('Empathy as method'), in F.Haug, *Erziehung und gesellschaftliche Produktion: Kritik des Rollenspiels*, Frankfurt/M. 1977.

15. See for example the work of the *Argument* project on automation and qualification, Projekt Automation und Qualifikation, *Entwicklung der Arbeit, AS 19*, Berlin/W. 1978.

16. Chapter III, Section 1, 'Sexuality and Power'.

17. Cf. Frigga Haug, 'Erfahrung und Theorie,' *Das Argument 126 11/12, and 'Frauen und Theorie', Das Argument 132 3/4*, Berlin/W 1982.

18. E.A.Rauter, *Vom Umgang mit Wörtern*, München 1978.

19. Doris Lessing, *The Summer Before the Dark*, Harmondworth 1975.

20. For a more detailed discussion of this point, see D.Sölle, 'Feministische Theologie', in *Das Argument 129, 9/10, Berlin/W. 1981*.

21. Cf. Luce Irigaray, *Speculum de l'autre femme*, Paris 1974.

22. Frigga Haug, 'Erf. u. Theorie' (op.cit) & 'Frauen u.Theorie' (op.cit.) 1982; also Projekt Frauengrundstudium, *Frauen Grundstudium, Argument Sonderheft 57*, Berlin/W 1982.

23. The work of Bertolt Brecht is particularly illuminating on the autonaturalization of social relations. See for example his *Seven Deadly Sins of the Petty Bourgeoisie, Collected Plays Vol.2, Part III*, ed. John Willett & Ralph Mannheim, London 1979.

Chapter II. Displacements of the Problem

Section 1. *Introduction to the projects*

1. Cf. Chapter II, Section 1, 'Sexuality and Power'.
2. Cf. the 'Legs Project' later in this chapter.
3. Cf. the 'Body Project' later in this chapter.
4. See Irigaray's excellent critique of Freud, in *Speculum*, 1974.
5. There is a review of the literature referred to here in the preliminary section of Chapter III, Section 3, 'Women and Bodies'.
6. Cf. the 'Legs Project' later in this chapter.
7. Cf. Chapter III, Section 1, 'Sexuality and Power'.
8. Erving Goffmann, *Stigma: Notes on the Management of Spoiled Identity* Harmondsworth 1968, p.153.

Section 2. *The Hair Project*

1. R.Schittenhelm, *Man wird dich lieber haben. Anstandsbuch für junge Damen* ('Learning to be liked: a book of etiquette for young ladies'), 5th ed., Stuttgart 1967.
2. For a more detailed account of the history of witches and witch-burning, we refer the reader to Becker, Bovenschen et al., *Aus der Zeit der Verzweiflung*, Frankfurt/M. 1977: also Barbara Ehrenreich and Deirdre English, *For her own good: 150 years of the experts' advice to women* London, 1979; and T.Hausschild, H.Staschen, R.Troschke, *Hexen. Katalog zur Ausstellung*, Hamburg 1979.
3. For a more detailed discussion of the process of individualization, see Chapter III, Section 2, 'Sexuality and Power'.

Section 3. *The Body Project*

1. For discussions of the way the notion of the average itself is socially constituted, see Chapter III.
2. There is a more developed discussion of the notion of submission in Projekt Ideologie-Theorie, *Theorien über Ideologie AS 40*, Berlin/W 1979; also F.Haug, *Frauenformen*, Vol.1, and W.F.Haug, 'Kritische Psychologie und Theorie des Ideologischen', in Haug (ed.), *Ideologie, Warenästhetik, Massenkultur. Entwürfe zu einer theoretischen Synthese. Argument Sonderheft 33*, Berlin/W. 1979.
3. M.Maron, *Flugasche*, Frankfurt/M. 1981, p.62.
4. Cf. in this context Chapter 1, 'Memory-work'.
5. This point is discussed more fully in the introductory section to this present chapter.
6. For further development of these terms, see Chapter II, Section 5, 'Legs Project'.

Section 4. *The Slavegirl Project*

1. Interview with Roland Barthes, *Tageszeitung*, 4.1.82.

2. W.F.Haug, 'Kritische Psychologie', p.44.
3. Cf. the introduction to this present chapter.
4. Helga Novak, *Vogel federlos*, Darmstadt 1982.
5. Heidi Hartmann, 'The Unhappy Marriage of Marxism and Feminism', in Lydia Sargent (ed.), *Women and Revolution*, London 1981.
6. Luce Irigaray, 'That Sex which is not One', in Paul Foss and Meaghan Morris (eds.), *Language, Sexuality and Subversion*, Darlington, Australia 1978, p.166.
7. For a more extended discussion of these and similar resistances to a story in the course of group analysis, see Chapter I, 'Memory-work'.
8. Robert Musil, *Der Mann ohne Eigenschaften*, Hamburg 1981.
9. Sigmund Freud, *Civilization and its Discontents*, transl. Joan Riviere, London 1982, pp.82-83.

Section 5. The Legs Project

1. L Röhrich, *Lexikon der sprichwörtlichen Redensarten*, Freiburg/Basel/Wien 1979, p.111.
2. Ibid.
3. Ibid., p.518.
4. Cit. M.von Boehne, *Die Mode, Bd.8. Menschen und Moden im 19. Jahrhundert 1878–1914*, München, 3rd.ed., 1963, p.158.
5. Ibid.
6. Ibid., p.160.
7. Ibid., p.162.
8. *Szene Hamburg*, April 1872, p.12.
9. Ibid.
10. 'So sind Sie gut auf den Beinen', in *Brigitte* 23, 1981, pp.42-46.
11. Ibid., p.44.
12. Cf. also the 'Body Project'.
13. *Brigitte* 23/81, p.44.
14. R.Schittenhelm, *Man wird dich lieber haben. Anstandsbuch für junge Damen.*, Stuttgart, 5th ed., 1967, p.89.
15. Cf. Also Chapter III, Section 4, 'Women and Bodies'.
16. Cf. also the 'Body Project'.
17. Cf. also the 'Slavegirl Project'.
18. As did Bertolt Brecht, in *The Mother*, transl. Steve Gooch, London 1978.
19. Translator's note: this is given in the original as 'Nemitz 1983', but there is no corresponding reference in the bibliography. I am writing to the authors for clarification.
20. Cf. 'The legs that were too long', in 'The Body Project'.
21. Cf. also 'Introduction to the Projects' and the 'Body Project'.
22. W.F.Haug, 'Der modellierte Männerkörper als ideologische Macht im Faschismus. Ein Diskussionsbeitrag zu Breker' in Projekt Ideologie-Theorie (PIT), *Faschismus und Ideologie 3. Argument Sonderheft 80*, Berlin/W.1983; also 'Medizin und Psychiatrie als ideologische Mächte im Faschismus und ihre Mitwirkung an den Ausrottungspolitiken', in PIT, op.cit (Quotes in the following are taken from the unpublished manuscript of this second article).
23. Cf. our discussion in the 'Body Project' of 'pulling in the tummy'.
24. W.F.Haug, 'Medizin und Psychiatrie', in PIT, *Faschismus und Ideologie*, Berlin/W. 1983.
25. Ibid.

Section 6. 'Notes on Women's Gymnastics'

1. For a discussion of counter-arguments to the women's team leadership, see R. Prinz, *Die Entwicklung des Kunstturnens der Frauen nach 1945,* Finals dissertation, Berlin/W. 1982.

2. Sophie Dapper, 'Kritische Nachschau auf die deutschen Meisterschaften im Frauenturnen', in *Deutsches Turnen, Jg. 96,* No.9, 1951, p.4.

3. Sophie Dapper, 'Höchstleistung und Wettkampf im Frauenturnen', in *Deutsches Turnen, Jg. 98,* No. 5, p.5.

4. Dapper, 'Kritische Nachschau. . . ', DT 96/9/*51, p.4.*

5. Inge Heuser, 'Wohin führt der Weg im Frauenturnen?', in *Jahrbuch der Turnkunst, Jg. 51* 1957, p.74.

6. Dapper, 'Unser Frauenturnen. Die internationalen Wettkampfanforderungen im Frauenturnen', in *Jahrbuch der Turnkunst, Jg. 40* 1954, p.67.

7. Cf. *Jahrbuch der Turnkunst, Jg.49* 1955, p.39.

8. Cf. for example Chapter II, Section 5, 'The Legs Project'.

9. Heuser, 'Wohin führt. .?', JdT 1957, p.74.

10. Dapper, 'Unser Frauenturnen. . .', JdT 1954, p.60. Emphasis RP.

11. Heuser, 'Wohin Führt. . .?', JdT 1957, p.76. Emphasis RP.

12. L.Niemeyer, 'Die deutschen Meisterschaften im Frauenturnen 1959: Der Durchbruch ist gelungen!', in *Deutsches Turnen, Jg.104,* No.9 1959, p.170.

13. *Deutsches Turnen, Jg. 100,* No.20 1955, p.20.

14. Inge Heuser, 'Was sagt die DTB-Frauenführung zum Beschluss von Oberwerries?', in *Deutsches Turnen, Jg.105,* No.23 1960, p.450. Emphasis RP.

15. C.Ackermann, 'Die 2. Europameisterschaften der Turnerinnen', in *Jahrbuch der Turnkunst, Jg.54,* 1960, p.60. Emphasis RP.

16. Barbara Otto, 'Gegensätze zwischen deutschem und internationalem Frauenturnen', in *Deutsches Turnen, Jg.105,* No.24 1960, p.473.

17. *Frankfurter Allgemeine Zeitung* 2.9.72.

Chapter III. Constructions of the Domain

Section 1. Sexuality and Power

1. Sigmund Freud, *New Introductory Lectures on Psychoanalysis,* transl. James Strachey, Harmondworth 1973, p.152.

2. Wilhelm Reich, *The Sexual Revolution. Towards a self-regulating character structure,* transl. Therese Pol Farrar, New York 1974, p.25.

3. Ibid., p.64.

4. Ibid.

5. Ibid., p.66.

6. Reimut Reiche, *Sexuality and Class Struggle,* Transl. Susan Bennett & David Fernbach, London 1972, p.70.

7. Herbert Marcuse, *One-dimensional man,* London 1972, p.70.

8. Luce Irigaray, *Speculum,* Paris 1974, pp.9-10. (Tr. here by EC).

9. Cf. H.Woetzel & M.Geier, 'Sprachtheorie und Diskursanalyse in Frankreich' in *Das Argument 133* 1981, pp.386ff.

10. For Foucault's own discussion of method, the reader is referred to M.Foucault, *The Archaeology of Knowledge,* transl. A.M.Sheridan Smith, London 1972.

290

11. Ernesto Laclau, 'Diskurs, Hegemonie und Politik', in *Neue Soziale Bewegungen und Marxismus*, Berlin/W. 1982, pp.6-23: here, p.15 (transl. EC).

12. Michel Foucault, *The History of Sexuality*, transl. Robert Hurley, Harmondsworth 1981, p.37.

13. Ibid., p.38.

14. Ibid.

15. Cf. Foucault, 'Historisches Wissen der Kämpfe und Macht' (Historical knowledge of struggles and power), Lecture of 7th Jan. 1975, in *Dispositive der Macht. über Sexualität, Wissen und Wahrheit*, Berlin 1978, p.95.

16. Foucault, *History of Sexuality*, Harmondsworth 1981.

17. Foucault, 'Ein Spiel um die Psychoanalyse' (Playing around psycho-analysis): Foucault in conversation with members of the Departement de Psychanalyse at the University of Vincennes, Paris, in *Dispositive der Macht*, Berlin 1978, p.187.

18. Ibid. (own translation).

19. Cf. Chapter III, Section 2, 'The Church and Sexuality'.

20. Foucault, *History of Sexuality*, Harmondsworth 1981, p.17.

21. Ibid., p.108.

22. Ibid.

23. For a more detailed discussion of this point, see a later sub-section entitled 'The deployment of sexuality on firmer ground'.

24. Foucault, *History of Sexuality*, Harmondsworth 1981, p.96.

25. Ibid., p.86.

26. Cf. Louis Althusser, 'Ideology and the Ideological State Apparatuses', in *Lenin and Philosophy and other essays*, transl. Ben Brewster, London 1977.

27. Cf. Frigga Haug (ed.), *Frauenformen I*, Berlin/W, 1980, and PIT, *Theorien über Ideologie*, Berlin/W. 1979.

28. *Frankfurter Allgemeine Zeitung*, 19.10.82.

29. A critique of this same point can be found in N. Poulantzas *State, Power, Socialism*, transl. Patrick Camiller, London 1978; cf. also M.Jäger, 'Kommunismus kommt von kommunal' in *Aktualisierung Marx AS 100* Berlin/W 1982.

30. For a more extended discussion of auto-naturalization, see also Projekt Automation und Qualifikation, *Automationsarbeit. Empirie 2.*, Berlin/W.1981, pp.363ff.

31. Cf. also Chapter II, 'Displacements of the Problem'.

32. Foucault, *History of Sexuality*, Harmondworth 1981, p.157.

33. Cf, also Chapter I, 'Memory-work'.

34. Cf. G.Bonacchi, 'Gibt es eine feministische Theorie?' in W.F.Haug & W.Elifferding (eds.), *Neue soziale Bewegungen und Marxismus. AS 78*, Berlin/W 1982.

35. B.Heintz & C.Honegger, 'Weibliche Widerstandsformen und Verweigerungsstrategien im 19. Jahrhundert' in *Beiträge 5 zur feministischen Theorie und Praxis*, München 1981, p.99.

36. Ibid., p.100.

37. Ovid, *Metamorphoses*, Harmondsworth, 19th edn. 1984, and Giovanni Boccaccio, *The Decameron*, transln G.H.McWilliam, Harmondsworth 1972.

38. Foucault, 'Das Abendland und die Wahrheit des Sexes' (The Occident and The Truth of Sex), interview in *Le Monde*, 5/11/76. Here, from *Dispositive der Macht*, Berlin 1978, p.114.

39. Foucault, *History of Sexuality*, Harmondsworth 1981, p.156.

40. Cf. Chapter III, Section 2, 'The Church and Sexuality'.

41. Ovid, *Metamorphoses*, pp.102-4.

42. Viz. the work of William Masters and Virginia Johnson, *Human Sexual Inadequacy*, London 1970.

Section 2. The Church and Sexuality

1. Karol Wojtyla, *Love and Responsibility*, trans. H.T.Willetts, London 1981, p.200.
2. Ibid., p.22.
3. Ibid., p.22.
4. Ibid., p.23.
5. Ibid., p.24.
6. Ibid., p.27.
7. Ibid., p.28.
8. Ibid., p.29.
9. Ibid., p.29-30.
10. Ibid., p.31.
11. Ibid., p.36.
12. Ibid., p.38.
13. Ibid., p.41.
14. Ibid., p.42.
15. Ibid., p.42.
16. Ibid., p.46.
17. Ibid., p.47.
18. Ibid., p.49.
19. Ibid., p.49.
20. Ibid., p.80.
21. Ibid., pp.50-51.
22. Ibid., p.51.
23. Ibid., p.52.
24. Ibid., p.53-54.
25. Ibid., p.54-55.
26. Ibid., p.55-56.
27. Ibid., p.57.
28. Ibid., p.59.
29. Ibid., p.60.
30. Ibid., p.66.
31. Ibid., p.75.
32. Ibid., p.78.
33. Ibid., p.79.
34. Ibid., p.80.
35. Ibid., p.81.
36. Ibid., P.82-83.
37. Ibid., p.85.
38. Ibid., p.81.
39. Ibid., p.90.
40. Ibid.
41. Ibid.
42. Ibid. p.95.
43. Ibid., p.97-98.
44. Ibid., p.100.
45. Ibid., p.122-123.

292

46. Ibid., p.128.
47. Cf. in this context our discussion of psychoanalysis in Chapter III, 'Constructions of the Domain', as well as of linkages to the body in the body projects, and in the opening chapter on 'memory-work'.

Section 3. Women and Bodies

1. R. Reitz, *Wechseljahre. Ermutigung zu einem neuen Verständnis,* Hamburg 1981, p.33.
2. Ibid., p.104.
3. Boston Women's Health Book Collective (BWHBC), *Our Bodies Ourselves,* US 2nd. ed., New York 1973, p.13.
4. Ibid.
5. Ibid.
6. Reitz, *Wechseljahre,* Hamburg 1981, p.20.
7. BWHBC, *Our Bodies Ourselves,* US 2nd ed., New York 1973, p.11.
8. Ibid., p.18.
9. Ibid., p.24.
10. L.Boltankski, *Die soziale Verwendung des Körpers,* in D.Kamper and V.Rittner (eds.) *Zur Geschichte des Körpers,* München/Wien 1976, p.131.
11. For a critique of the concept of illness in industrial medicine, see Projekt Automationsmedizin, Berlin/W.1981.
12. Reitz, *Wechseljahre,* Hamburg 1981, p.65.
13. BWHBC, *Our Bodies Ourselves,* US 2nd ed., New York 1973, p.38.
14. Ibid.
15. Cf. Chapter III, Section 1, 'Sexuality and Power'.
16. BWHBC, *Our Bodies Ourselves,* UK 2nd ed., Harmondsworth 1978, pp.73-74.
17. BWHBC, *Our Bodies Ourselves,* US 2nd ed., New York 1973, p.222.
18. BWHBC, *Our Bodies Ourselves,* UK 2nd ed., Harmondsworth 1978, p.71.
19. Cf. introduction to this chapter.
20. BWHBC, *Our Bodies Ourselves,* UK 2nd ed., Harmondsworth 1978, p.41.
21. Frigga Haug (ed.), *Frauenformen I,* Berlin/W.1980, p.41.
22. Ibid.
23. BWHBC, *unser körper unser leben,* Reinbek 1980, p.38 (quotation taken from preface to West German edition).
24. Cf. Chapter I, 'Memory-Work'.
25. BWHBC, *unser körper,* Reinbek 1980, p.49 (preface).
26. Bertolt Brecht, *Me-ti/Buch der Wendungen* in *Gesammelte Werke Bd.12,* Frankfurt/M 1967.
27. *Courage-Sonderheft 6, Jg.4,* p.40.
28. Ibid., p.12.
29. Ibid.
30. Ibid., p.58-59.
31. BWHBC, *Our Bodies Ourselves,* UK 2nd ed., Harmondsworth 1978, p.66.
32. BWHBC, *Our Bodies Ourselves,* US 2nd ed., New York 1973, pp.59-60.
33. BWHBC, *unser körper,* Reinbek 1980, p. 40 (preface).
34. A.Tüne, *Körper, Liebe, Sprache: über die weibliche Kunst, Erotik dar-*

zustellen, Berlin/W 1982, p.7.
35. Cf. Chapter II, 'The Body Project'.
36. Tüne, *Körper, Liebe, Sprache*, Berlin/W.1982. p.8.
37. M.Baumgarten, 'Spuren lesen', in Tüne, op. cit., p.1982, and Tune, *Körper, Liebe, Sprache*, Berlin/W, 1982, p.37.
38. Cf. for example Tüne, *Körper, Liebe, Sprahce*, Berlin/W 1982, p.7.

Section 4. Marxism and Sexuality

1. A. Menzel, 'Gedrängel im Bett', in *Rote Blätter 11*, 1982.
2. Cf. eg. Projekt Ideologie-Theorie, *Theorien über Ideologie*, Berlin/W.1979, pp.178ff.
3. Nebride 1980.
4. Brecht, *Me-Ti*, Frankfurt/M.1967, p.55.

Bibliography

Preface & Chapter I

Theodor W. Adorno et al., *The Positivist Dispute in German Sociology*, transl. Glyn Adey & David Frisby, London 1976.

R.Benedict, 'Kontinuität und Diskontinuität im Sozialisationsprozess', in Kohli (ed.), *Soziologie des Lebenslaufs*, Darmstadt 1978.

Walter Benjamin, *Berliner Kindheit um Neunzehnhundert. Gesammelte Werke, Bd.IV.1*, Frankfurt/M.1972.

— *One-way street and other writings*, transl. Edmund Jephcott, Kingsley Shorter, London 1979.

Bertolt Brecht, *Kleines Organon für das Theater, Schriften zum Theater 7. 1948 - 1956*, Frankfurt/M 1962.

— *The Seven Deadly Sins of the Petty Bourgeoisie, Collected Plays Vol. 2, Part III.*, ed. John Willett & Ralph Mannheim, London 1979.

W.Deppe, *Drei Generationen Arbeiterleben. Eine soziobiographischge Darstellung, Studienreihe des soziologischen Forschungsinstitutes Göttingen*, Frankfurt/M 1982.

Andre Gorz, *Farewell to the working class: an essay on post-industrial socialism*, transl. Michael Sonenscher, London 1982.

Donna Haraway, 'I'd rather be a Kyborg than a Goddess', in *Argument Sonderband 105*, Berlin/W 1984.

K. Hartung, 'Die Repression wird zum Milieu. Die Beredsamkeit linker Literatur', in *Literaturmagazin 11*, Hamburg 1979.

Frigga Haug, *Erziehung und gesellschaftliche Produktion: Kritik des Rollenspiels*, Frankfurt/M. 1977.

— 'Dialektische Theorie und empirische Methodik', in *Das Argument III 9/10*, Berlin/W. 1978.

— (ed.) *Frauenformen. Alltagsgeschichten und Entwurf einer Theorie weiblicher Sozialisation. AS 45*, Berlin/W. 1980.

— 'Erfahrungen in die Krise führen', in *Die Wertfrage der Erziehung. AS 58*, Berlin/W.1981.

— 'Männergeschichte, Frauengeschichte, Sozialismus', in *Das Argument 129*, 9/10, Berlin/W. 1981.

— 'Erfahrung und Theorie', in *Das Argument 136*, 11/12, Berlin/W 1982.

— 'Frauen und Theorie', in *Das Argument 132*, 3/4, Berlin/W 1982.

— 'Morals also have genders', *New Left Review 143*, London 1984.

— 'The Victim-Actor debate', in *Education Links*, Sydney, Australia, August 1985.

W.F.Haug, 'Der Körper und die Macht im Faschismus. Zur Analyse einer Faszination am Beispiel Brekers', in *Sammlung 4, Jahrbuch für antifaschistische Literatur und Kunst*, Frankfurt/M. 1982.

— 'Standpunkt und Perspektive materialisticher Kulturtheorie', in *Materialistiche Kulturtheorie und Alltagskultur*. AS 47, Berlin/W 1980.

H. Hermanns, *Das narrative Interview in berufsbiographisch orientierten Untersuchungen. Arbeitspapiere des Wissenschaftlichen Zentrums für Berufs- und Hochschulforschung an der Gesamthochschule Kassel*, typescript.

Ch.Hoffmann-Riem, 'Sozialforschung, Lebenswelt und Erzählung', in *Soziologische Revue* No.2.

K.Holzkamp, *Grundlegung der Psychologie*, Frankfurt/M. 1983 U.

Holzkamp-Osterkamp, 'Unterdrückung oder Selbstunterwerfung? Zu Frigga Haugs "Opfer-Täter"-Konzept', in *Das Argument 136*, 11/12, Berlin/W. 1982.

Luce Irigaray, *Speculum de l'autre femme*, Paris 1974.

Ursula Krechel, 'Leben in Anführungszeichen. Das Authentische in der gegenwärtigen Literatur', in *Literaturmagazin 11*, Hamburg 1979.

F. Kröll, 'Biographie. Ein Sozialforschungsweg?', in *Das Argument 126*, 3/4, Berlin/W1981.

F. Kröll, J.Matthes & M.Stosberg, 'Zehn Thesen zur Einbeziehung biographisch orientierter Konzepte in soziologische Forschung', in Mattes et al (eds.), *Biographie in handlungswissenschaftlicher Perspektive*, Nürenberg 1981.

Doris Lessing, *The summer before the dark*, Harmondsworth 1975.

J.Manthey (ed.), *Literaturmagazin 11. Schreiben oder Literatur*, Hamburg 1979.

Karl Marx & Friedrich Engels, *The German Ideology*, transl. C.J. Arthur, London 1970.

I.A.Morisse et al, 'Unsicherheit in der Politik – Gewerkschafterinnentagebuch', in *Das Argument 135* 9/10, Berlin/W 1982.

Chantal Mouffe, 'The Sex-Gender System and the Discursive Construction of Women's Subordination', in *Rethinking Ideology*, AS 84, Berlin/W 1983.

Detlef Peukert, 'Arbeiteralltag – Mode oder Methode?', in Haumann (ed.), *Arbeiteralltag in Stadt und Land. Neue Wege der Geschichtsschreibung*, AS 94, Berlin/W. 1982.

H.P.Pitwitt, 'Plädoyer für den Gelegenheitsschriftsteller', in *Literatur-*

magazin 11, Hamburg 1979.

Projekt Automation und Qualifikation, *Entwicklung der Arbeit, AS 19*, Berlin/W 1978.

Projekt Frauengrundstudium, *Frauengrundstudium*. *Argument-Sonderheft (SH) 44*, Berlin/W 1980.

— *Frauen-Grundstudium 2. SH 57*, Berlin/W. 1982.

Projekt Ideologie-Theorie (PIT), *Faschismus und Ideologie 3, AS 80*, Berlin/W. 1983.

— *Bereichstheorien. AS 70*, Berlin/W. 1983.

— *Theorien über Ideologie, AS 40*, Berlin/W. 1979.

E.A. Rauter, *Vom Umgang mit Wörtern*, München 1978.

Ruth Rehmann, *Die Leute vom Tal*, Frankfurt/M. 1968.

— *Der Mann auf der Kanzel*, München/Wien 1979.

Michael Rutschky, 'Ethnographie des Alltags. Eine literarische Tendenz der siebziger Jahre', in *Literaturmagazin 11*, Hamburg 1979.

D. Schmidt, 'Gegen die Placebo-Literatur. Eine Vorbemerkung', in *Literaturmagazin 11*, Hamburg 1979.

P. Schuster, 'Sinnlichkeit und "Talent". Zu einer Hauptbedingung des Schreibens', in *Literaturmagazin 11*, Hamburg 1979.

D. Sölle, 'Feministische Theologie', in *Das Argument 129*, 9/10, Berlin/W 1981.

W. Thomczyk, 'über das schreiben hinaus. . . .erfahrungen mit dem andauernden versuch, über das ziel eines schriftstellers hinauszukommen', in *Literaturmagazin 11*, Hamburg 1979.

S. Tretjakow, *Die Arbeit des Schriftstellers*, Hamburg 1972.

Brigitte Wartmann, 'Schreiben als Angriff auf das Patriarchat', in *Literaturmagazin 11*, Hamburg 1979.

Paul Willis, *Learning to Labour. How working-class kids get working-class jobs*, Farnborough, Hants. 1977.

Christa Wolf, *A model childhood*, transl. Ursula Molinaro & Hedwig Rappolt, London 1983.

Chapter II. Displacements of the Problem

C. Ackermann, 'Die 2. Europameisterschaft der Turnerinnen', in *Jahrbuch der Turnkunst, Jg.54*, 1960, pp. 60-62.

Michele Barrett & Mary McKintosh, *The Anti-Social Family*, London 1982.

Becker, Bovenschen et.al. *Aus der Zeit der Verzweiflung*, Frankfurt/M. 1977.

Max von Boehne, *Die Mode, Bd.8. Menschen und Moden im 19. Jahrhundert 1878 - 1914*, 3rd ed., München 1963.

Bertolt Brecht. *Gesammelte Werke 12*, Frankfurt/M. 1967.

— *The Mother*, transl. Steve Gooch, London 1978.

Brigitte, 'So sind Sie gut auf den Beinen', No.23 1981,pp.42-46.

Sophie Dapper, 'Kritische Nachschau auf die deutschen Meisterschaften

im Frauenturnen', in *Deutsches Turnen, Jg.98*, No.5 1951, pp. 4ff.
— 'Höchstleistung und Wettkampf im Frauenturnen', in *Deutsches Turnen, Jg.98*, No.5 1953, p.5.
— 'Unser Frauenturnen. Die internationalen Wettkampfanforderungen im Frauenturnen', in *Jahrbuch der Turnkunst, Jg.40*, 1954,pp.67-70 *Deutsches Turnen, Jg.100*, No.20, 1955, p.20.
Duden Etymologie, *Herkunftswörterbuch der deutschen Sprache*, 1963.
Barbara Ehrenreich & Deirdre English, *For her own good. 150 years of the experts' advice to women*, London 1983.
Frankfurter Allgemeine Zeitung, 2.9 — 6.5.1972.
Frauenredaktion, Projekt Frauenbewegung und Arbeiterbewegung (eds.), *Frauenpolitik – Opfer – Täter–Diskussion 2. Argument Studienhefte 56*, Berlin/W. 1982.
Sigmund Freud, *Civilization and its Discontents*, transl. Joan Riviere, London 1982.
Erving Goffmann, *Stigma: notes on the management of spoiled identity*, Harmondsworth 1968.
Heidi Hartmann, 'The Unhappy Marriage of Marxism and Feminism', in Lydia Sargent (ed.), *Women and Revolution*, London 1981.
Frigga Haug (ed.), *Frauenformen I.*, Berlin/W 1980.
— 'Männergeschichte, Frauenbefreiung, Sozialismus, Zum Verhältnis von Frauenbewegung und Arbeiterbewegung', in *Das Argument 129*, Berlin/W. 1981.
W.F.Haug, 'Kritische Psychologie und Theorie des Ideologischen', in W.F.Haug, *Ideologie, Warenästhetik, Massenkultur. Entwürfe zu einer theoretischen Synthese. SH33*, Berlin/W 1979.
— 'Standpunkt und Perspektive materialistischer Kulturtheorie', in *Materialistische Kulturtheorie und Alltagskultur Argument-Sonderband 47*, Berlin/W 1980.
— 'Der modellierte Männerkörper als ideologische Macht im Faschismus. Ein Diskussionsbeitrag zu Breker', in Projekt Ideologie-Theorie, *Faschismus und Ideologie 3. AS 80*, Berlin/W. 1983.
— 'Medizin und Psychiatrie als ideologische Mächte im Faschismus und ihre Mitwirkung an den Ausrottungspolitiken', in Projekt Ideologie-Theorie, *Faschismus und Ideologie 3, AS 80*, Berlin/W. 1983.
T.Hausschild, H.Staschen, R.Troschke, *Hexen Katalog zur Ausstellung*, Hamburg 1979.
Inge Heuser, 'Wohin führt der Weg im Frauenturnen?' in *Jahrbuch der Turnkunst. Jg. 51*, 1957, pp.73-79.
— 'Was sagt die DTB-Frauenführung zum Beschluss von Oberwerries?', in *Deutsches Turnen, Jg.105*, No.23 1960, p.450.
B.Hinz, *Die Malerie im deutschen Faschismus*, München 1974.
Luce Irigaray, 'That Sex which is not One', in Paul Foss & Meaghan Morris (eds.), *Language, Sexuality and Subversion*, Darlington, Australia 1978, pp.161-171.
— *Speculum de l'autre femme*, Paris 1974.
Jahrbuch der Turnkunst, Jg.49, pp.38ff.

D.Kamper & V.Rittner (eds.), *Zur Geschichte des Körpers*, München/ Wien 1976.

D.Kamper & Ch.Wulf (eds), *Die Wiederkehr des Körpers*, Frankfurt/M 1982.

M.Maron, *Flugasche*, Frankfurt/M. 1981.

Anja Meulenbelt, *Für uns selbst*, München 1981.

Robert Musil, *Der Mann ohne Eigenschaften*, Hamburg 1981.

L. Niemeyer, 'Die deutschen Meisterschaften im Frauenturnen 1959: Der Durchbruch ist gelungen!', in *Deutsches Turnen, Jg.104*, No.9 1959, pp.170ff.

Helga Novak, *Vogel federlos*, Darmstadt 1982.

Barbara Otto, 'Gegensätze zwischen deutschem und internationalem Frauenturnen', in *Deutsches Turnen, Jg.105*, No.24 1960, p.473.

Renate Prinz, *Die Entwicklung des Kunstturnens der Frauen nach 1945*, Finals Dissertation, Berlin/W 1982.

Projekt Ideologie-Theorie, *Theorien über Ideolgie*, Berlin/W.1979.

L.Röhrich, *Lexikon der sprichwörtlichen Redensarten*, Frieburg/Basel/ Wien 1979.

R.Schittenhelm, *Man wird dich lieber haben. Anstandsbuch für junge Damen*, 5th ed., Stuttgart 1967.

Szene Hamburg, April, 1982.

Chapter III. Constructions of the Domain

Louis Althusser, 'Ideology and the ideological State apparatuses', in *Lenin and Philosophy and other essays*, transl. Ben Brewster, London 1977.

M. Baumgarten, 'Spuren lesen', in Anna Tüne, *Körper, Liebe, Sprache: über die weibliche Kunst, Erotik darzustellen*, Berlin/W. 1982.

Giovanni Boccaccio, *The Decameron*, transl. G.H.McWilliam, Harmondsworth 1972.

L.Boltanksi, 'Die soziale Verwendung des Körpers', in D.Kamper & V.Rittner (eds.) *Zur Geschichte des Körpers*, München/Wien 1976.

G.Bonacchi, 'Gibt es eine feministische Theorie?', in W.F.Haug & W.Elfferding (eds.) *Neue soziale Bewegungen und Marxismus, Argument- Sonderband 78*, Berlin/W. 1982.

Bertolt Brecht, 'Me-Ti/Buch der Wendungen' in *Gesammelte Werke Bd.12* Frankfurt/M 1967.

The Boston Women's Health Book Collective, *Our Bodies Ourselves*, US 2nd ed., New York 1973, and UK 2nd ed., Harmondsworth 1978: also Preface to German translation, *unser körper unser leben. ein handbuch von frauen für frauen*, Reinbek 1980 pp.27-31.

F. Ewald, in D.Kamper & V.Rittner, *Geschichte des Körpers*, Munchen/Wien 1976.

Michel Foucault, *The Archaeology of Knowledge*, transl. A.M.Sheridan Smith, London 1972.

300

— *Dispositive der Macht. über Sexualität. Wissen und Wahrheit* ('Deployments of Power. On Sexuality, Knowledge and Truth: a collection of lectures, essays and interviews), Berlin/W.1978.
— Interview, in D. Kamper & V.Rittner (eds.), *Geschichte des Körpers*, München/Wien 1976.
Sigmund Freud, *On Sexuality. Three Essays on the theory of Sexuality and other works*, Harmondsworth 1977.
Gruppe Offensivs Altern, *Courage Sonderheft 6, Jg.4*, Berlin/W. no date.
Frigga Haug (ed.), *Frauenformen I*, Berlin/W. 1980.
W.F.Haug, 'Umrisse zu einer Theorie des Ideologischen', in Projekt Ideologie-Theorie (PIT), *Theorien über Ideologie*, Berlin/W. 1979.
— 'Standpunkt und Perspektive materialistischer Kulturtheorie', in *Materialistische Kulturtheorie und Alltagskultur. AS 47*, Berlin/W. 1980.
B.Heintz & C.Honegger, 'Weibliche Widerstandsformen und Verweigerungsstrategien im 19. Jahrhundert', in *Beiträge zur feministischen Theorie und Praxis 5*, München 1981.
Luce Irigaray, *Speculum de l'autre femme*, Paris 1974.
Michael Jäger, 'Kommunismus kommt von kommunal,' in *Aktualisierung Marx. AS 100*, Berlin/W. 1983.
Ernesto Laclau, 'Diskurs, Hegemonie und Politik', in *Neue soziale Bewegungen und Marxismus*, Berlin/W. 1982.
Doris Lessing, *The Golden Notebook*, London 1973.
Herbert Marcuse, *One-dimensional man*, London 1972.
William Masters & Virginia Johnson, *Human Sexual Inadequacy*, London 1970.
W. McBride, *Zeig mal! Ein Bilderbuch für Kinder und Eltern*, Wuppertal 1980.
A. Menzel, 'Gedrängel im Bett', *Rote Blätter 11*, 1982.
Maurice Merleau-Ponty, *The Phenomenology of Perception*, New York 1962.
Ovid, *Metamorphoses*, 19th edn., Harmondsworth 1984.
N. Poulantzas, *State, power, socialism*, transl. Patrick Camiller, London 1978.
Projekt Automation und Qualifikation, *Automationsarbeit. Empirie 2*, Berlin/W 1981.
Projekt Ideologie-Theorie, *Theorien über Ideologie*, Berlin/W.1979.
Wilhelm Reich, *The Sexual revolution. Towards a self-regulating character structure*, transl. Therese Pol Farrar, New York 1974.
Reimut Reiche, *Sexuality and Class Struggle*, transl. Susan Bennett & David Fernbach, London 1972.
R.Reitz, *Wechseljahre. Ermutigung zu einem neuen Verständnis*, Hamburg 1981.
Anna Tüne, *Körper, Liebe, Sprache. über die weibliche Kunst, Erotik darzustellen*, Berlin/W. 1982.
Paul Willis, *Learning to Labour. How working-class kids get working-*

class jobs, Farnborough, Hants 1977.

H.Woetzel & M.Geier, 'Sprachtheorie und Diskursanalyse in Frank-reich', in *Das Argument 133*, 1981.

Karol Wojtyla, *Love and Responsibility*, London 1981.